CASE STUDIES IN EXISTENTIAL PSYCHOTHERAPY AND COUNSELLING

WILEY SERIES
in
EXISTENTIAL PERSPECTIVES ON
PSYCHOTHERAPY AND COUNSELLING

Editor

Emmy van Deurzen

Case Studies in Existential Psychotherapy and Counselling
Editor: Simon du Plock

Existential Time-Limited Therapy: The Wheel of Existence
Freddie Strasser and Alison Strasser

Further title in preparation

Paradox and Passion in Psychotherapy:
An Existential Approach to Therapy and Counselling
Emmy van Deurzen

CASE STUDIES IN EXISTENTIAL PSYCHOTHERAPY AND COUNSELLING

Edited by

Simon du Plock

Regent's College, London, UK

JOHN WILEY & SONS

Chichester · New York · Weinheim · Brisbane · Singapore · Toronto

Copyright © 1997 by John Wiley & Sons Ltd,
Baffins Lane, Chichester,
West Sussex PO19 1UD, England

National   01243 779777
International (+44) 1243 779777
e-mail (for orders and customer service enquiries):
cs-books@wiley.co.uk
Visit our Home Page on http://www.wiley.co.uk
or http://www.wiley.com

Other Wiley Editorial Offices

John Wiley & Sons, Inc., 605 Third Avenue,
New York, NY 10158-0012, USA

Wiley-VCH Verlag GmbH,
Pappelallee 3, D-69469 Weinheim, Germany

Jacaranda Wiley Ltd, 33 Park Road, Milton,
Queensland 4064, Australia

John Wiley & Sons (Asia) Pte Ltd, 2 Clementi Loop #02-01,
Jin Xing Distripark, Singapore 129809

John Wiley & Sons (Canada) Ltd, 22 Worcester Road,
Rexdale, Ontario M9W 1L1, Canada

Library of Congress Cataloging-in-Publication Data

Case studies in existential psychotherapy and counselling / edited by
    Simon du Plock.
        p.   cm. — (Wiley series in existential psychotherapy and
    counselling)
        Includes bibliographical references and index.
        ISBN 0-471-96192-2 (cloth : alk. paper). — ISBN 0-471-97079-4
    (pbk. : alk. paper)
        1. Existential psychotherapy—Case studies. I. Plock, Simon du.
    II. Series.
    RC489.E93C37   1997
    616.89'14—dc21   97-8659
                                                                               CIP

British Library Cataloguing in Publication Data

A catalogue record for this book is available from the British Library

ISBN 0471-96192-2 (cased)
ISBN 0-471-97079-4 (paper)

Typeset by Dorwyn Ltd, Rowlands Castle, Hants
Printed and bound in Great Britain by Bookcraft (Bath) Ltd, Midsomer Norton, Somerset
This book is printed on acid-free paper responsibly manufactured from sustainable forestation, for which at least two trees are planted for each one
used for paper production.

CONTENTS

ABOUT THE EDITOR

Simon du Plock is an Associate Fellow of the British Psychological Society and Head of MA Programmes at Regent's College School of Psychotherapy and Counselling. He is a Registered Existential Psychotherapist and Chartered Counselling Psychologist with a background which includes experience in the UK National Health Service, the independent sector, and therapeutic communities. He teaches on the psychotherapeutic and counselling psychology doctoral programme of the University of Surrey and has contributed to several texts on counselling psychology and psychotherapy. He is the author of a number of papers and journal articles, primarily on existential–phenomenological therapy and supervision (in which he maintains a private practice), is Co-editor of the *Journal of the Society for Existential Analysis* and Editor of the *Universities Psychotherapy Association Review*. At present he is engaged on research into clinical supervision from an existential perspective.

ABOUT THE AUTHORS

Zack Eleftheriadou BA, MSc, MA, Dip. Infant Mental Health, CPsychol, UKCP Registered is a psychotherapist at NAFSIYAT Intercultural Therapy Centre, London, where she works with children and adults. She is the Coordinator of the Cross-cultural Counselling and Psychotherapy Specialist Certificate at Regent's College, London, UK. She also has a private practice in North London. She lectures widely and has published widely in the field of cross-cultural counselling and psychotherapy. Her publications include the book *Transcultural Counselling*.

Harriet Goldenberg BA, MA, MSc, CPsychol is a course leader and part-time tutor at the School of Psychotherapy and Counselling, Regent's College, London, UK, and Editor of the *Newsletter of the Society for Existential Analysis*. She has a private practice in psychotherapy and counselling. Her two main areas of interest revolve around the therapeutic applications of the work of Martin Buber and society's responses to "marginality". In addition, she is Chair of a national human rights campaigning organization.

Dr Bo Jacobsen is a research psychologist and an existentially-oriented psychotherapist who is Head of Research, Centre for Human Science Research in Health and Ageing, at the University of Copenhagen, Denmark. Having done a PhD (educational studies) and a DPhil (psychology) he is currently responsible for a number of existentially-oriented research projects in Denmark. Among these are: existential problems in cancer patients; the phenomena and treatment of crises in an existential light; existential dimensions of ageing. Dr Jacobsen has written a number of books and articles on educational and psychological subjects. He is presently completing a book on existential psychology.

Dr Arthur L. Jonathan is a UKCP Registered Existential Psychotherapist in private practice. Originally a Senior Lecturer in Education at Goldsmiths'

College, London, UK he subsequently completed an MA in Psychotherapy and Counselling and the Advanced Diploma in Existential Psychotherapy at the School of Psychotherapy and Counselling, Regent's College, London, where he is now a Senior Lecturer. He is a founding member of the Society for Existential Analysis and is a former Chair of the Humanistic and Integrative Psychotherapy Section of the United Kingdom Council for Psychotherapy.

Alessandra Lemma is a Chartered Clinical and Counselling Psychologist and UKCP registered psychotherapist. She works as Clinical Tutor on the Doctorate in Clinical Psychology at University College London (UCL) and as a clinical psychologist in the National Health Service, UK, with people with long-term mental health problems. She also has a private practice as a psychotherapist. She is presently the UK Academic Advisor to the UCL–Dhaka University project which is running the first clinical psychology training in Bangladesh. She is the author of several books: *Starving to Live: the Paradox of Anorexia Nervosa* (Central Publishing), *An Invitation to Psychodynamic Psychology* (Whurr) and *An Introduction to Psychopathology* (Sage).

Martin Milton CPsychol, AFBPsS, is a Chartered Counselling Psychologist and works primarily within the National Health Service, UK, although he is a clinical affiliate for an employee assistance programme and has a private practice. He has taught on HIV-related psychotherapy at Regent's College School of Psychotherapy and Counselling and in other settings. He has previously written on an existential approach to HIV-related psychotherapy. His research interests are in the area of lesbian and gay psychologies. In addition to this he is on the Standing Committee for Scientific Affairs and the Standing Committee for Professional Affairs of the British Psychological Society Division of Counselling Psychology, for whom he is currently researching psychologists' practice with lesbian and gay clients.

Lucia Moja-Strasser MA, AdvDipExPsych, UKCP Registered is a practising existential psychotherapist and supervisor. She is a lecturer on the Diploma and Advanced Diplama programmes in Existential Psychotherapy and Counselling at Regent's College, London, UK. She has been working as an honorary psychotherapist at the Munro Clinic at Guy's Hospital, London. She has also lectured at University College London and City University and has given numerous workshops in London, Birmingham, Berkshire, Windsor College, Durham, Brighton, Warwick University and Queen's College Cambridge. She has also given workshops at Conferences held by the British Psychological Society, BAC, the

Society for Existential Analysis and UKCP. She is one of the founding members of the Society for Existential Analysis. Her special interests are philosophy, music, poetry and meditation.

June Roberts began her working life in Fry's chocolate factory, UK, from where she progressed to approved schools as a housemother, and to Family Service Units as a family caseworker. She studied social administration and applied social studies at Bristol University and went on to specialise in family work and mental health. In 1980 she undertook a study of the management of parasuicide patients in the National Health Service, UK, and also embarked on psychotherapy training with the Institute of Psychotherapy and Social Studies. She is now deeply involved in the theory and practice of time-limited psychotherapy, owing much to Laing and Esterson, John Weakland and James Mann. She gives workshops throughout England and Wales.

Dr Freddie Strasser is a course leader, tutor and clinical supervisor at Regent's College School of Psychotherapy and Counselling, London, UK. He is particularly interested in the application of existential concepts to practice in existential brief therapy.

Dr Steve J. Ticktin BA, MA, MD, MRCPsych is a Canadian psychiatrist and psychotherapist who has held a number of hospital posts in the NHS (1978–91). In addition he has acted as personal assistant to David Cooper (1974), studied with the Philadelphia Association (1978–80) and was apprenticed in psychotherapy with R.D. Laing (1982–84). In 1983–84 he helped establish the British Network of Alternatives to Psychiatry and the Supportive Psychotherapy Association and from 1987 onwards he has been London editor for *ASYLUM*, a magazine for democratic psychiatry. Since 1991 he has been working as a freelance psychiatrist and psychotherapist, dividing his time between London and his native Toronto. He is presently visiting lecturer at the Regent's College School of Psychotherapy and Counselling, London, UK, and registered as an existential therapist with the UKCP. He is interested in philosophical and political critiques of traditional psychiatry and psychotherapy, particularly the works of R.D. Laing and David Cooper.

Dr Christopher Wurm studied medicine at the University of Adelaide and undertook postgraduate training in family medicine in South Australia, New South Wales and the UK, becoming a Fellow of the Royal Australian College of General Practitioners in 1987. He also trained in logotherapy and existential analysis at the Institut für Logotherapic und andere Methoden der Psychotherapie in Vienna, and was made a Corresponding

Member of the Gesellschaft für Logotherapie und Existenzanalyse in 1988 at the recommendation of Professor Viktor Frankl. He now lives in Adelaide, South Australia, where he works as a general practitioner in a group practice, and as a psychotherapist in private practice. He is involved in the training of general practitioners and holds an honorary position as Clinical Lecturer at the National Centre for Education and Training on Addiction. He has presented papers at seminars and conferences in Australia, Canada, Austria, Sweden and Thailand. He enjoys cinema, gardening, cooking and reading.

SERIES PREFACE

Emmy van Deurzen

It is very telling that this series should be launched at a time when dramatic social and cultural changes accompany the turn of the millennium. As people contend with a sense of crisis and confusion, they search for clarity and new ways of living. Increasingly they turn to the professions of psychotherapy and counselling to help them address crucial existential issues.

It is no longer sufficient to talk with clients and patients about their problems as if these were purely functions of intrapsychic mechanisms. In an increasingly complex world, people need to be able to see their own difficulties in relation to the overall contradictions and dilemmas that bedevil human living. They have to be able to make sense of themselves within their own contexts. Many human troubles are generated by living with technology, bureaucracy and social alienation. Other problems are as old as humanity itself and become more understandable when looked at from a philosophical angle.

The existential perspective on psychotherapy and counselling makes it possible to re-evaluate personal problems in the light of human wisdom. It pays attention to the philosophical, social, cultural and political dimensions as well as to the personal and the interpersonal. It encouragespeople to examine their lives and rediscover meaning. It makes room for paradox and the acceptance of the inevitable. It allows for questioning and re-evaluation.

Existential psychotherapy has been in existence for close to a century and the theories in which it is rooted go back to the nineteenth century philosophies of freedom of Kierkegaard and Nietzsche and the twentieth century philosophies of Heidegger and Sartre, amongst others. Indirectly it draws on a much longer lineage, in that all of

Western and Eastern philosophy are relevant to such a reappraisal of everyday life.

The approach has not been well documented until quite recently, as many existential practitioners abhor formalisation and technology and few have wanted to write about their work, let alone systematise it. This is a pity, for psychotherapists and counsellors need to inform each other of their findings about human life in order to progress in understanding the complex situations their clients are caught up in.

It is therefore delightful to me that the present series of books, with their focus on the application of the existential approach, will remedy this situation. Here are a number of practitioners documenting their own particular brands of existential work and showing them to be utterly relevant to their clients.

The present volume provides us with much needed practical applications and illustrations of existential psychotherapy. There are here a number of different existential psychotherapists, each conveying their personal interpretation of the existential approach as it is worked with in their everyday practice.

Their various contributions cover a wide range of situations and issues and each throws a little bit of light on the human dilemma as experienced by all. A book with case illustrations has long been needed in this field, which has often remained very theoretical and abstract. The illustrations show existential psychotherapy to be a down-to-earth approach that is relevant in many different situations. The book also demonstrates the fact that there is no single, true form of existential practice, but a plurality of forms, each one particular to the specific therapist and client working together. Sometimes what the existential therapist does is not so different to what therapists of other orientations might have done, which demonstrates that good therapy is often less denominational and more simply human and relational. Increasingly other forms of therapy adopt existential principles, in order to be able to deal efficiently with their client's life issues. The present volume will provide much food for thought in this respect.

PREFACE

The great majority of texts intended to provide psychotherapists, coun-sellors and other mental health professionals with examples of thera-peutic client work employ the case study as a device to describe specific clinical problems, show how these are to be understood and treated, and discuss their epidemiology and aetiology. This text departs from this traditional model, asserting that while it can give a greater understanding of the medical/scientific approach to psychological distress, it often serves to widen the gap between clients and those who seek to assist them. In either case, the client more or less vanishes, to be replaced by the presenting problem.

Case Studies in Existential Psychotherapy and Counselling is intended as a response to the increasing need of practitioners who question the efficacy of the medical/scientific approach for a text which offers a different perspective: one which enables and encourages them in their efforts to engage more fully with the clients themselves in a joint exploration of their world. The experienced practitioners who have contributed to this text recognise, too, that psychological distress is increasingly endemic to modern societies. Such a reconceptualisation of the problem requires a new understanding which may be more readily provided by the existential–phenomenological approach with its insights into what it is to be human.

Each chapter of the text addresses a different "problem of living" and shows the way in which an existential–phenomenological therapist works with the client's experience. Moreover, the book attempts to redefine the concept of a case study, arguing for something more akin to studies of the manner in which individual therapists and clients come to engage with these "problems of living".

Simon du Plock

<table><tr><td>

1

</td></tr></table>

INTRODUCTION

Simon du Plock
Regents College, London, UK

The vast majority of texts specifically designed to provide mental health practitioners with examples of work with clients focus almost exclusively on the problem which the client presents, since they take the case study as a mnemonic device to illustrate abstract theoretical and research issues. As such the case study serves a threefold purpose: (a) to describe a specific clinical problem; (b) to show how such a problem is viewed by experts in the field and how they treat it; and (c) to provide a place to discuss the epidemiology and aetiology of the problem.

Astute readers will no doubt have noticed that the individual client has more or less disappeared, to be replaced by a presenting problem. At its most clumsy, this medical/scientific approach can view clients themselves as the problem and as nothing other than the problem so that, for example, the person experiencing particular anxieties, behaving in compulsive ways or having hallucinations comes to be viewed as a neurotic, an obsessive compulsive or schizophrenic, and treated as such.

This might be all well and good if these experiences, like physical illnesses such as influenza, could be fully understood using a disease model. If we get 'flu we know that the illness will follow a particular course, that there are a certain number of actions which we can take to aid recovery and that after a relatively specific period of time we are likely to return to health. Mental health problems do not seem to be like this, not least because the relationship between mental activities and the symptoms we observe is not understood to the extent that the connection

Case Studies in Existential Psychotherapy and Counselling. Edited by S. du Plock
© 1997 John Wiley & Sons Ltd

between infection and physical signs of illness are. Similarly, while physical health may be defined as the absence of physical disease, mental health is certainly not merely the absence of mental illness—however defined. As Joyce McDougal (1990, p. 484) recognized in her book *Plea for a Measure of Abnormality*, to be "over-reasonable and over-adapted is no more desirable than the dominance of unleashed instinctual forces. The point at which [the norm] becomes the straightjacket of the soul and the cemetery of the imagination is a delicate one to define".

Such case study texts are frequently to be found, when not under the rubric of psychoanalysis, in the abnormal psychology stable—thus ensuring from the outset that we understand what is to follow as deviations from the normal and, implicitly, amenable to and requiring treatment. Mental health workers have been asking for many years, "What is normal?". In recent years this question has been accompanied by the debate as to whether any human behaviour or experience can be said to be normal, beyond the somewhat limited concept of a statistical norm—and even this has been called into some doubt by our increasingly sophisticated understanding of such factors as the impact of the observer's consciousness on empirical data.

The search for normality, then, and the wish to move "transgressors" towards it, appears increasingly pointless and, at worst, enormously destructive. We have only to recall for a moment the appalling violence of aversion therapy visited upon unhappy gay men, the chemical coshing of the depressed (and particularly depressed women) in Western society, and the still widespread use of electro-convulsive therapy in psychiatric institutions, to see the absurdity of the scientific pursuit of normality and the deadening of the human spirit which is held up as evidence of health and stability. I shall never forget my horror, when first working on a geriatric ward of a large psychiatric hospital in the mid-1970s, on discovering that almost half the female patients had been lobotomized. These feelings were compounded when I was told by senior staff that many of these patients had been committed as "moral degenerates" in the 1920s and 1930s, having had illegitimate babies. What I was witnessing was not so much damaged lives as lives which had never been allowed to come fully into being—and it was impossible to know the impact of this on the children involved. It might be argued that these people are the fall-out of a blunt-instrument psychiatry which has become more humane and intelligent in the intervening years. Physical lobotomy is now out of favour, but stereotactic psychosurgery—a technique which uses electrodes to melt certain areas of brain tissue—has to some extent replaced it. In any case, as Breggin (1993) has pointed out in his book *Toxic Psychiatry*, ECT and chemical interventions are also grossly intrusive and frequently have irreversible effects.

While the medical establishment has made strenuous attempts over the years to compile diagnostic manuals, the illness categories enshrined in them, far from becoming more certain, have changed and moved in and out of fashion in ways which clearly indicate their social construction. New syndromes have come into existence (or at least into print) with alarming regularity: their astonishing concentration on smaller and smaller aspects of human life may owe much to innovation and market creation, but the seriousness with which they are received must surely tell us something about a deeper social malaise and a wish to grasp any promise of certainty and control. In the 1980s many members of the middle class obtained a feeling of well-being by selling their houses to each other. In the 1990s they are more creative—they go on courses and learn to "therap" each other.

Definitions of madness and sanity have varied greatly throughout history, between cultures and even between classes within national cultures. Those in receipt of psychiatric labels are drawn disproportionately from the inner city poor, and especially from ethnic minorities. The debate about the reasons for this is too complex to enter into here, but it is perhaps worth noting that, while much has been written by psychiatrists about the concentration of the mentally distressed in run-down urban areas, this phenomenon has been generally understood to be a result of the gravitation of such people towards a poorer lifestyle as their condition worsens. Certainly there is evidence of the mobility of many of these people from paid employment on the outskirts of cities to unemployment in their centres, but much of this, like their shift in socio-economic status, is surprisingly limited: it is rare for affluent young white professionals to find themselves on the streets and labelled schizophrenic.

As Foucault (1963) recognised, the mental health institutions function in complex ways to regulate and control "deviant" behaviour, and members of more privileged social groups have correspondingly greater chances of avoiding or rejecting pejorative labelling. The fact that diagnostic tools such as the DSM-IV, which are intended to be scientific, actually tend to take as their main criterion the effectiveness of an individual's ability to adapt in the face of life problems, immediately alerts us to the myth of fixed and immutable illness categories. This is not, of course, to deny that people experience emotional problems and that they may benefit from some form of therapy, but it is important to recognise that the meaning we give to this experience—indeed the meaning, or lack of meaning, the sufferers themselves are able to attribute to it—is socially constructed. What may in one context be considered harmless eccentricity or appropriate go-getting executive behaviour may be seen in another as dangerous and mad.

It is tempting to go along with the views of such critics as Thomas Szasz (1961), who claim that there is no such thing as mental illness, but this too would be an error since a libertarian approach simply lets society off the hook as regards provision of mental health care: if the psychologically distressed are just malingerers or criminals, the only logical options are to ignore or imprison them. Recent government closures of psychiatric hospitals in favour of the misnomer "community care" have been given a measure of comfort by such arguments, although it is doubtful whether government policy, in the UK at least, is driven by philosophical rather than economic considerations.

While the dominance of the medical model is likely to continue for some time, it is increasingly challenged by a more educated rights-conscious public. Paradoxically—and the existential approach is ideally suited to working with paradox—the emphasis on the customer, and their choice and consumer status, however hollow this turns out to be (and in the case of community care it has proved very hollow indeed), has enabled many service users to air their dissatisfaction with expert scientific knowledge. Those who are financially able have increasingly sought out alternatives from among the numerous different approaches available in the private health care market place. What such people have in common is a desire for individual attention for their own very personal distress, something which a philosophical approach such as existential therapy is able to offer. Expressed most simply, the existential–phenomenological approach acknowledges as its premise the plea of very many clients faced with mental health care practitioners: namely, that the individual who seeks a consultation is just that—an individual and not a "case". It does so for not merely political or humane reasons, although many clients and practitioners in the UK and Europe, and to a lesser extent in the USA, have been drawn to a broadly existential perspective as a result of reading the work of R.D. Laing, a Scottish psychiatrist whose major books *The Divided Self* (1960) and *The Politics of Experience* (1967) did much to challenge the worst pathologising aspects of the medical model.

While critics have attacked Laing on a number of grounds, not least that he generalised too broadly from a very small number of patients and that he romanticised the experience of psychological distress, there can be little doubt that he tapped into the needs of both clients and practitioners for a way of working which fully acknowledges the experience of the individual. As regards the continuing influence of his work, this is evidenced by the fact that many of his books remain in print—no small achievement in a field in which the number of publications each year seems to grow exponentially and publishers' lists are rigorously pruned of dead wood.

The existential approach is grounded in a view of the human being as constantly changing, flexible and always in the process of becoming. This view owes much to the work of the German philosopher Edmund Husserl. Husserl (1913, 1929) argued that natural sciences are based on the assumption of a split between subject and object and that this kind of dualism should be replaced by a method of investigating the world in which all prejudice and assumptions are put aside in order to meet the world directly through intuition. Rather than explain or analyse things, we must describe and understand them.

Husserl's work was taken up and developed by his pupil Heidegger, who applied this method of phenomenological investigation to reflect on the meaning of being. In 1958 Heidegger was invited by the psychiatrist Binswanger to give a series of lectures, which have become known as the Zollikon lectures (Boss, 1988), to trainee psychiatriasts in Switzerland. Binswanger had become increasingly disillusioned with Freudian psychoanalytic theory. As he expressed it:

> The existential research orientation in psychiatry arose from dissatisfaction with the prevailing efforts to gain scientific understanding in psychiatry . . . psychology and psychotherapy as sciences are admittedly concerned with "man", not at all primarily with mentally *ill* man but with *man* as such. The new understanding of man, which we owe to Heidegger's analysis of existence, has its basis in the new conception that man is no longer understood in terms of some theory—[be it] a mechanistic, a biological or a psychological one.
>
> (May et al., 1958, p. 4)

Many of the insights of existential exploration and of phenomenology have been taken up by humanistic psychology in the UK and USA and have in this way become widely known, although considerably diluted and distorted. This text is not a "how to" manual which the reader can imbibe in order to get round these distortions to learn how existential–phenomenological therapists actually work, since there are as many ways as there are practitioners, and the fact that the existential–phenomenological approach is primarily about relationship—the relationship between the therapist and the client in each therapy, indeed in each session and moment to moment—will be unique in ways more fundamental than is the case for other approaches. Neither is this book intended as a "Here's one I made earlier" style of text in which a carefully edited piece of work by an expert is presented to a group of novices and admiring onlookers. Such exercises are frequently more about the self-importance of the therapist than a generous sharing of knowledge. The early days of psychiatry and psychoanalysis have left us any number of such thaumaturgical firework displays. While Freud's case studies are generally models of openness and exploration (or at least appear as such), many of his followers have reverted to the safety and irrelevance—for the rest of us—of the expert. The days of the thaumaturge are numbered and the expert position more and more alienating and difficult to maintain in the face of increasing public awareness of mental health issues, and a correspondingly burgeoning wish for a greater degree of support rather than treatment, as people go through the numerous life problems which we all encounter at the turn of the millenium.

If the reader will not discover here the wise words of experts, they will, I hope, find themselves witness to the struggles of a range of therapists to arrive at a way of working which takes fully into account the experiences of their individual clients. These efforts are rarely cut and dried, just as life is not cut and dried; they may sometimes appear more poetic or literary than we have come to expect such accounts to be. They will certainly not read as scientific experiments. Sometimes readers may find themselves frustrated by the material or by what they perceive the therapist to be doing with the material the client brings. Inevitably they will feel frustrated that they have only a snapshot, or impression, of a larger piece of work. My own study is possibly the exception in that a single session constitutes the entire therapy. While the usual case study often maintains the illusion that all of the important aspects of the client's life can be contained within its parameters—that all the relevant aspects of the client's life prior to entering therapy can be summarised and that the client's future can be predicted on the basis of the changes which have come about during therapy—the reader's frustration is, perhaps, something of a given with an approach which does not permit the practitioner to parcel up the client's life neatly.

It would do violence to the richness and complexity of the client's life if we were to pretend that we are able to capture it in a handful of printed pages. The frustration, though, is in itself a valuable thing, since it reminds us that others are not reducible to illness categories, or any other categories for that matter, and are not, finally, knowable. This unknowable quality, which is sometimes thought by non-existentialists to be rather bleak, encourages us not just simply to wonder about people's motivations in an everyday manner, or even to wonder with a client about their behaviour—in the way that most, probably all, therapists would recognise themselves as doing—but to wonder about the human condition and about the nature of being itself.

Notwithstanding the various ways in which practitioners utilise the existential–phenomenological approach, it is possible to outline certain assumptions which these therapists are likely to see as the foundation of their therapeutic work:

1. Human beings are 'thrown' into the world in the sense that they find themselves in a given situation over which they have not exercised

choice. A baby cannot choose to be born into one family, with its concomitant circumstances, rather than another, or to be born with particular physical attributes and genetic make-up. Similarly, as we are all born so shall we all die; as Heidegger (1962) terms it, "our being is a being unto death". Although we cannot choose the givens of our existence, we can choose our response to them and in so doing we create our own values and our own life. As Sartre (1943) expresses it, human beings are condemned to be free. While this may appear obvious, many clients (indeed all of us at certain points in our lives) resist the responsibility that such a view of their place in the world entails, preferring instead to attribute the shape of their life to fate, chance, economics, upbringing, or a hundred other "external" factors which can be pressed into service. *In extremis* almost anything can be taken up by clients and used as the explanation for their current misery or dilemma.

2. Since human beings are thrown into the world it makes no sense to attempt to understand them separate from their context—if indeed such a thing were possible. This is necessarily so within the therapeutic relationship: neither client nor therapist are present as just client or therapist. As Cohn (1994) expresses it: "When we see a client, his/her family, partner, social nexus, etc. are also present in the room. For the existential therapist, there is in fact no 'individual' therapy". This pertains as much to the therapist as it does to the client, although care must be taken to prevent their context from impinging inappropriately on the client's work. In existential therapy, as distinct from psychoanalytic or psychodynamic therapy or those mental health interventions where the practitioner assumes an expert role, it is understood that the therapist should not, indeed cannot, be a blank screen.

3. Since it is the phenomenon—that which appears—which is of concern in existential work the therapist takes care to maintain his/her openness to this and to engage with it as fully as possible. The therapist tends to stay in the present of the client's experience rather than import normative theories or gather evidence from previous sessions to support the hypotheses which such theories entail. In doing so the therapist encourages clients to experience themselves in relation to the therapist and to engage directly with their material rather than couch it in terms exclusively of their past or of their aspirations for the future.

4. Of course, just as clients bring their context into therapy, so they bring their pasts and their hopes and fears for the future, as well as their experiences of the present moment. Existential therapy has often been misunderstood as discounting the past, but this is not so: what it does

reject is the reductionistic notion frequently encountered in therapy that the past 'causes' the present, since such a deterministic approach denies the ability of humans to be creative and to make choices about their lives. Clients often restrict themselves to living almost exclusively in the past, or the present, or some imagined future, and where this occurs much of the therapeutic work will be concerned with enabling them to experience themselves in relation to all three. The client, for example, who has experienced an abusive childhood and who gets by in life by adopting the role of victim—however understandable this may be—will be poorly served by a therapist who fails to clarify the meaning of this choice for the client, its advantages and disadvantages and the way it is manifested in the therapeutic session. When such work is undertaken with care, past and future become part of the present therapeutic encounter.

5. The existential approach is concerned with the being of the client in its entirety and therefore rejects such dichotomies as mind and body, or psyche and soma, since the way we relate to our bodies cannot be split off from any of the other dimensions in which we encounter the world.

6. Since we are able to choose our response to those aspects of our lives which are given, it follows that we can also fail to choose or to make choices which do not really reflect our needs. The types of anxiety and guilt which we experience in the face of this need to choose how we will "be" are quite distinct from neurotic anxiety or guilt. They are the result of our attempts either to act authentically or to evade authenticity and since they are clearly of a specifically existential nature—that is, to do with existence itself—they must be approached as such if they are to be worked with effectively.

It would be inaccurate to deny that other approaches to therapy, including the psychoanalytic, have moved a considerable distance away from situating pathology in particular individuals or groups, but it is the existential–phenomenological approach which most readily addresses the problems of living which beset us today. As van Deurzen, a leading British practitioner, has noted:

A lot of distress is generated by post-modern society, now that humankind has reached a position of potential self-destruction through atomic war or overpopulation of the planet. Mass communication increasingly rules, endangering personal relationships, whilst little solace is expected from the old structures that used to safeguard human values. People often feel that they have a choice between either becoming commodities themselves as slaves in

the production process or focusing so much on achievement in pro-
ducing more commodities that they will not have time to enjoy the
commodities that they have accumulated.

(van Deurzen-Smith, 1994, p. 7)

It is an interesting paradox that, at a time when everything seems to
conspire to make life easier and our range of choice greater, our individual ability to choose ourselves has never been in greater jeopardy.

The contributors to this book, in the examples they provide of their
engagement with individual clients—we might perhaps call them "studies" rather than "case studies"—show not how to act in response to
different types of pathology, but how to engage with the problems of
living which their clients bring to them.

In Chapter 2 the first contributor, *Dr Steve Ticktin* offers an existential
approach to working therapeutically with adolescents and young people,
as they struggle to discover how they want to live their lives and make
sense of the alternatives which they find among their family and friends,
and promoted in wider society. Ticktin, a psychiatrist who trained with
R.D. Laing, illustrates in his client work an existential attitude of "being
with" the client in an open and honest way, rather than "doing something to them". He suggests that this experience of a good relationship is,
in itself, therapeutic.

Dr Freddie Strasser, in Chapter 3, is also struggling to make sense of his
client's life, this time in a foreign culture. His focus is primarily on what
he calls his client's "sedimented value system" and the part this plays in
preventing her from living out fully into the world.

Martin Milton, in Chapter 4, shows how he makes use of an existential–
phenomenological approach in his work with clients with HIV and AIDS.
In doing so, he focuses on the existential givens of death, freedom, isolation and meaninglessness which are present in all our lives but which can
come into the foreground in this particular field, and shows how his
relationship with a client helped to restore a sense of meaning and personal integration.

Zack Eleftheriadou's Chapter 5 is an exploration of cross-cultural counselling. The case study illustrates the complexities of "adjusting" to a
different country to one's origin. It illustrates how some people lose a
sense of self when they have moved from their familiar familial or
cultural framework. This creates an inner confusion which needs careful
exploration during the counselling encounter before a person can feel
able to relate to the new context and, indeed, him/herself again.

In Chapter 6, I have attempted to do two things: first, to reinforce the
central message of Ticktin's case study, that young people are more often
assisted in their struggles with life's problems by a good relationship,

rather than a theoretical explanation of their "pathological" behaviour, (and by "good relationship" I mean one which enables them to clarify their own feelings about what troubles them)'; and second, to suggest that a philosophical approach can be employed in even so pressured and demanding an area as student counselling. Indeed, it is the ideal approach whenever people are seeking to make sense of their lives.

Alessandra Lemma's Chapter 7 is particularly interesting for two reasons: first, because she writes about the way in which an existential crisis may arise as a direct result of a sudden need to come to terms with a change in our physical relationship with our world; and second, because the chapter provides a fascinating attempt to combine aspects of psychoanalytic and psychodynamic therapy with existential therapy.

Harriet Goldenberg's Chapter 8, "Who Am I, if I Am not a Mother?", charts the story of one woman's struggle with infertility. Her life predicament highlights core existential issues, in particular issues of meaning (and meaninglessness) and choice. The case study demonstrates that working existentially is particularly appropriate for clients having to reconsider the meaning and direction of their lives.

Lucia Moja-Strasser, in Chapter 9, compares an existential–phenomenological approach to dreams with the psychoanalytic model which tends to underpin much therapeutic work in this area and illustrates her own way of exploring dreams with a client.

Dr Arthur Jonathan's Chapter 10 is about working existentially with a client who is presenting with what may be generally termed a mid-life crisis. In this chapter he illustrates how the existential approach is especially suitable to throw light on, confront and work with the problems, concerns and issues people find in their lives when externally they appear to all intents and purposes to be very successful.

Dr Christopher Wurm, in his Chapter 11 on working with alcohol dependence, provides an interesting illustration of the way in which an existential approach can be applied in the context of a general medical practice in Australia. As general practitioners in the UK are increasingly looking to provide counselling services, it seems probable that many more existentially-trained therapists will become involved in this provision.

In Chapter 12, on "Working with Existential Groups", *Dr Bo Jacobsen* from Denmark discusses therapy and workshops with groups. He advocates the integration of existential–phenomenological thinking with the so-called systemic approach in order to grasp what happens in groups. He then reports experiences from two types of group work: existential–analytic therapy and a new method of existential workshops. Dr Jacobsen points to the numerous promising—until now unexplored—possibilities in existential group work.

The final chapter in this book is by *June Roberts*. In it she shows how three major tenets of the existential approach were played out in a therapeutic alliance between two women in middle life. The writer has used self-reflection and some hindsight to examine the interaction democratically, and as far as possible phenomenologically, giving equal weight to meaning and to the dynamics of the felt emotions.

REFERENCES

Boss, M. (1988). Martin Heidegger's Zollikon Seminars. In K. Hoeller (ed.) *Heidegger and Psychology*. Seattle, WA: Review of Existential Psychology and Psychiatry.

Breggin, P. (1993). *Toxic Psychiatry*. London: Fontana.

Cohn, H. (1994). What is Existential Psychotherapy? *British Journal of Psychiatry*, **165**, 699–701.

Foucault, M. (1963/1973). *The Birth of the Clinic* (transl. A Sheridan). London: Tavistock.

Foucault, M. (1965). *Madness and Civilization: A History of Insanity in the Age of Reason*. New York: Harper.

Husserl, E. (1913/31). *Ideas* (transl. W.R. Boyce Gibson). New York: Macmillan.

Husserl, E. (1929/1960). *Cartesian Meditations*. The Hague: Nijhoff.

Laing, R.D. (1960). *The Divided Self*. Harmondsworth: Penguin.

Laing, R.D. (1967). *The Policies of Experience and the Bird of Paradise*. Harmondsworth: Penguin.

May, R., Angel, E. and Ellenberger, H. (1958). *Existence*. New York: Basic Books.

McDougal, J. (1990). *Plea for a Measure of Abnormality*. London: Free Association Books.

Sartre, J.P. (1943/1956). *Being and Nothingness—An Essay on Phenomenological Ontology* (transl. H. Barner). New York: Philosophical Library.

Szasz, T.S. (1961). *The Myth of Mental Illness*. New York: Harper.

van Deurzen-Smith, E. (1994). Can counselling help? Durham: Occasional Paper, Durham University School of Education.

2

FRIENDSHIP, THERAPY, CAMARADERIE—AN EXISTENTIAL APPROACH TO THERAPY WITH YOUNG PEOPLE

Steve Ticktin
Regent's College, London, UK

INTRODUCTION

This chapter explores the use of a Laingian-inspired existential therapy with young people (aged 16–25). The author is both a psychiatrist and psychotherapist who has worked in a number of NHS settings offering therapeutic programmes to adolescents and young adults in distress. In addition he did a personal apprenticeship in psychotherapy with R.D. Laing between the years 1978–84. He is critical of the psychodynamic nature of the therapy that is offered in the NHS, feeling that it is often not user-friendly and, at times, can even replicate the abusive relations that drive young people crazy in the first place. Arguing that what they are looking for, primarily, in the therapeutic setting is the experience of a good relationship (akin to that of a good friendship) rather than a theoretical explanation of their so-called "pathological behaviour", he puts forward the case that a more existentially-oriented therapy (and one

Case Studies in Existential Psychotherapy and Counselling. Edited by S. du Plock
© 1997 John Wiley & Sons Ltd

particularly inflected and informed by the work of R.D. Laing), which highlights the being and relational qualities of the therapeutic encounter, lends itself more readily to being something felt to be of value by young people in their search for identity, autonomy and good relationships. The author explores this theme in relation to one young person whom he has called Ellen North-North-West, to whom he was introduced via R.D. Laing when she was 20 years old and residing in one of the therapeutic households sponsored by the Philadelphia Association, and who came to see him in a state of distress provoked by problematical interpersonal relationships. The work was conducted over a 5-year period and, through it, the themes of therapy, friendship and camaraderie were highlighted.

> Now ain't it good to know,
> You've got a friend,
> People can be so cold
> (James Taylor, American folk singer)

Adolescence and young adulthood is often a time of great turbulence and turmoil. The young person, to borrow from Heidegger, is "thrown" into a troubling and disturbing world not of his/her own making and given the arduous task of carving out an autonomous existence within it. During this period of great transformation, the individual is beset on all sides by a number of existential concerns pertaining to one's burgeoning emotional, sexual, social and intellectual life that entail some hard-wrought decision-making, as well as some exquisitely painful moments of being. Often relations with family members are fraught as the result of changing perceptions, in which the parents are no longer seen as ideal models of emulation and their failings and shortcomings come more to the fore. These early familial relations tend to inform those that are established outside with teachers and peers, often in terms of a search for what was lacking at home.

When I came to London in the late 1970s to study and work with R.D. Laing, I simultaneously continued my more traditional psychiatric training and held several hospital posts in the process.[1] Laing, in fact, encouraged me in this endeavour and saw nothing contradictory between this activity and my involvement in the Philadelphia Association (PA),[2] the organization which he helped found in the mid-1960s. One of my jobs entailed working in an NHS regional adolescent unit for disturbed young people between the ages of 16 and 20. The unit was structured along the lines of a therapeutic community and there were various combinations of different kinds of therapy, including individual, group and family. All of the adolescents who came into the unit were given twice-weekly individual psychotherapy. All of the psychotherapists were psychodynamic. My own supervisor was Kleinian!

My experience of the kind of therapy that was offered in this institutional setting was that it was problematic in a number of respects. In the first instance it partook of the medical model of psychiatry and sought to explain the young people's behaviour as the "acting out" of different kinds of "psychopathology". In the second place, with its emphasis on the anonymity and blank screen-ness of the therapist, I felt it was not experienced by the recipients of "user-friendly" and often tended to replicate the same cold and distant kinds of relations that young people were seeking an antidote to. To be confronted by someone who might spend the hour with you in virtual silence, revealing nothing of themselves, and offering only the occasional, theoretically-informed interpretation of your behaviour that, more often than not, didn't make any sense to you anyway, did not seem to me to be a very welcome (or welcoming) kind of experience. More and more, I began to feel that what a young person was looking for was not so much an explanation, but an experience of a good relationship akin to that of a good friendship. In this regard, Ernesto Spinelli's recent and highly recommended book *Demystifying Therapy* (1994) points out that what is felt to be a very significant, albeit non-specific, factor in effective psychotherapy is the quality of the relationship between client and therapist.

> As to the therapeutic process itself, clients identify the quality of the relationship as being of central defining importance in that it fosters both acceptance and understanding . . .
>
> (Spinelli, 1994, p. 78)

As a result of all the above, it was during this time that I began to evolve a more existential approach (and one particularly informed by the work of R.D. Laing) which, as Spinelli points out, emphasises the being and relational qualities of the therapeutic encounter. I thought this kind of approach had more to offer young people and would be felt by them to be of value in their search for identity, autonomy and good interpersonal relationships.

The existential approach in therapy and the philosophy on which it is based have been described over the past decade by a number of practitioners and contributors in the field (e.g. van Deurzen-Smith 1988; Spinelli, 1989; May, 1983; Hoeller, 1990). Although there are probably, in some sense, as many existential therapies as there are existential therapists, there are a number of shared assumptions which, as Hans Cohn (1994) has pointed out, are likely to be in play in their practices. The emphasis, as van Deurzen has described, is always on the individual person's experience of his/her world and the aim is to facilitate the clarification of the person's thoughts, feelings, values, etc. without imposing one's own (i.e. the therapist's) theoretical explanations and moral beliefs. The person is therefore approached with respect and as someone quite capable of making decisions and taking responsibility for his/her life (i.e. able to respond to the givens and limitations of the human condition). Existential therapy at its best does not pathologise human dilemmas, neither does it offer technical solutions to them:

> The existential approach is well known for its anti-technique orientation. It prefers description, understanding and interpretation of reality to diagnosis, treatment and prognosis.
>
> (van Deurzen-Smith, 1990, p. 13)

It is to the existential tradition that Laing (1960), on the first page of his first book, *The Divided Self*, acknowledges his intellectual debt. Although he drew, in his own practice, upon a number of disciplines (particularly Eastern philosophies and spiritual traditions) and at one point considered describing his approach as "integral" (see Mullan, 1994), there is no doubt in my mind that the existential and phenomenological attitude (spirit) informed his work. He was always at pains in therapy to approach someone as a person to be accepted rather than an object to be changed. In his practice, he stressed the importance of providing a good presence for the other person (often someone in great distress) and attending[3] to his/her predicament. As Adrian Laing (1994) has pointed out in his recent biography of his father:

> Treatment, in Ronnie's eyes, meant how people treated other people. Listening to people was therefore treatment. Seeing patients as people was treatment.
>
> (Laing, 1994, p. 50)

And treating the other person as another *person*, with the full range of human capacities and vulnerabilities that that implies, was at the heart of his practice.

My own approach to therapy reflects what I have described in the preceding two paragraphs. It is an existential approach, but one highly influenced by Laing's writings, practice and being. It is, I believe, a more user-friendly approach to adolescents; one which can be experienced by them as akin to a good friendship. This was particularly highlighted in my work with one young woman called Ellen North-North-West.[4]

CASE STUDY

I first met Ellen informally in the summer of 1984.[5] At that time she was living in a West London therapeutic household sponsored by the

Philadelphia Association. One evening, Laing had been invited by the residents of the community to come for a meal and, on this occasion, he asked me to join him. My recollection is that it was quite a convivial get-together spent initially in round-table dinner discussion, followed by a musical melange in which Laing played piano and I played guitar. Ellen appeared to me as a tall thin young woman with long brown hair, who seemed to be an integral part of the community, but simultaneously exuded a fey and fragile quality that reminded me very much of the character "Nina" in Chekhov's *The Seagull*. I recall being struck by her capacity to harmonise well with some of the songs that I sang, particularly the ones by Simon and Garfunkel. I also remember her showing Laing, myself and the other five members of the house some of the paintings she had been doing at the time. I left with a feeling of an evening well spent and was invited back, over the course of the following year-and-a-half that the house lasted, on several occasions, to repeat the experience.

It was not until the beginning of 1985, shortly after her twenty-first birthday, that Ellen officially consulted me as a therapist. She was depressed about the way things had gone for her in the PA household. A couple of months before she came to see me she had taken an overdose of amitriptyline, resulting in her being hospitalised locally for a few days. (She had been discovered unconscious by Mary Barnes,[6] who happened to be staying in the community at that time.) The overdose followed the departure from the house of a young English male resident with whom she had been sexually involved for a few months after she had moved into the house in the Autumn of 1983. Initially the relationship had gone well but then, at a certain juncture, he seemed to turn on her, as well as the other residents of the community, and would threaten her with physical violence unless she continued to have sex with him. Ellen felt frightened, hurt and shaken by this experience and found it very difficult to cope with the very raw emotions it had engendered.

Shortly after she moved into the community Ellen began to see the house therapist for individual therapy sessions. However, she became progressively disillusioned with him over the course of her first year there. She felt, essentially, that he was hypocritical and weak and that when there was a real crisis in the household he didn't want to get involved. She thought that he had mishandled the situation with the young man mentioned above, and that he hadn't acted to properly protect her or the other residents from his violent behaviour. She finally decided to stop seeing him after he charged her father (who had been paying for Ellen's therapy) what she felt to be an exorbitant amount of money for visiting her at the hospital at the time of the overdose. Ellen took this as a sign that he was ultimately mercenary in his intentions, and didn't really care about her well-being at all. It was subsequent to these events that she came to see me. She had liked the contact she had with me on the few occasions I had been to the household and hoped that I would be able to really listen to her and understand her in a way that the other therapist had not.

Although Ellen's depression at the time she consulted me had been precipitated by the difficult inter-personal relations which were extant in the household, it had actually been in existence for some years previously. Probably the most emotionally significant event for her, in this regard, had been the death of her mother when Ellen was 17. She had died from a brain tumour (probably a craniopharyngioma) which had affected her speech and vision and left her partially paralysed. She had really been ill from the time Ellen was 11 years old, and during the last year of her life, Ellen, who had been close to her mother while she was alive, helped to look after her at home, and had been responsible for administering her medicine.

Ellen's mother was a Canadian of Scottish descent with a Presbyterian background. Her father was an Englishman, and they had met in Canada in 1946 and had married about a year later after returning to England. They had three children, Ellen being the youngest, with a brother (Paul) 9 years older and a sister (Marjory) 13 years her senior. Ellen was born on the east coast of England, but spent her early years living in Edinburgh. She described her mother as being a very warm, patient and creative woman, who had been a piano teacher before she married. She had also played the violin and painted in oils. Ellen felt that her mother had sacrificed a lot for the marriage and often suffered silently in it. She thought that the family revolved around her father's career (he had been a high-ranking officer in the armed forces). She recalled several occasions when she saw her mother in tears, and she was aware that her mother had been taking antidepressants for a number of years before she fell ill.

Following her mother's death, Ellen's father took early retirement and moved from the suburbs of North London to a small village near Cambridge. Ellen was not happy living with him during this period of time. He was overcome with grief at the death of his wife and, when confronted with any new difficulties, his pre-existent tendency to drink became full-blown. While under the influence of drink he was increasingly maudlin and depressed. This put an enormous strain on their relationship which, as Ellen pointed out, had always been problematic.

Her father was a proud and authoritarian man who had lived for his career. In this upper-middle class environment, he expected his children to behave in a disciplined manner and to avoid any family scandal which might be damaging to his reputation or career. Ellen told me that she often felt that he was treating her just like one of his subordinates. She had been quite rebellious during her teenage years, truanting from school, experimenting with soft drugs and just generally, as she put it, "being a constant thorn in his side". Ellen concedes that she felt an admixture of fear and hatred for her father during the periods of her later childhood and adolescence. Her dislike of anything connected with the military remains with her to this day.

Ellen's relationship with her brother Paul had been the one good experience during her early teenage years. He had, she felt, been a good friend to her. Paul's relationship with their father was equally fraught, and he moved away from the family setting when Ellen was 16, a year before their mother died. Ellen's sister Marjory was not around very much during this period of time. She had married (when Ellen was 11) and emigrated with her husband to Canada. While Ellen did visit her sister in Canada every 2 years or so, Marjory remained a distant figure during Ellen's adolescence.

Ellen's own early childhood and adolescence had been marred by serious illness. At the age of 5 it was discovered (following an emergency admission to hospital after an episode of gastro-internal bleeding) that she had a blocked portal vein, causing an enlargement of the liver and spleen as well as varices in the oesophagus, which resulted in recurrent and often life-threatening episodes of haematemesis (vomiting up blood) and the destruction of the blood cells and platelets (due to splenomegaly). This condition was thought to have been caused by an infection (possibly occurring around the time when the umbilical cord was cut) in early infancy.

Between the ages of 5 and 16, Ellen had multiple admissions to hospital, and this (combined with her father being restationed every 1–2 years) caused major disruptions to her education and early interpersonal relationships. She recalled feeling very distressed during one of her stays on a children's ward, because at that time it was not the hospital policy to allow parents to stay overnight there. At the age of 16, Ellen underwent surgery at a teaching hospital in North-west London. This procedure (oesophageal transectomy) successfully prevented any further major haemorrhages from recurring. In the months before she had surgery, she took an overdose of aspirin, which resulted in her being referred to the hospital child and adolescent psychiatrist, who then followed her up until she was 18. Ironically enough, she was considered for referral to the very adolescent unit where I was working at that time. She had a consultation with my Kleinian supervisor. However, the institutional atmosphere of the unit led her to reject this option.

Ellen had her first consultation with R.D. Laing at the age of 17 (a few months after her mother's death). He told her that there was very little he could do, because she was still a minor, and he advised her to go back to see him after her eighteenth birthday. She went to Canada for 6 months and when she returned in the Autumn of 1982, she saw him for a second time. On this occasion he referred her to a colleague, a woman therapist working in South London. Ellen saw her over the course of the next year, until the therapist recommended her to the Philadelphia Association household. After she moved in she stopped seeing this therapist, as she felt that the therapist's interpretations were often at odds with Ellen's own self-understanding.

By the time Ellen came to see me, then, she had had several bad experiences of psychotherapy and a number of negative encounters with psychiatrists, as well as being the object of scrutiny by numerous medical students because of her rare and anomalous medical condition. I felt, therefore, somewhat intuitively, that what she was looking for in the therapeutic relationship with me was something in the nature of a corrective experience that would offset the previous negative ones. Indeed, her desire was to find a therapist who would be like a trustworthy companion, i.e. someone who would attend to her, understand her and really care about her. This was at the heart of her search and was highlighted in one particular session which occurred toward the end of the therapy, and which I will describe anon.

The therapeutic work with Ellen lasted, essentially, for 5 years (from early 1985 to early 1990). It seemed to have three distinct phases. There was the initial period of the first year, in which Ellen continued to live in the PA household until its closure at the end of 1985. This was followed by the years 1986–8, in which Ellen felt strong enough to return to complete her education (she had left school at the age of 16 without any qualifications) and gain several "O" and "A" levels. Then there was the final part, in which she decided to continue her studies, enrolling in a BA programme in Literature and Philosophy at one of the North London Polytechnics (now a University). At this juncture, I made the decision to return to Canada, my native land.

During the first year of the therapeutic relationship, Ellen's approach to me was quite tentative and her appointments irregular, so that I had some doubts as to whether the therapy with her was going to "take". I also had some uncertainties and anxieties about her level of disturbance, which was exacerbated by her telling me that she had pulled a gun (thankfully a fake replica of a police revolver as it turned out!) on her previous therapist. (Unfortunately, being a resident in a Laingian community often carried with it the assumption of "psychotic" until proven otherwise. But I was to discover that Ellen was not "mad", but simply very angry.) Accordingly, in that first phase of our contact, in order to somehow galvanise our relationship, we would often end a session by singing a song together, as we had done when we first met at the household.

The focus in those early sessions was on the exploration and clarification of the often difficult emotions that arose in relation to the various people she lived with in the PA household, including her previous therapist and the male resident who had assaulted her. Ellen emerged in those meetings as a very sensitive soul with high ideals who often found it difficult to reconcile other people's behaviour with their stated beliefs. She couldn't understand these contradictions in others, and they appeared to her as hypocritical. Only gradually was she able to turn the lamp of scrutiny inward and begin to discover some of the same contradictions within herself, which were indeed very difficult for her to assimilate.

Another area of concern that revealed itself early on and caused deep existential anxiety was her physical being. Her body was at best unreliable, at worst, a living time bomb. As she said:

It is just like having the sword of Damocles hanging over my head—I never know when I am going to have another haemorrhage or when they are going to find something else wrong with my body.

Because she was exposed from a very early age to life-threatening illness, she was very much aware of her physical vulnerabilities and limitations (of her own mortality), and she felt that she really had no control over this dimension of her being.[7] Ellen's state of mind was particularly understandable since she had witnessed the long illness and early death of her mother. In addition to arousing anxiety about dying prematurely, this existential "given" (i.e. her illness) also led her to feel that she was unable to lead an ordinary life and would be incapable in the future of pursuing a career. Given all of the above, it was no wonder that the inevitable medical interventions (i.e. frequent blood transfusions, endoscopies, colonoscopies, sclerotherapy, etc.) were, more often than not, experienced by Ellen as being intrusive assaults on her body, mind and spirit.

Once Ellen had left the PA household and embarked on furthering her education, her concerns moved on. The second phase of our work together then ensued. One important area we discussed was Ellen's attraction to older men. Ellen had had one or two boyfriends in her late teens and early 20s, although the experience with the young man who had been resident in the PA household, had "put her off men" for some time. However, she often described older men in her circle of friends whom she was very fond of and liked. This attraction came to the foreground when Ellen was attending a college of further education (1986–8). One day she came to her session and told me that sometime during the previous week, she had been to see the school counsellor to ask his advice about some study-related problems she had been experiencing. She asked me if I had any objections to her seeing him from time to time. I replied that if she felt that seeing him would contribute to the new supportive network that she was trying to establish, then that was fine by me. What emerged out of this new situation was a growing attraction to this counsellor, who was a white male of 50 years old. Subsequently we spent many hours talking about the painful emotions that this situation brought up, and what might be the best way for Ellen to deal with these feelings. She thought that the attraction to this man (and older men in general) might be connected with her disappointing relationship with her father, and that she was attempting to make up for the affection she felt she had been deprived of or denied in her early life. During this period I pointed out to her that, given the nature of their contact, he was unlikely to reciprocate her feelings, or to act on them even if he did. Likewise, I stressed the ultimate uncertainty of life, especially in the area of human relations, as we do not have the same control over people as we have over other things.[8] I described to her my own experience of being in a context of unrequited love which, I believe, both made me a more real person to her and also gave her the feeling she was in the presence of someone who understood the particular nature of her suffering. Although there were times when she would ask me direct questions, such as, "Steve, what should I do?", I was always at pains to reflect this back to her and to point out that, difficult as the situation was, it was going to involve some hard decision-making on her part. Certainly I would explore with her what the existential possibilities were in this scenario, as well as the respective repercussions. But how she responded, was, in the end, ultimately her choice—I couldn't decide for her.

Ellen finally found the courage to tell the counsellor how she really felt about him. He responded by telling her that he was flattered, but also revealed to her that he was gay and had a partner of his own. However, he said that he was certainly willing to continue seeing her within a professional context if she so desired. Although she felt hurt, Ellen acknowledged to me that she thought that he had handled the situation very well. By the time she had completed her studies at this college, and was ready to leave, she decided that the best thing was simply not to have any further contact with him. This was a painful decision for her and occupied us for some time in subsequent sessions, but she gradually emerged the stronger for it.

During the final period of our therapeutic work together (1989–90), I made the decision to return to Canada. Ellen had enrolled on a BA programme in Literature and Philosophy in North London, and her life was moving on. She was sorry to hear that I was leaving. She felt that I had been a great help to her in her struggles and, in some sense, had enabled her to restore her faith in the psychiatric and psychotherapeutic professions. She told me that she was going to miss me a lot. For my part, I felt Ellen had really grown (even blossomed!) during the 5-year period of her therapy with me, and that the young woman who said good-bye to me in early 1990 was most definitely changed. She had certainly gained confidence in herself, especially in her capacity to face the often depressing and negative exigencies of life, and survive!

In one session toward the end, Ellen came in and told me that she was thinking of seeing a psychotherapist! There was something in the manner in which she said this which took me aback, and made me wonder how she had been perceiving me for the last 5 years. When I tried to explore this further with her, her response was immediate; "Why, Steve . . . you're my friend". On a superficial level it might be easy to discern why Ellen experienced me in this way—in some respects my behaviour toward her appeared no different than that of some of her ordinary acquaintances. But, upon refection I felt that she was really making a profound statement—that in her relationship with me, she had found something akin to a good friendship. And that that experience, i.e. of good friendship (albeit unidirectional), had been of great value to her (she was certainly aware that I had been her therapist).

DISCUSSION

This search on the part of young people for a therapeutic relationship akin to friendship is one that makes sense to them. It is my belief that an existentially-oriented psychotherapy (and one particularly informed by the writings of Laing) can go a long way toward meeting this need and, therefore, can be felt to be of value to them in their search for identity, autonomy and good relationships. Unfortunately, the notion of "therapist as friend" is one that generally does not sit well in the minds of most psychotherapists. Surely, it is argued, psychotherapy is something quite different from friendship and, besides, the latter doesn't require any professional training. Anyone can be a friend.

To a certain extent this is true. But what I am proposing is a re-examination of the generally held assumption of this difference and a reconsideration of the affinities that might exist between therapy and friendship. For if we are to take Spinelli's project of the demystification of psychotherapy seriously (as well as, I would equally argue, the task of its humanization),[9] then we need to be careful that our very professionalisation does not take us too far afield in the diametrically opposed direction.

R.D. Laing (1985) has argued in his last published book, *Wisdom, Madness and Folly*, that:

It seems to me that what is professionally called a "therapeutic relationship" cannot exist without a primary camaraderie being present and manifest

(Laing, 1985, p. 28),

and Rollo May (1967) has pointed out that:

One of my own teachers, the late Dr Freida Fromm-Reichman, used to have a tremendous ability for relating as one existence communicating to another. What she used to tell us analytical students was that the patient does not need an explanation, he needs an experience

(May, 1967, p. 10)

Might not this experience at the end of the day be something akin to friendship?

POSTSCRIPT

In the process of preparing for this chapter, I decided to contact Ellen to let her know that I was planning to write about my work with her and to get her permission for doing so. Through what Marcus Aurelius might have described as a strange concatenation of fortuitous circumstances, I discovered that she was now living in my home town—Toronto, Canada! She had completed her BA in Literature and Philosophy and had decided to embark on a two-year MA programme in information sciences at the university there. She was planning to stay there for another year and then return to England. She was living in the postgraduate residence and, on the whole, felt reasonably all right, except that she wondered how I had survived all those cold winters there during my youth. Relations with her father had improved, and she was now concerned that he was getting older, living on his own, and had no-one there really to look after him.

She was still single but had become emotionally involved with one of the tutors from her previous BA programme. She felt it wasn't a good situation as he was married and unlikely to leave his wife. She was in the process of gradually trying to extricate herself from the relationship, which was proving to be particularly difficult as this tutor actually reciprocated her feelings and was writing her letters from England declaring his love for her. However, the distance of Canada and the pressure to apply herself to her second year of postgraduate studies were abetting the process. She was glad to hear from me, thanked me again for all the help I had given her in the past and freely agreed to my writing about her.

I thanked her, in my turn, for her permission to do so and wished her the best for the future.

DISCUSSION WITH THE EDITOR

SIMON: I'm interested in your reaction to the psychotherapy you saw on offer in an NHS adolescent unit in the late 1970s, as I was involved with a therapeutic community in the mid-1980s and found the therapy available then to be very much about treatment rather than assisting someone to negotiate a problem of living. Do you think that things have moved on in recent years or does a medical model approach still hold sway?

STEVE: My experience of psychotherapy in the NHS in general, and in the adolescent unit where I worked in particular, was that it presented itself, very much as you describe it, as treatment (or cure)-oriented, and also, I would add, as somewhat conformist in nature. The medical model very much held sway and I don't think things have changed much in this regard. I suppose this is not surprising if you keep in mind the nature of the setting and the fact that the therapy on offer was predominantly psychodynamic. Historically, psychoanalysis has always subscribed to the notion of "psycho-pathology" (e.g. Freud's "General Theory of the Neuroses" in his *Introductory Lectures on Psychoanalysis* being a case in point), and doesn't seem to have found the concept of "mental illness" intrinsically problematic. Within the existential/phenomenological tradition I think there has been some ambivalence about this matter, so that you find therapists like Medard Boss, Rollo May, and Irving Yalom still utilising psychopathological concepts. This is where the work of Laing and Cooper, here in England, has been most instructive, as they were really the first existential psychiatrists to clearly question the medical model. This is why I have found the writing of more recent existential/phenomenological therapists like Emmy van Deurzen and Ernesto Spinelli refreshing, as they both seem to eschew notions of "treatment" and "mental illness".

SIMON: What do you make of the concept of "acting out"? I have always found it rather odd and something which distances the therapist from the client.

STEVE: In this regard, I find a concept like "acting out", drawn from the pschoanalytic tradition, unpalatable, because it again presupposes the concept of "psychopathology" (which is what is assumed to be "acted out"). I agree that the concept is distancing, but what is even more so is pathologising tendency which underlies it and creates a huge divide between the supposedly "healthy therapist" who doesn't "act out" and the "mad" (if not bad) client who behaves in ways that are alienating and disturbing to the therapist and has to suffer the latter's judging disapproval (disguised as a psychoanalytic interpretation).

SIMON: I very much like the idea that the client needs an experience rather than an explanation. It seems to me that we therapists are very rarely in a position to explain anything to our clients. While we might assist them to clarify their thoughts and feelings to the point that they are able to achieve new, perhaps "better" explanations for themselves, in general when we offer explanations our motivation is to do with our fear of being with clients and our wish to keep a distance by taking the "expert" role, Ellen, already sensitive to anything hypocritical, would, I'm sure, have picked up on this in a trice.

STEVE: I think this is why I came to the conclusion, while working as a psychiatric registrar in the adolescent unit, that what young people were looking for in therapy was much more in the nature of an experience than an explanation. More often than not they found it hard to relate to someone who seemed cold, distant and unfriendly, and only offered them psychoanalytic interpretations of their supposedly "acting out" behaviour which didn't make a lot of sense to them anyway. They seemed to be looking for the kind of relationship in which they felt accepted, validated and understood.

SIMON: Is such a relationship just for adolescents and young people—couldn't we all benefit from it?

STEVE: Yes, in a sense, this may be what we are all looking for, but I think it applies most poignantly in adolescence and young adulthood, where family and friends may be found wanting and experiences of therapy few and far between.

SIMON: There is a tension, though, isn't there, between being a friend and being a therapist? The way you met Ellen seems to have helped you to forge a more friendship-like relationship. My sense is that when people are referred or self-refer to me they are not looking for a friend and neither am I, so to go down a friendship road would be unauthentic. At the same time I find your notion of camaraderie enormously appealing, not least because it conjures for me the idea of fellow-travellers on a journey of exploration.

STEVE: It strikes me that this kind of relationship, for which a young person is looking with the therapist, comes close to what that person would call a "good friendship". This does not imply (and here I would agree with you) that when someone comes to see me in therapy I'm looking to become friends with them. Certainly *my* desire for friendship needs to be suspended. But the other person may experience my therapeutic attention as friendship. And I think this is what happened with Ellen. In me she found someone who treated her as another human being, not as an alien object needing to be cured of "psychopathology". As a result of my attentiveness to her she found she could open up to me, and her experience of this, which she found helpful, led her to feel that I was her friend.

But perhaps it is here that the notion of camaraderie takes on a certain importance and may be the more appropriate term. For it does conjure up, as you say, the notion of a fellow-traveller, someone with whom you feel a certain connection, who shares something in common with you.

There is a discipline at the heart of therapy which I believe (as did Laing) is very much connected to these notions of "camaraderie" and "attending to" (somewhat like Spinelli's notions of "being with" and "being for" the client) and which should stand as the centrepiece of all existential psychotherapy.

NOTES

1. I had also spent a year (1974) as personal assistant to David Cooper, one of Laing's colleagues. It was Laing and Cooper who, in the 1960s, had provided the most trenchant critique of traditional psychiatry here in England and were identified as the country's foremost existential psychiatrists.
2. Now based in London NW3.
3. The Greek word *therapeia*, from which our modern-day term "therapy" is derived, has this connotation of "attending to".
4. The reference here is both to Ludwig Binswanger's study, "The case of Ellen West", in R. May et al. (1958), *Existence*. New York: Simon and Schuster; and to Shakespeare's *Hamlet*: "I am mad north-north-west, but when the wind blows southerly, I can tell a hawk from a handsaw".
5. In Laingian circles it was not uncommon to meet a prospective client in such circumstances as these and also to continue to have some form of social contact, e.g. at seminars, house parties, etc. For an interesting discussion of this, see Haya Oakley's chapter in R. Cooper (1989). *Thresholds in Philosophy and Psychoanalysis: Papers of the Philadelphia Association*. London: Free Associations.
6. Mary Barnes was one of the first residents in Kingsley Hall, the first therapeutic community sponsored by the Philadelphia Association. Her experiences are recounted in M. Barnes and J. Berke (1972) *Two Accounts of a Journey Through Madness*. Harmondsworth: Penguin; and M. Barnes (1988) *Something Sacred*. London: Free Associations.
7. This dimension is subsumed by Binswanger's term *Umwelt*.
8. See Jean-Paul Sartre's (1956) discussion of the essential distinction between "Being-in-itself" and "Being-for-itself", in Chapter 1 of *Being and Nothing*. New York: Pocket Books.
9. I believe we need to make the therapeutic encounter as human (as distinct from humanistic) as possible.

REFERENCES

Cohen, H. (1994). What is existential psychotherapy. *British Journal of Psychiatry*, **165**, 699–701.

Hoeller, K. (1990). *Readings in Existential Psychology and Psychiatry*. Seattle: REPP.

Laing, A. (1994). *R.D. Laing: A Biography*, p. 50. London: Peter Owen.

Laing, R.D. (1985). *Wisdom, Madness, and Folly*, p. 28. London: Macmillan.

Laing, R.D. (1960). *The Divided Self*. Harmondsworth: Penguin.

May, R. (1967). *Existential Psychotherapy*, p. 10. Toronto: CBC.

May, R. (1983) (1983). *The Discovery of Being*. London: W.W. Norton.

Mullan, B. (1994). *Mad to be Normal: Conversations with R.D. Laing*, p. 327. London: Free Associations.

Spinelli, E. (1989). *The Interpreted World*. London: Sage.

Spinelli, E. (1994). *Demystifying Psychotherapy*, p. 78. London: Constable.

van Deurzen-Smith, E. (1988). *Existential Counselling in Practice*. London: Sage.

van Deurzen-Smith, E. (1990). *Existential Therapy*, p. 13. London: Society for Existential Analysis Publications.

3

THE CASE OF BERNADETTE—THE TYRANNY OF "SEDIMENTATION"

Freddie Strasser
Regent's College, London, UK

INTRODUCTION

"Sedimentation" is an unusual word. In its everyday meaning, "sediment" is described as "the matter that settles at the bottom of the liquid" (*Webster's International Dictionary*), while "sedimentation" means the action or process of depositing those sediments.

Sedimentation for existential therapy is a concept derived from phenomenology. Essentially, it is the way we humans become stuck or fixed in certain beliefs and behaviour patterns. These patterns deposit themselves deep down in our belief system in the way that sediment settles at "the bottom of the liquid". Our value and behaviour patterns may become integrated into the way we operate on a day-to-day basis and may become "sedimented" to such a degree that they appear immovable. Since most of the time we are unaware that these patterns exist, they can be extremely difficult to unlearn. Yet, according to the phenomenological perspective, no sedimented patterns needs to be immutable. Spinelli writes:

Case Studies in Existential Psychotherapy and Counselling. Edited by S. du Plock
© 1997 John Wiley & Sons Ltd

Novelty implies temporality. With the passage of time and, possibly, with the lessening of the anxiety that externally imposed novelties induce, the novelty may become accepted, even highly valued, and itself become part of a new sedimented framework.

(Spinelli, 1989, p. 52)

Part of the process of brief existential therapy is to facilitate clients to challenge their own sedimentations and, by doing so, enable them to change, if necessary, their exaggerated sedimented behaviour patterns. It is important, however, to remember that sedimented behaviour patterns and values do not necessarily impute negative meanings. On the contrary, most of them can be positive. They could be equated so strongly embedded habits that are culturally imposed on us. For example, sedimented values that are culturally prevalent, such as loyalty, honesty, ambition, perfection and material well-being, can be very helpful to achieve successes, ambitions and skilful interaction within society. It is when those sedimentations become so rigid and exaggerated that they become compulsive, that they become serious impediments in our lives.

THE CLIENT

The case of Bernadette is such an example. She was an attractive young woman in her 30s. I ushered her into my consulting room and she leaned back in her chair, silent, not knowing what to say. I waited, preferring her to choose the opening. After a minute's silence, I began to talk about what I believed the first meeting should be concerned with, seeing that she felt it more appropriate that I begin the session. I explained that this meeting was an exploratory session where we could both decide whether we could work together and how we could best do this. We would also examine our expectations of the outcome and she was free to ask any questions about the process of therapy.

During the first few sessions Bernadette soon revealed her life story. She was the second child of a family of three siblings. She had been brought up in a conservative, religious family in a European Mediterranean country. While her initial mannerisms did not reveal any trace of religious fervour, there remained a strong residue of religious faith that manifested itself in unquestioningly accepting the dictates of the patriarchal hierarchy. There was an underlying inference that she expected total submission to some kind of authority, be it a person or a more nebulous "something". Although she avoided speaking about God's wishes and power, there was a strong belief in the background of an omnipotent authority that would reward good behaviour.

Her father's profession meant that he was constantly away from home, while her mother, in the Mediterranean fashion, looked after the children. Nevertheless, her mother came across as a mere appendage to her husband, who left Bernadette feeling neglected. At this point she spoke with respect and understanding, rationalising her father's behaviour towards her. Yet, I also had the impression that she felt unjustly treated and believed he loved her less than her two sisters. I believed that relationships within the family were underpinned to some extent by the cultural ethos of the environment in which she grew up. It was quite natural for her that her father spent very little time at home, that in spite of this he was the authority in the house and that her mother was only carrying out her husband's wishes.

As a child, Bernadette felt ostracised and an outsider within her family. This was backed up by several revelations that also exposed some of her raw feelings. For example, she felt picked on when her father was at home, whereas he always approved and acknowledged her sisters' behaviour. She remembered distinctly that her older sister Sarah was particularly bright at school and a good communicator with both her parents and her peers. Bernadette, on the other hand, was just the opposite. She was constantly reprimanded in her elementary school for not following the lessons, and she felt a subordinate and an inadequate member of the family. By the age of 10 she felt utterly excluded from her home, her siblings and her peer groups.

One vivid memory was Bernadette's encounter with "a big, stern and very elegantly dressed man in black attire—the doctor". This was a psychiatrist she had been taken to see. By the time she returned from her examination she knew, without a doubt, that she was "psychotic". For her, at the early age of 11, this was not only a confirmation that she was a peculiar child, but in addition she had the label of an ill child. This one visit to the doctor had given her the reason for her rejection and seclusion from others. Between the ages of 11 and 17 Bernadette attended high school, where she experienced similar difficulties to those at home. The sense of rejection by her peers and problems with her schoolwork helped to maintain her feelings of low self-esteem and her perception of herself as an outsider. Despite this, Bernadette managed to keep her spirits up and scraped through her exams. Yet by the time she reached the end of High School she broke down and attempted suicide. She was subsequently taken to hospital and referred to a psychotherapist. The relationship between Bernadette and her therapist developed into a very deep, caring and understanding one. She describes the therapy, which lasted for two years, as "One of my best experiences of love and caring".

However, the therapy had to be abruptly curtailed when the therapist was admitted to a mental hospital.

Bernadette manifested her strengths again, for in spite of all her trials, she managed to get into university. After several unsuccessful relationships, she met Jose, a fellow student, and married him at the age of 21, while she was studying. Jose decided to study for his PhD in London and Bernadette joined him. She found work teaching foreign languages, which she greatly enjoyed.

When Bernadette talked about her presenting problems, she became noticeably more tense and nervous. Her life seemed burdened with fears. She feared talking to people, being in the dark, and she was terrified of nightmares. Her presenting issues centred on her anxiety, having left her husband and established a new relationship. She had met Malcolm, who, she felt, was the first person to understand her and with whom she might have her first real loving relationship. She left her marriage in spite of Jose's endeavour to keep her. Jose could not comprehend the situation, but he eventually accepted it and they divorced.

After the early "honeymoon" period, however, the relationship between Bernadette and Malcolm deteriorated rapidly. The first serious crisis occurred after Bernadette had an abortion, which left her deeply depressed. This was very much exacerbated by Malcolm's neglectful attitude towards her and the fact that he hardly visited her in hospital. All these issues threw her into a deep abyss and she suffered from insomnia. She felt rejected once again.

It took two sessions for Bernadette to recount her narrative. It usually takes me one or two sessions to agree the frame and the contract for the therapy. I consider this process as the preliminary (buffer zone) to therapy. Since Bernadette and I had not concluded the contract yet, I explained to her that there was still a need to discuss such questions of payment, commitment, frequency, and any questions she might have. I also told her that I felt that we could work together, but left it to Bernadette to consider my suitability for her therapy. Following this, we discussed the way in which we would work and the expectations we both had of the therapy. In answer to one of her questions, I explained to Bernadette that she could disclose, in confidence, everything and anything that was troublesome or problematic for her; she should also try to be open and honest and treat me as if I were her alter ego. My interactions would help her explore and illuminate her thinking and illustrate any discrepancies and contradictions that might arise. This in itself might initiate a process of self-inquiry that she could continue between sessions and after the termination of the therapy. After a few more questions and her agreement to commit herself we agreed on every point.

THERAPY

The Search for Bernadette's Value System

During the next six sessions Bernadette spoke of her fears and the isolation she had experienced in her early youth. Yet, when isolated fragments of certain events emerged, Bernadette had a habit of becoming side-tracked. For example, she talked about an event when her father had come home from work and had reprimanded Bernadette on her eating habits. She felt that he was simply picking on her, which was in direct contrast to the treatment that Sarah, her older sister, received. Sarah was always praised. When I prompted Bernadette to expand on this and to express her feelings, she changed the subject very skilfully. She began to talk about her husband and when this became too difficult she switched to yet another topic. Using this evasive technique, she was able to bring a whole host of issues into one session and yet none of them could be properly explored. I constantly challenged this behaviour pattern by pointing out what she was doing and gradually she began to focus on one issue at a time.

During this phase, Bernadette routinely demanded answers and advice. For example, she was experiencing great difficulties in her relationship with Malcolm. He would not allow Bernadette to stay in his flat, but expected to stay at Bernadette's house. Bernadette was hesitant to accept this and insisted on getting a clear-cut direction from me. After many challenges and reiterating that my advice was not part of our contract, I asked her to put herself in my position and to try to answer her own questions. This method was successful, and Bernadette arrived at her own conclusion that my advice would only mean a collusion with her behaviour and would perpetuate her reliance on me and on others. She added that advice "can be dangerous because nobody knows better than myself the risks involved". This incident brought us somewhat closer to one another.

Bernadette then embarked on an exploration of her problems by clarifying and looking at each of them from various angles. At around the sixth session, she began to focus on her feelings of isolation and loneliness. She connected this to her fear of communicating and recollected how terrified she had been when her father flew into a rage because she had not or could not behave as he wanted. Bernadette could not study well and found it difficult to mix with her peers. Yet, through her parental influences she began to believe in the same value judgements; that to be accepted and liked one had to be a good student, an obedient child and jovial company. In spite of vigorous attempts Bernadette could not live up to this standard.

Indeed, the more she could not conform the more pressure was exerted on her to comply with her family's values. It was therefore no surprise that since her early youth, Bernadette had felt ostracised and rejected by her family and others. This feeling was accentuated by that ominous visit to the psychiatrist which reinforced her belief that she must be psychotic. She felt utterly lost and isolated.

The Coping Strategy

In order to survive, Bernadette withdrew into her private world and strived to keep others out of her life. Externally, however, she made every effort to comply with her family's value system. She tried to be pleasant and cheerful within the family, yet the more she endeavoured, the more she felt excluded. This in turn threw Bernadette into a deeper depression, a depression marked with feelings of loneliness and a low sense of self, akin to being in a bottomless black hole. It is not surprising that at the age of 17 she attempted suicide by overdosing on the tablets her psychiatrist had given her seven years previously and which she kept in her cupboard. There then ensued a period of 18 months of a caring relationship with the very "nice and kind" psychiatrist, which only came to an end with his admission to hospital. Bernadette was forced to separate from the only person from whom she had experienced real care and love.

The Sedimentation of Values

In the process of relating the event of her attempted suicide and separation from her therapist, she revealed a great deal of emotion. The sessions became very painful for Bernadette. She cried and showed her anger towards me when I challenged her to stay with her emotions. There were moments when I felt uneasy and feared that I had overloaded her with challenges. I was afraid that she would leave therapy. Nevertheless, Bernadette diligently continued to work hard, both in clarifying and describing her feelings.

She gradually realised that her anger towards me reflected her own defence mechanism that she used to avoid painful disclosures. At around the same time, Bernadette also began to discuss her value system, namely that to be an accepted person she should be "sociable" and a "good student". She saw how these values had gradually and imperceptibly become more rigid and dogmatic until they became her only accepted way of being a "good" person. When this happens, as described above, they are called, in phenomenological terms, "sedimented values".

Sedimentation of Coping Habits

During the following sessions Bernadette discussed her continuing fear of expressing her needs and the way she always submitted to others, especially those people who represented figures of authority. This was not only exemplified in her relationship with me, but also in her sexual submissiveness with Jose. We discussed at length through many sessions her difficulties in expressing her needs, even to me. She had realised that she simply could not tell Malcolm what she desired and what she wanted from him. Following this, she began to speak freely of her sexuality and that she felt something was missing in terms of her love life. While Malcolm was more considerate in his sexual approach to Bernadette than anyone before him, she still found it difficult to reach orgasm. I began pointing out the contradictions of both wanting a perfect relationship and checking herself from expressing her emotional and physical needs. These two desires were mutually exclusive.

Gradually, Bernadette began to realise that her patterns of withdrawal, pleasing others and ignoring her own needs were so ingrained in her behaviour that she was not only unaware of them happening, but also that they served to prevent the recurrence of her depression, loneliness and to some extent low self-esteem. Through pleasing others and withholding her own needs Bernadette managed to stave off rejection and thus maintain her self-esteem. Her sedimented coping strategy was also apparent in the therapeutic relationship and as I carefully guided her through this, she became aware of her difficulty in expressing any disapproval towards me. Nevertheless, however much these behaviour patterns and belief systems are rigidly sedimented, they can be always opened up and unlearned. As Spinelli states:

> . . . phenomenological investigation demonstrates that, once our sedimented outlook is "opened up", numerous perceptual possibilities become available which can be repeatedly turned to for experiential verification.
>
> (Spinelli, 1989, p. 55)

While Bernadette was ready to challenge her outlook at this stage of her therapy, she was, however, not ready as yet to change her behaviour patterns.

Self-concept

Between the sixteenth and twentieth sessions it became increasingly apparent that she was unable to communicate her needs. I continually challenged Bernadette to contemplate what would happen if she had the courage to disclose her desire to develop a closer relationship with Malcolm. She was terrified of rejection, which she described in terms of total annihilation, loneliness, disconnectedness and a self-concept that would amount to nil. I felt that this period was the most difficult for Bernadette. She remembered many of her painful experiences and the hurt she had felt. I, too, found it difficult to extricate myself from being totally devastated. I felt her isolation and utter disconnectedness from the world. It was hard for me to disentangle myself from Bernadette's pain and to view the situation from another perspective. I knew it was important for me to understand Bernadette's world, but also to be objective in order to open up her perception of the world. This was vital for me if I was to hear the discrepancies and contradictions that were emerging, and to point them out to Bernadette.

Compulsion

In the following sessions it transpired that although her compulsion to please others and her feelings of disconnectedness continued, there was a noticeable difference in that she was aware of what she was doing.

During the twentieth session she spoke of her impending holiday, during which she would visit her family. She felt apprehension about meeting her father. She was afraid of rejection, not only by her father but also by Malcolm. When I asked her whether she could hypothetically imagine a state of loneliness that would be desirable, she announced, after two minutes of silence: "If only I could do that, then I would be totally free". This led us into an exploration of how her depression and loneliness might have a positive function.

Rollo May has an interesting view of such despair. He says:

> When a person has hit bottom—i.e. when he has reached ultimate despair—he then can surrender to eternal forces; this is the dynamic of all authentic conversions. I would describe this process as giving up the delusion of false hopes and, thus, acknowledging fully the fact of destiny. Then and only then can this person begin to rebuild himself. It is a superb demonstration of the hypothesis that freedom begins only when we confront destiny.
>
> (May, 1989, p. 236)

The holiday proved to be disastrous. She decided that she would be more open and told her father about her relationship with Malcolm. He reacted by announcing that unless she either married or ended the relationship, he would have nothing more to do with her. This threw Bernadette and she was plunged into depression. Three weeks later she arrived with a large parcel containing a striking portrait of a woman. As she took out the painting she said, "Now I know that even if I am in the depth of my aloneness I am not alone, I still have myself". I was astonished to hear this paradoxical existential statement. We referred very often to this revelation during the remainder of the course of therapy. Bernadette had decided to pursue her desire to paint and had begun taking evening classes. She had always known that she could paint, but had never dared, as she was afraid that her family "would find her work ridiculous". She found solace in her painting and furthermore realised that it served an additional purpose, in that it made her less lonely.

She had also plucked up enough courage to speak to Malcolm about her needs and had decided that she would only stay with him if he could work towards meeting them. She was asking for a different emotional and more permanent relationship. Malcolm behaved ambiguously towards Bernadette. On the one hand he told her that he loved her and could not live without her, on the other hand he had started to visit her less frequently and still did not allow her to stay overnight in his flat.

Ending

This was the period during which Bernadette challenged herself about her fear of separation and loneliness. She and Malcolm finally separated and she found that the loneliness was not as hard to endure as she had expected, finding solace in her painting and our weekly sessions. She used this time to express her feelings through her paintings and in the process gained a new energy. In its turn this was expressed on canvas.

We also talked about discontinuing the therapy, agreed on a date for that and moved from weekly to fortnightly sessions. Bernadette realised that our parting was her choice and not a rejection. Four sessions before the end she met Kevin, who not only lived out of town but was a workaholic; to see him she would have to travel. They fell in love and Bernadette spent much time discussing Kevin and our impending separation.

Between one of our sessions, Bernadette telephoned me one day, wanting to see me urgently. Although I argued with her to wait until our next session, she insisted on visiting me as soon as possible. I hesitated, but agreed to see her the following day. She arrived in a state of agitation and recounted how she had discovered that Kevin was having an affair with his landlady. Following a long telephone conversation with him she decided to visit at the weekend, making it clear that she would stay in a hotel. Although Bernadette was very upset, we were still able to explore her relationship with Kevin from a number of angles. She argued with herself whether or not to visit him, and related this to another possible rejection and her dread of the consequent loneliness. It was a difficult session for Bernadette, but she was prepared to take the risk in refusing to visit Kevin, even if it might result in a separation and subsequent loneliness.

In our next session she told me she had telephoned Kevin to say that she had decided not to visit him. Instead, if he wanted to talk to her, he could come to London. Kevin decided to come and they had spent time exploring and discussing their relationship.

Two sessions later we concluded the course of therapy.

DISCUSSION

First, I would like to point out my own existential/phenomenological approach to this case. I hope that my description of it demonstrates how much of the therapy revolved around clarification and exploration of phenomena that emerged from the client, and that all my interventions were strictly those of either prompting or challenging phenomenologically her perceptions. I tried as far as possible to avoid interpretations that were coloured by my own issues and prejudices. I attempted to suspend all my assumptions and to intervene only when I believed it to be in Bernadette's interest. This approach is in harmony with the phenomenological rule of "époque" or "bracketing". In keeping with the process of exploring through phenomenological investigation, my expectation of the therapeutic outcome was for Bernadette to clarify certain issues both during the therapy and between sessions, as well as after the termination of therapy.

Bernadette was able to clarify her values and her world-views. She realised that already in her early youth she had developed a fixed, relatively stagnant view of the world in order to feel accepted. During therapy we established an open and trusting relationship by which Bernadette felt comfortable in challenging her value system and her coping strategies (her paradoxical behaviour patterns, withdrawing or pleasing others). These had both become part of her sedimented belief system to such an extent that they were totally ingrained in the way she presented herself to the outside world. It was also intensely difficult for Bernadette to accustom herself to the process, because her one initial aim had been to eliminate all her anxieties through getting explicit directions from me as her therapist. This was obviously an unrealistic objective.

Although our journey was characterised by great difficulties, and included pain and joy, we both consciously entered into a special relationship—a relationship that is best described by Martin Buber's "I–Thou" sense of being. This is a reciprocal relation where we both influence and change each other. Buber describes that we are: "Inscrutably involved, we live in the currents of universal reciprocity" (Buber, 1960). Emmy van Deurzen in *Existential Counselling in Practice* (1988), explains this in the light of a therapeutic relationship. This is an endeavour to establish an I–Thou therapist–client relationship to facilitate clients "to build an I–You relationship with themselves". This is a unifying project that the author calls an "I–Me" relationship (1988). van Deurzen describes:

> In the unity of the shared project individual differences become unimportant for the moment. All that stands out is the awareness of an underlying motive that binds people together. The energy and enthusiasm generated in such a moment of merging with an absolute notion of one's own destiny can be considerable. Many religions, especially more primitive ones, build their ceremonies around this type of experience. Healing rituals do the same thing.
>
> (van Deurzen-Smith, 1988, p. 209)

In the process of therapy Bernadette challenged and began to come to terms with her fear of loneliness and loss of self-esteem. She acknowledged her pain and connected this to her total sense of nothingness and her fear of annihilation. Through this sense of despair she gradually realised that she did have choices: it was within her power to choose her attitude towards her sense of nothingness and to choose her coping strategies, the way she regarded her values and her life as a whole.

It is interesting to note that Bernadette in some way needed to plunge into the abyss, to dive into the depths of nothingness in order to emerge as an "authentic" person. This type of emergence from nothingness to authenticity is described in detail by Heidegger (1962) in *Being and Time*, where authenticity and our awareness of our finitude are closely related. Death is closely related to nothingness. Heidegger says that by accepting the encounter with nothingness, we can muster and organise our possibilities in life. In other words, at this point we can then project ourselves into the future.

Although Bernadette entered therapy expecting an instant cure and explicit advice, she gradually realised that these were unrealistic hopes. Therapy is comparable to a learning process of self-exploration; to a journey that does not terminate, but continues long after the therapy concludes. Bernadette realised that ending need not mean rejection, for she acknowledged that concluding our sessions did not mean that I had stopped caring about her.

DISCUSSION WITH THE EDITOR

SIMON: This concept of "sedimentation" seems to have appeared in the existential literature quite recently but it has clearly filled a gap in our terminology and many practitioners now use it as a matter of course. What was its genesis?

FREDDIE: "Sedimentation" and "époche" (bracketing) both stem from the original concept that was originated by Brentano and taken over by Husser (1960). Both these questions are closely related to the concept of "intentionality".

"Intentionality" represents the relationship between our consciousness and what extends beyond it. In other words, Brentano argued that for human beings, consciousness is always to be conscious of something. Husserl has accepted this notion, from Brentano, and has suggested also that the most basic interpretative action of our consciousness is to identify something. He further expanded this notion and suggested that every act of intentionality consists of two sides of a correlation. Sedimentation and bracketing, "intentionality", Brentano's and Husserl's connection, are explained by Mary Warnock (1970); Raymond McCəll (1983) and Ernesto Spinelli (1994).

Ihde (1986) discusses the phenomenological investigation of that which Husserl termed as "noema" or a "noematic correlate" (that which is experienced) and for the mode of experiencing it he used the terms "noesis" or "noetic correlate". Ihde (1986, p. 43) wrote, "If I experience at all, I experience something in some way". In other words, when a human being experiences something, then the correlate of *what* is experienced is the noema. On the other hand, noesis is the correlate of *how* it is experienced. The important factor, however, again as Ihde (1986) states, is that "the experience has its directional and referential focus, it is intentional".

Furthermore, a human being can, in a noetic context, experience objects in different ways. For example, the Rubin's vase/face object can be experienced as either only a face, only a vase, or both. When a belief focuses only on one possibility, Ihde called this a sedimented belief, which can or cannot be abandoned. On the other hand, a view that is allowing experience of both the vase and the face, is called "polymorphic". Ernesto Spinelli (1984) writes: Sedimental beliefs may provide (illusory) security and a (seeming) order to our world views, but it is polymorphic-mindedness which allows for personal and cultural advancements" (Spinelli, 1989, p. 53).

To answer your question about the genesis of sedimentation, I would refer you again to the work of Ernesto Spinelli (1989) in his *Interpreted World*, where he deals extensively with this notion. The onset of the notion, however, I believe, stems from Husser (1960) and Merleau-Ponty (1962). van Deurzen (1997) writes in her book *Everyday Mysteries*:

> Sometimes truth gets defined by use as if it were set and definite and, again following Husserl's work, Merleau-Ponty refers to this process as sedimentation: the acting as if truth is stagnant and knowable. Sedimented truth is the quasi-truth that has become deposited as if it were solid.
>
> (van Deurzen, 1997)

van Deurzen (1997, p. 66) goes further than that when she speaks of Merleau-Ponty's concept of projection that emphasises the opposite of sedimentation, redefines it in terms of future use and experience of the world.

SIMON: Can you remind me what "époche" and "bracketing" refer to—they are obviously key concepts in the existential way of working.

FREDDIE: Husserl rejected the concept that a meaningful understanding of knowledge can be deduced from the accumulation of facts, theories, classifications and hypotheses. According to him, scientific predictions or improvement of technologies do not bring us nearer to an understanding of the world. Husserl believed that there is an original insight through which undistorted things reveal themselves, and that phenomenology offers us access to such an insight. The route is via a strict discipline of transcendental reduction ("époche") whereby one suspends, puts aside or "into brackets", all the given empirical facts: the results of science; the very existence of the world; other people and, even, one's own ego.

This type of reduction, according to Husserl, to free oneself from all prejudices concerning both the world and the subject, was a necessary operation on the way to reach certainty. Through "bracketing", the world and the ego are reduced and as such became devoid of values, judgements and dichotomy, which are inescapable in an empirical world. Husserl maintained that such a reduction gives us access to direct intuition or in Kolakowski's terms, "to unshakeable evidence of certitude" or, in Husserl's (1960) own words: "to return to an intuitive experience". Husserl, in *Cartesian Meditations* (1960, p. 25) writes:

> But phenomenological époche . . . inhibits acceptance of the objective world as existent, and thereby excludes this world completely from the field of judgement.

In practice terms, needless to say, in therapy the aim for the therapist is to try to suspend all the his/her prejudices, judgements and preconceived ideas as far as possible. I believe, and maybe you could agree with me, that total époche is impossible to achieve, yet I also hold that bracketing can help therapists to stop and think before interventions.

REFERENCES

Buber, M. (1960). *I and Thou*. Edinburgh: T. & T. Clarke.

Heidegger, M. (1962). *Being and Time*. Oxford: Basil Blackwell.

Husserl, E. (1960). *Cartesian Meditations*. The Hague: Nijhoff.

Ihde, D. (1986). *Experimental Phenomenology*. New York: State University of New York Press.

Kolakowski, L. (1975). *Husserl and the Search for Certitudes*. Chicago: University of Chicago Press.

Merleau-Ponty, M. (1962). *Phenomenology of Perception* (transl. C. Smith). London: Routledge and Kegan Paul.

May, R. (1989). *Freedom and Destiny*. New York: Delta.

McCall, R.J. (1983). *Phenomenological Psychology*. London and Madison: University of Wisconsin Press.

Spinelli, E. (1989). *The Interpreted World*. London: Sage.

Spinelli, E. (1994). *The Demystifying Therapy*. London: Constable.

van Deurzen-Smith, E. (1988). *Existential Counselling in Practice*. London: Sage.

van Deurzen, E. (1997). *Everyday Mysteries*. London: Routledge.

Warnock, M. (1970). *Existentialism*. Oxford: Oxford University Press.

4

ROBERTO: LIVING WITH HIV—ISSUES OF MEANING AND RELATIONSHIP IN HIV-RELATED PSYCHOTHERAPY

Martin Milton
Department of Psychology, University of Surrey, Guildford, UK

INTRODUCTION

In this chapter I describe some work that was undertaken with a young man who was trying to accustom himself to several different changes. He hadn't long been diagnosed as HIV-positive and had recently settled in London. I understood the work to be primarily about helping him clarify what his experiences, both past and present, meant. In doing so we faced issues of impending death, acceptance and rejection, social stigma and prejudice. These are issues that seem to arise in HIV-related psychotherapy on a regular basis.

THE "GIVENS" OF EXISTENCE

Yalom (1980) provides a useful understanding of the "givens", or limits, of existence. He names four; "death", "freedom", "isolation" and

Case Studies in Existential Psychotherapy and Counselling. Edited by S. du Plock
© 1997 John Wiley & Sons Ltd

"meaninglessness", and offers us a view of how people attempt to protect themselves against the anxieties that accompany them. In this chapter, I will illustrate how the use of these defences can permeate the experience of living with, or working with, HIV.

van Deurzen-Smith (1988) provides a thorough and clear description of the different "worlds" or dimension that we exist in. I would express these as:

- The "natural world", which includes our experiences of our bodies and the physical world.
- The "public world" includes relationships with others, such as work and play.
- The "private world" includes the experiences of intimacy and close interpersonal relationships.
- The "ideal world" is the spiritual world and the world of personal ethics and values.

These concepts will be used throughout the chapter. The effects of HIV on the "public" and "private" worlds will be particularly highlighted.

The phenomenological approach is a disciplined and reflective way of interacting in order to try and understand the experience of another as best we can. Spinelli (1989, 1994) gives a thorough and clear explanation of this method. For me, this approach is summarised by three distinct "rules":

- *The rule of bracketing*, or putting aside (as best we can) our own assumptions in order to clear our perceptions and actually hear what the other person is expressing.
- *The rule of description*—it is considered important to describe what you have heard and not try to explain it theoretically.
- *The rule of horizontalisation*—the therapist is asked to apply no judgement, but initially to try to hear everything before allowing importance to be attributed to any aspect of the experience.

HIV is an abbreviation for human immunodeficiency virus, the virus which is believed to lead to the development of AIDS. People can be HIV-positive, i.e. be infected with HIV for a long period of time, before it has any obvious physical manifestations. HIV appears to have powerful psychic, social and emotional consequences, to both those infected and those affected. HIV is known to be transmitted between people via such bodily fluids as blood and semen, thus adding a new dimension to intimacy and the ways that people affirm life.

AIDS is an acronym for acquired immune deficiency syndrome. Medically, AIDS is considered to be a syndrome of infections rather than any one illness. A diagnosis of AIDS is given when certain medical criteria are met. These include infection with HIV and the presence of at least one of the various AIDS-defining illnesses.

The existential approach is appropriate for working with the issues that arise in HIV-related therapy since, as I have found in my own work, the "givens" of death, freedom, isolation and meaninglessness permeate the experience of living with HIV in the following manner:

> Death, because people experience periods of ill-health, face their own or others' impending death and many people do go on to die of AIDS at a young age. Freedom, because HIV can force us to explore the freedom that we do have and how this is affected once the effects of HIV are felt. Meaninglessness, as HIV doesn't play by many of the rules that we have grown to expect. It affects many young people, and has been a cause of many young people dying, it is passed on through sexual contact which is the means of expressing caring and starting life. Isolation is also relevant for HIV as many people have experienced abuse, stigma and people drawing away from those infected.
>
> (Milton, 1994a)

I shall focus on the issue of meaning and the concept of relationship, and will describe how the experience of HIV and of meaninglessness led to the client searching for answers in other people, a search for the "ultimate rescuer". This dynamic was central in the formation of the world of this client in which different dimensions and experiences were dissociated from each other. I hope to show how the phenomenological method and an awareness of existential theory and philosophy interact to provide a powerful and productive psychotherapeutic arena, in which the experience of separate worlds of existence is brought together. The therapy shows that the relationship with the therapist is important in helping to restore a sense of meaning and personal integration.

I will discuss the therapy in terms of its initial, middle and final stages. The study will follow the headings that Levson (1974) suggests characterise the dynamics of the therapeutic relationship in these stages: "being together", "staying together" and "leaving behind". In line with the interpersonal nature of existential psychotherapy, the author's subjective experiences will be discussed.

ROBERTO: LIVING WITH HIV*

"Being" Together

Roberto was a healthy young man in his early 20s, quite characteristic of many people currently living with HIV (Public Health Laboratory Service, 1995). He came from Switzerland and we had different first languages. He was away from home, he'd left home after being diagnosed as HIV-positive, and had left without sharing this information with any family members. To Roberto, London had meant an escape from restrictions and a chance to start over again with a new freedom.

Roberto was isolated and depressed and this was one of the reasons he considered starting therapy. I asked him to elaborate on this and he was able to tell me that there were certain areas of his life that caused him discomfort (i.e. his relationship with his parents, his past and his homosexuality), and that it was time to explore these areas before deciding "what to do" about them. This way of viewing life fits well with an existential approach to therapy, which sees the highlighting of the values and assumptions that we live by to be very important. On the level of the public world, Roberto was adjusting to living in a foreign country, speaking a different language and trying to develop a new network of friends. On the level of his natural world, he had to adjust to the concept of being well and healthy, yet having HIV which for him meant illness and death.

Roberto suggested early on in the first session that he had difficulty in discussing "serious" issues such as his HIV infection and his sexuality. In fact, he'd usually managed to veer away from these issues. Another piece of information that Roberto shared was that in the past he had often come to depend heavily on significant male figures in his life, having had a "crush" in his late teens on a priest to whom he'd turned for help. I felt that this information might be significant as he came to tell me about this in the first session, and also as he appeared embarrassed as he told me. However, I tried to keep the "rule of horizontalisation" in mind and not jump to conclusions or pre-assign value, in line with the phenomenological method.

The structural issues of therapy were discussed and an initial series of six sessions were negotiated, with the understanding that we could review and evaluate at the end of that time. Sex and sexuality became an early focus. I came to see that Roberto held a number of assumptions

---

* All names and identifying details have been changed to preserve anonymity.

and beliefs that I thought contradicted each other, making it difficult for Roberto to understand or integrate his view of life. Two of these beliefs were that "Men want sex all the time"—it was seen as a natural appetite—yet "Sex is a sin". His "natural" and "ideal" worlds were at odds. Another pair of conflicting views was that "Being gay is very positive", yet he accepted the conservative view suggested by some editions of the DSM & the ICD psychiatric classification systems, that his sexuality was officially a pathological condition. Sex was a lot of fun and a source of intimacy, yet it was also the means whereby he had become infected with HIV and now felt alienated from others.

HIV was the focus of conflicting viewpoints. He was a young, healthy, attractive, HIV-positive man. Yet HIV meant to him death, illness, isolation and ugliness. I had to remember that we weren't only talking of psychological concepts, but of real and powerful issues that people with HIV have to contend with earlier than and differently from the way people may contend with these issues in other circumstances. The two views he held were hard for him to reconcile and he spent much time exploring his thoughts and the experiences he'd had and what they all meant for him. However, HIV, as a concept, did not present overtly as a central theme in this stage of therapy.

During the first few sessions my interventions were geared mainly to increasing my view of his world and, hopefully, allowing him to gain clarity. I was hoping to keep from distorting his description of his world and thus was trying to "bracket" any theoretical ideas or assumptions that I had about any "correct" technique, or the issues of HIV, AIDS or sexuality. I was trying to listen attentively, and offered reflective comments pointing out the picture that I was getting, in an attempt to remain with a descriptive intervention, rather than an explanatory one.

At times this was difficult work, since I felt that Roberto was struggling between allowing himself to trust me and share with me, while also needing to pull away in order to limit his dependency on others. I experienced this as a closeness with him during some sessions, while in others he felt withdrawn. This added to the picture that I was getting that Roberto was coping with life by living in separate worlds—that relationships were a source of some anxiety.

Towards the end of the six sessions, I put it to Roberto that what he was reporting highlighted a tension he experienced between taking care of his own needs and desires, and dealing with those of others. In life he would be close to people until his own needs were contrary to what he felt others wanted, then he would withdraw to take care of his own needs. This occurred with lovers, with medical practitioners, with his parents and at times in the sessions with me. He'd come into the session and spend the first few minutes telling me of his concerns or of his week, and then become nervous and embarrassed. His fear, he said, was that I would find him repetitive and uninteresting. I commented on this dynamic in our relationship and I tried to do this in a way that was descriptive. Roberto had asked me what I thought, and I wasn't sure whether he meant about the content of the session or about my thoughts of him. I offered a summary of the session content, and he was silent. I asked:

MARTIN: Is that what you wanted or was it something more personal?
ROBERTO: Yes . . .
MARTIN: I see you as being open and honest with both me and yourself.
   You are trusting and no, I don't find you repetitive and uninteresting.
ROBERTO: Really?
MARTIN: Yes.
ROBERTO: Really? . . . No, it's OK, I'll stop asking.
MARTIN: It seems difficult to accept such a view of yourself.

Roberto reported a dream during our fifth session—he was in a forest with a lot of men. He was caught by soldiers who had taken him away and asked him whether he wanted to be kept in a Nazi camp or an American one. When he replied that he would choose the American one, two old women said, "No, you can't go to the American camp, you must go to the Nazi camp". He had no response to this and awoke, very scared.

We spent some time exploring the assumption he had that the dream was linked to sexuality. I was curious and wondered about the meaning of the dream. I noted the experience I had and my question. Was I being told that there was a lack of meaning in his sexuality? Was I being told that the meaning was hard to communicate, or that there is risk involved in relating to men? I understood the gist of the dream to be that he had two experiences of his sexuality. In the public world his sexuality was related to confusion, isolation, and was experienced as offensive to others, punishable. Risk and relationship were linked. This was different to the manner in which he experienced sexuality in his natural world. As Roberto struggled to find a definite meaning for the dream, he asked what I felt it meant. I explained my thoughts as: "You seem to be saying that your sexuality is difficult to accept in social settings. I know that this is different to the way you experience it in more private settings and the dream seems to be showing that difference".

He considered this and moved on to talk about his sexuality further. As I noted this move I remembered him saying that he found it difficult to talk about serious issues such as sexuality and his infection—but this was in fact what he was now risking. Considering the dream in this way had helped him continue to look at the serious issue of sexuality. I wonder what a more theoretical understanding would have offered. I wouldn't have been sure that any theoretical material I could consider (e.g. about sexuality or dream theory) would have been more important than his experience.

Early in the therapy Roberto had asked me my views on his needs and the work that he was doing, "What do you think of me?" he would ask. "Am I schizophrenic, paranoid, neurotic . . .? I thought that these questions were related to his search for meaning. Life was very confusing on so many levels and he was grasping for answers. I wondered whether he felt he might be able to live more authentically, with a fuller sense of himself, if he could name himself, if he could express a sense of who he was? I wondered whether this dynamic was an illustration of the defence that Yalom (1980) called the "ultimate rescuer"? Was he looking to me to rescue him from the discomfort he was experiencing? This is a dynamic often encouraged in medical settings, which value the "compliant patient" (Milton, 1994b). I responded by letting him know that I didn't feel a psychiatric diagnosis was needed. I also described how I found his desire for a label to be of importance.

When I reviewed Roberto's use of relationships I noticed the theme of difference. He was different from his closest friends (most of whom were not HIV-positive) and from his father. He felt that this led to his feelings of depression and hopelessness. An existential understanding of psychological disturbance, according to van Deurzen-Smith (1995), is that life is being lived by attempting to evade one side of life and to live solely in the other, thus trying to avoid the anxieties and hoping to live only in the good. Spinelli (1994) has referred to this as a "dissociated, or divided consciousness". Roberto had been attempting to live in separate worlds and his deliberations suggested an effort to modify this. As he did this he came to question many things, including therapy. "Is this worth it?" he asked, "or is it just wanking?". Even in the midst of therapy he was swamped by confusion and a lack of clear meaning which he found distressing. The themes of meaning and isolation became quite central during the penultimate session and we ended the session by acknowledging that in our next meeting we would consider the options available. Despite the session ending on such a practical note, I realised that my preoccupation was about what other questions were coming my way. I was wanting to know something definite, and finding the uncertainty difficult. I recognised that this is a dynamic in therapy where meaninglessness is faced, but I also recognise the central place it has in work with HIV. I thought that there was a parallel: we were both pondering, and becoming preoccupied with, questions and the search for answers.

During the final session, Roberto talked about his week. There was no mention of the ending that was facing us. As the session progressed I became aware that we needed to discuss overtly the arrangements that we would be making about the therapy, i.e. were we going to meet further, and if we were, what form would this take, what would it mean to us both—would it be a temporary relief from isolation, or would it allow the creation of any significant and lasting meaning? Would it be interaction and engagement, or would it just be "wanking"? I was also asking questions, and seeking my own meaning in the uncertainty. This was an illustration of the interpersonal nature of the search for the "ultimate rescuer", and how the therapist is involved in its development and maintenance.

I asked Roberto what his thoughts were on the fact that we had arrived at our last scheduled session. He responded with ambivalent feelings regarding the setting (a medical milieu) and how it continually reminded him of his HIV status. He also returned to the important question he'd raised earlier, and that I had been mulling over, "Would talking help?" I didn't know anything for sure about the "success", but I offered this to Roberto. "I have no way to know what will come out of the therapy if we continue. I'll be responding to things as they occur in the same way. I need to hear whether you want to continue to meet, or whether it would feel like wanking?" I used his own phrase at this point to indicate that I understood the pleasant, but limited gratification he experienced in masturbation, and he was wondering whether relating to me might remain short-term and with some limited comfort, while not being as intense as the experience he might expect from relating to someone in greater depth. It was important to reflect the actual situation that Roberto was experiencing, including his uncertainty and questions about value. "Wanking" implied a pseudo-closeness, with some elements being open and others needing to be hidden—and this led to questions about the true value of relationships and his part in them. I wondered whether it was related to the HIV infection—The implication of the infection being that he was only *somewhat* approachable, *somewhat* loveable.

The discussion resulted in a commitment to 12 further sessions, which I felt to be a significant development for Roberto. He had considered engagement, he had engaged in these considerations with me—risking having his uncertainties aired to another. He then chose to engage further than we had done before, and this in defiance of his usual urge to avoid uncertainty and anxiety. I felt that he had chosen to take the risk of being more involved.

Summary

In the early phase of therapy Roberto was able to face some of the concerns that having HIV has raised for him, and the manner that he has used to cope with them—i.e. putting his belief in the skill, ability, luck of another. The relationship between the therapist and Roberto is important in this regard, since it is through this relationship that the hopes and disappointments that inevitably occur when depending on others can be experienced and reflected upon.

"Staying Together"

"I can't do anything right". This is how Roberto began the seventh session, and I wasn't clear exactly what he was referring to and wondered whether it was related to the return to therapy. ". . . What would be right?", I asked. "Getting married, having children and a nice home".

It felt quite sad. I noted that these right things were complicated by his sexual orientation, and to his HIV infection. In this session he seemed very aware of the two worlds he inhabited—the one wherein he couldn't do anything right, was sexual, had HIV and was depressed, and the one in which he managed to be good, to comply with the requirements of others and to gain reassurance from others. Again the "natural" and "public" worlds were at odds.

Roberto soon made an important statement regarding his view of HIV. In a period where he was facing a number of difficult practical problems, he said, "I don't know if I'm tired because of being positive, or because I think I should be tired!" The power of assumptions, and their meaings, was brought clearly into focus. It struck me that even when processing his experience, uncertainty abounded, and that he now linked it with his infection. HIV had actually been a topic on the periphery so far, but this suggested that he was attributing more to it than he was discussing in sessions.

This phase of therapy was characterised by further uncertainty and I was facing a quandary about where to focus my attention, what could I "do" for this man? The urgency he experienced was beginning to resonate with me. I noted the effects on his view on work ("Why do it, if I'm going to get sick?"); death ("The end of everything, although I like to think of heaven"); and his view of himself as either depressed and negative or good and special. My own resonances meant that I had to work harder, and be more disciplined, to stay in a phenomenological frame of mind and avoid rescuing, teaching, or "doing" things. These developments seemed different from earlier in the therapy, as now he could move between the "natural" and "social" dimensions with greater ease and with a greater sense of fulfilment. I wondered whether it was an attempt to live with less of the "dissociated consciousness" that abounded earlier.

As time passed, Roberto found that he was able to bring more "serious" issues into therapy, despite his initial concerns. One of these he had highlighted at the beginning of therapy—sexual behaviour. He talked about it and again showed how difficult it was to find a single meaning. Anonymous sex was more than "just wanking", at least there was someone else involved and it offered an uncomplicated relationship. I remembered Roberto using these words earlier, and that I felt they were related to assumptions about value. As we explored what it was that was important to him in the realm of sex he went on to talk about the after-effects of a relationship and how it related to his HIV infection:

ROBERTO: I miss my ex-boyfriend. He told this guy that I was HIV-positive. That wasn't nice.
MARTIN: What wasn't nice?
ROBERTO: Telling him nasty things about me.
Martin: Saying that you have HIV, is saying something nasty about you?

Roberto appeared hurt at this point, and sad.

ROBERTO: To hear people say that I'm gay or that I'm positive . . . to hear my daddy say that it's a sin, that it's evil . . . I don't like being gay.
MARTIN: One side of you knows that you have HIV and that you are gay, the other doesn't like it.

He seemed to consider himself "nasty", both because of the HIV and because he is gay. This affected his relationship with himself and with others. In his sexual world it kept him from relating closely to people he had sex with, or from having sex with those he felt close to. It was evident that we were working with the conflicting dimensions of his experience almost simultaneously.

There seemed to be three distinct ways in which he allowed himself to experience his sexuality, which limited the fulfilment he could experience. They seemed to reflect a continuum of meaning. Firstly, in the relative safety of not knowing a partner he could have some sexual engagement, but once it was over it seemed to be a rejection. However it was a rejection that was not too difficult to get over—it had minimal meaning since it involved little in relating to another. Sex with another person was "75–100% better than wanking". Secondly, there was the notion of sex within a relationship, and the concomitant pressure he felt of needing to disclose his HIV status. In this case he expected rejection of a more painful and damaging kind. Thirdly, there was masturbation ("wanking"), which felt safe. Rejection wasn't a part of wanking, although he experienced it as a reminder of his lack of relationship.

Roberto was risking engagement more and more with me. He was now able to bring his intimate fantasies for exploration. This seemed important as it both suggested the increased level of engagement, but also was a clear description of the way in which he linked sex and the infection. His sexual fantasies were central to experience orgasm—he had to fantasise about specific people and specific, meaningful relationships, if he was to reach orgasm. But regardless of fantasy, at this point in time, Roberto experienced orgasm as impossible during intercourse. I wondered whether this was the behavioural manifestation of the link he had talked about between sex and HIV infection. I wondered whether it acted as protection from passing on the virus—regardless of the use of condoms. He was only relaxed enough to reach orgasm when he was assured that he wouldn't pass on the virus.

Throughout the experience of working with his more intimate world, Roberto would return to the issue of sex and its meanings time and again. This was particularly the case when a new relationship began. Roberto would ask whether his new partner and he "could . . . have 'No Sex' in our relationship", whether he could have a relationship where intercourse was excluded. Roberto wondered whether he could keep a relationship going in any other ways, with HIV in the picture? What would either of these types of relationship mean? As I listened to these questions, I noted that they sounded different to his previous questions. His English seemed less clear than usual, and there seemed to be less of a demand for answers. In fact his whole presence seemed to change somewhat. He seemed more engaged in that he would now lead the session more spontaneously, and with greater enthusiasm. He appeared more at home with the uncertainty and more confident in reflecting on his questions, becoming more at east physically.

Summary

In this stage of therapy Roberto seemed increasingly able to bring conflicting experiences to therapy and to consider their implications. This allowed him to explore the meanings each had for him, and to discover whether they were as incompatible as they seemed when he attempted to keep them apart. By engaging in this process with the therapist, Roberto in effect worked with these issues in a different manner to the solitary attempts he usually made, and there interaction seemed to allow a wider range of possible understandings to be gained of his experience.

"Leaving Behind"

The growing ability to reflect on conflicting experiences simultaneously was particularly noticeable within 3 weeks of the agreed end of therapy. I thought about how Roberto would be experiencing this countdown, and how he would experience the end of therapy itself. Would it be a liberating experience? Would it be full of anxiety? I reflected on the form of my questions and realised that, like Roberto, I was not pressuring myself to come up with the answers, but was reflecting on the situation with an interest and a confidence in our ability to survive the "not knowing".

In this series of sessions, it was again I who raised the issue of the ending. I asked Roberto about the impact of the impending end to our relationship and what it might mean to him. He said:

> I feel different towards you than I did towards my "spiritual father". I've not fallen in love with you, not like you do with psychologists.[1] It's interesting here, and it's mature. Also there are days when I'd rather not be here.

I felt he was saying that he was now viewing relationships as more than unidimensional, he didn't have to live in either the "good" or the "bad" feelings, he could live with them together. I described it as:

> You could have warm feelings, and cooler ones . . . towards the same person?

He thought about this for a second and smiled before saying "Yes".

The penultimate session saw us revisit uncertainty about endings, although Roberto didn't mention the end of the session directly. He talked about concerns that his boyfriend might leave him, about his separation form his family and about death. The end of our relationship seemed to be reminding Roberto of painful feelings about other meaningful relationships that had ended. I wondered whether the ending was also posing a significant challenge to Roberto's attempt to challenge his search for an "ultimate rescuer". By ending we would be acknowledging that my assistance was limited and that we were confident that he had the ability to live in a more fulfilling manner by accepting his own strengths and responsibilities to cope with the risks that life and encounters with others creates.

Endings may create or highlight concerns relating to death, and HIV has links to death. Death anxiety can therefore be heightened in living with HIV. This was the case for Roberto and can be seen in a preoccupation with youth (a theme from earlier in the therapy), which could now be seen as an attempt to defy death. All the time that he could stay young, and not grow up, he felt as though he could avoid dying. In our 17th session he said, with fear and in a tone that I thought was a sense of resignation, "I don't want to die, I want to live, I thought I was immortal". In this moment Roberto voiced a sentiment central to an existential understanding of life. Cohn

(1994) says, "The fear and denial of death as an undisputed certainty in our life is of crucial importance in existential therapy".

The last session we had was indicative of the work that Roberto had done, both in the content of what he said, and in the way that the session went and the emotional tone. He talked both about the shifts he had experienced in his perception of himself and his ability to be in relationship with another and also the concerns that he will had about this. A major development was being able to re-engage with his boyfriend after their split, and I wondered whether this was an indication that he was integrating his separate "worlds". I described his progress in therapy in this light. I said, "You've also seemed to accept your other feelings too, the fear of illness and death. You've found a place where all your feelings can sit with each other", and Roberto agreed. He suggested different examples of this in how he understood love and need, life with HIV and feeling closer to his parents although gaining a sense of autonomy. He was also experiencing both sex and love in his current sexual relationship. As he described these examples it seemed to me that Roberto was more at ease with expressions of emotion and was able to convey a sense of contentedness as well as the anxieties we were talking about. The description he gave also contained more fulfilling relationships, both with others, but also in his relationship with himself.

He continued to have some concerns related to the progression of his HIV infection. He seemed able to express both the warmth he was experiencing in his relationship and his fears about the progression of the infection. He also said, "all I needed to say has been said". Although an analysis of existence can theoretically go on throughout life (and probably does in some form for the majority of people), this need not be in psychotherapy. Roberto had taken responsibility for his explorations in the therapeutic relationship and it was important to allow him to take responsibility for the end of the therapy. I felt this ending was different to previous endings that he had talked about, as it was not premature, but was the completion of an agreed contracted relationship. I had the sense that HIV had taken a different place in his life. Rather than living as if he could banish parts of his life, he seemed to have accepted variety in life. HIV had its place, but so did work, relationships, family, sex, drugs and food.

REFLECTIONS

This case study illustrates that attention to the relationship between therapist and client is important. Roberto found a way to explore the anxieties he had about what HIV meant to him and about the risk that relationships involve. The experience of meaningless was distressing for Roberto, and could be seen in the conflicting views that were held at different times.

His distress was exacerbated by the difficulties that exist and which he experienced in understanding the origins of, reasons for, and dynamics of, HIV infection and AIDS.

The case study shows how this experience of meaninglessness led to the attempt to live in separate worlds; sex meant different things when he was with people and when he was alone, he held some differing views on his sexuality, some affirming and some negative. These separations led to both an experience of inner fragility and a tendency to form split relationships in life, dissociating those that were anxiety-provoking and idealising those that promised to rescue him from his difficulties. It is because of this that I feel that the relationship offered in therapy was of particular importance. Roberto did not only attempt to heal the split, but was able to do it through a relationship with another. As meaning was generated it seems that Roberto was able to use the experience in therapy to risk integrating the different dimensions of being in the world, particularly the natural world and the ideal world.

The interpersonal element of therapy is important in HIV-related psychotherapy, as many of the difficulties that people experience are related to the difficulties which they experience in the world. Roberto illustrates this. That his infection occurred in a context that was not particularly supportive created difficulties for him. He tried to cope with his anxiety by trying to separate it off, as he had done with many aspects of his previous experiences. However, HIV was a reminder of his anxieties due to the physical and practical implications that it has.

The existential–phenomenological model focuses explicitly on the relational dimension of existence, and is alert to this in the practice of therapy (Spinelli, 1994). This may not be possible if a therapy focuses too heavily on theory or on only one aspect of experience, e.g. thoughts in cognitive therapy or the unconscious in psychoanalytic work (Milton, 1994a). The phenomenological method also assists in helping us limit the dangers inherent in being led by theories (Spinelli, 1994).

The ability to reflect on one's own involvement in therapy is important for both the therapist and the client. As the therapist, I realise that at times I felt surges of anxiety and that my part in the therapy was also dynamic, with great variations. At times I "did" better than at other times. I know I felt the limitations of being human in this endeavour, and I hope that this meant that I was experienced as human.

DISCUSSION WITH THE EDITOR

SIMON: I know you have written a number of papers on working from an existential perspective in HIV-related psychotherapy; I wonder if you have always worked this way, and if not, how you came to use this approach.

MARTIN: No, I haven't always worked this way. I started out trying to apply what I had learned in my psychology training. This often had the sense that all that you needed to do was figure out the "truth" about a person's problem, their development, and then direct them in the way to unravel this—in other words, to take the view that therapists can be, and should be, "the expert". The more I worked with this assumption, however, the more I came to see that it is a false assumption. Therefore, I struggled for a few years to try and choose the "right" approach and through experience came to find that an existential approach makes sense—and this was during the time I was working with a number of people whose lives were affected by HIV. The more experience I've gained, the more I feel that reliance on theory, and notions of "truth", can only be a limited part of the therapeutic process. At times I think that its *main* function is to keep therapists feeling grounded.

SIMON: You talk about the way existential "givens" arise in this field, and it seems to me that the existential approach might be the most useful approach whenever we work with illness, impending death, or even with situations such as disability, in which the client is made aware of his/her mortality and limitations.

MARTIN: Yes, I would agree with you, but I think I might widen it too. I think that this approach can be very useful when people are struggling with issues of identity. Identity development often involves a change from perceiving oneself in one way, giving up that perception and developing another identity. All this occurs in relation to our values and in relation to other people. So the shift from being HIV-negative, or unaware of one's HIV status, to being HIV-positive can call for a major shift in identity. Other examples include leaving home and becoming independent, developing an identity as a gay man or a lesbian, or even choosing a career that others may not think appropriate—I think these are all areas that the existential approach can help clarify. And that's because of its focus on descriptive interpretation and the clarification of areas of relation.

SIMON: You seem to have covered a lot of ground in 18 sessions. I wonder if this number was recommended by the agency in which you worked and whether you find you are generally able to work successfully within these parameters. I have generally been limited to 16 sessions when working in medical settings but have found clients can move a great deal in this time. There is still, though, a tendency for medical staff to view the existential approach as "too philosophical", too little goal-oriented. Your chapter suggests that a philosophical approach can be utilized even when financial pressures have led to increasing emphasis on throughput and brief therapy.

MARTIN: You raise several issues here—brief therapy, relationship between therapist and funders and the notion of "outcome". At the time that the work in this case study was being undertaken, I wasn't under pressure from the agency to use any particular fixed number of sessions at all. I face that issue a lot more now. I supervise counsellors in primary care who are frequently expected to work within six or eight sessions. Where time is so limited, I feel it's particularly important to have dialogue regarding the expectations at the beginning of therapy, both expectations of the agency and of the client. I'm not necessarily "pro" or "anti" brief therapy; I think the danger is when a limit is imposed arbitrarily. There are people who need more time, and expecting therapy to *only* occur within very short periods of time can end up excluding people from psychotherapeutic services. What I have noted, though, is that when I, or my supervisees, work where there is flexibility, a great many people naturally seem to use a short period of therapy. Therefore I think the drive to "prescribe" a course of therapy from the outset is shortsighted and may not be necessary. Organisational issues are important in this regard as in the NHS, the issue of length of therapy is usually brought up by those with decision-making powers in relation to the yearly funding cycles, with management and medics wanting to talk in terms of "truth", "knowledge" and "certainty". It is this view that also demands the simplistic, prescriptive approach to the provision of therapy.

SIMON: This seems to be a particularly emotionally challenging area to work in as a therapist. I wonder how you find the experience of working existentially given that you are concerned to "be with" the client rather than hide behind the role of "expert"?

MARTIN: At times it has been very emotionally challenging—there have been times I've felt burnt out, or anxious; and at other times I have experienced great pleasure and contentment. I think that being involved with the client within the sessions is probably part of what makes therapy therapeutic, and that's supported if we look at the research on non-specific factors in therapy. I sometimes see clients who have been to the service before and left. The main reason people give for having left therapy previously, is that the therapist was perceived as not being involved. "They just sat there and didn't say anything". "They seemed too practical, and didn't really listen to what I was saying". I also notice the difference in sessions when the intervention I have made has been a natural one rather than a clever, or theoretically-based one. So basically, from a naive initial belief that my training had to produce an "expert", I've experienced attempts to be "expert" as phony and not particularly helpful. The attempts I've made to relate to my clients more authentically are the attempts that have seemed to provide something more therapeutic. In addition to this, because of the personal involvement, I think that good supervision is important, and by that I mean reflective supervision rather than just case management. Also, I think that having a range of personal interests outside of the professional arena is important.

ACKNOWLEDGEMENT

Special thanks are extended to "Roberto" for permission to use this material in the case study, and for reading drafts of the case study during preparation. Thanks also to Cathy Skinner, a colleague in the BPS and the field of HIV, for her sensitive editorial comments.

NOTES

1. When this therapy was being undertaken, the author was neither qualified as a psychologist, nor working as one. He was working as a Counsellor in a medical setting that had a separate, clearly identifiable psychology team.

BIBLIOGRAPHY

Cohn, H.W. (1994). What is existential psychotherapy?. *British Journal of Psychiatry*, **165**, 699–701.
Levson, L.L. (1974). The existential use of the self. *American Journal of Psychiatry*, **131**, 1.
McKusick, L. (1988). The impact of AIDS on practitioner and client:notes for the therapeutic relationship. *American Psychologist*, **43**(11), 935–47.
Milton, M.J. (1994a). The case for existential therapy in HIV-related psychotherapy. *Counselling Psychology Quarterly*, **7**(4).
Milton, M.J. (1994b). HIV-related psychotherapy and its existential concerns. *Counselling Psychology Review*, **9**(4).
Public Health Laboratory Services (1995). AIDS Centre CDSU and CD(S)U. *Communicable Disease Report*, **5**(33), August.
Spinelli, E. (1989). *The Interpreted World: an Introduction to Phenomenological Psychology*. London: Sage.
Spinelli, E. (1994). *Demystifying Therapy*. London: Constable.
van Deurzen-Smith, E. (1988). *Existential Couselling in Practice*. London: Sage.
van Deurzen-Smith, E. (1995). *Existential Therapy*. London: Society for Existential Analysis.
Yalom, I.D. (1980). *Existential Psychotherapy*. New York: Basic Books.
Yalom, E.D. (1989). *Love's Executioner and Other Tales of Psychotherapy*. Harmondsworth: Penguin.

5

THE CROSS-CULTURAL EXPERIENCE— INTEGRATION OR ISOLATION?

Zack Eleftheriadou
*NAFSIYAT Intercultural Therapy Centre and Regent's College,
London, UK*

INTRODUCTION

The purpose of this chapter is to explore the experience of leaving one's country of birth and moving to another using ideas from existential thinking, particularly ideas from R.D. Laing (1987) as well as ideas from John Bowlby's (1982) work on attachment. The psychological process involved in "integration" to the new environment is a very complex one and for many one that never becomes resolved. In many ways the notion of what Bowlby termed "attachment" and what is experienced when it breaks down or is not able to form can provide us with insight when working with immigrants. Attachment in this context is used to refer to the attachment between self and culture, body and context, psyche and environment, amongst many others, and their effect when this link is broken and people are faced with separation and loss. The loss experienced is of the familiar family, culture and environmental milieu to something which is not only new, but can often feel very hostile, rejecting and even continually

Case Studies in Existential Psychotherapy and Counselling. Edited by S. du Plock
© 1997 John Wiley & Sons Ltd

persecuting. If the person is unable to form an attachment to the new culture or the new culture reinforces these feelings of "foreignness", the person can end up feeling unable to function and as a result any coping mechanisms can break down. The case study illustrates the inner split that is often created within the person, as well as the societal pressures from the person's birth or parental culture and the new culture, and examines the implications for psychotherapeutic practice during the "acculturation" process.

Culture and the Individual

Culture is used to refer to the observable, concrete characteristics of our experience, such as religious images, buildings, the environmental layout and the more abstract characteristics such as values, attitudes, beliefs and the multitude of subtle messages we receive. Culture is something that exists both inside us and outside us; that is, we have an active relationship with the cultural context in which we are brought up. Culture changes through time, with the experiences of its members as well as the influx of others. There is a relationship with the world in which the individual or group abide by certain cultural norms that are meaningful to them. Phenomenological psychologists like Brentano and Husserl (see Spinelli, 1989) explain this process of gaining meaning through what they call "intentional interpretation" of our world. The world reflects back onto the mind and in turn meaning is created by interpretation of it. We interpret those events according to our subjective relationship with them. Some people find it important to hold onto the concrete characteristics of their culture whilst others may need less contact with concrete aspects for security. For example, for some people who move to another country it may be important to make an attachment with people from the same cultural background, near places that sell their cultural foods and other familiar people and objects. For others it may be exciting to try new types of foods and there is not the same need to find the familiar in the new country. There is no one correct way of adjustment.

The relationship between the self and the community can be seen as a continuum where, on one extreme, no deviation from the cultural group is allowed and there are punishments if this happens. For example, a strict religious group may have certain rules regarding the conduct of women and how they appear in public places. In some countries there is flexibility, whilst in others the rules are literal. At the other end of the self and community spectrum, individualism and freedom are emphasised. An example of the latter may be the individual who has looser ties with their familial or cultural context and can exercise more flexibility in partner choice, for example, and general way of living. Therapy is an exploration of one's choices and limitations in life within an already historically and socially created world. Whenever someone chooses a course of action, they are not only choosing a course of action for themselves, but are also choosing to some extent for those around them. They will in turn be influenced also, and the person who chooses holds that responsibility for any choice that is made (Macquarrie, 1972).

In existentialism, working towards gaining a sense of self can be achieved by taking the cultural context into account. If we do not understand the context or do not value it, the client will only present a "false self" (Laing, 1987) or, as one client said to me, "I am black on the outside and white on the inside". She explained to me that everyone treats her as the Indian woman, as if her racial characteristics determine her whole character, behaviours and expression. This can result in the formation of a "false self". This "arises in compliance with the intentions or expectations" (Laing, 1987, p. 98). The attachments are therefore not meaningful to the individual and have become rather functional, for example appearing to belong to a group or culture on a rather superficial level. The "true self" (Laing, 1987), or more meaningful part of the person, can be discovered only when the therapist brackets their own theoretical frame or even culture. Sometimes a client who has experienced discrimination may try to take on board all of the persecutor's values. In therapy the client may try to do this with the therapist.

These themes will be explored through the case of Leila, who came to me for counselling some years ago, presenting cross-cultural conflicts.

CASE STUDY

The Client

Leila came to Britain when she was 12 years old, when she was sent to an all-girls boarding school and then onto a British university, where it was thought she would gain the best education in the economics field. In her third year of the course she was referred to me by her tutor, who felt that she was losing weight and had become very withdrawn. When her tutor suggested psychotherapy she was hesitant at first, wondering whether someone else would really understand her Arab culture. She also made it clear that she did not want to go to an Arab therapist. She was referred to me as someone who was also Mediterranean and was familiar with the Arab culture, but was not Arab.

She explained to me that she had always wanted to return to her country of origin but now that her studies were coming to an end she was no longer sure. Her mother, however, had insisted that Leila return home to get married. When she first came to Britain she felt rather alienated and homesick. She viewed the new culture as her host culture for a few years, with a wish to gain its good aspects and not have any involvement in other areas, for example not to get involved in any relationships with men who were not Muslim. Leila had not had a relationship with a man until a year prior to the time she came to counselling. She confessed that she would not have been able to tell me had I been Arab. She struggled about whether she should break off this relationship, since the man was not a Muslim, or whether she should just continue and not tell her parents. She felt very guilty and the secrecy had become unbearable.

The Therapist and Client Relationship

A therapist's world-view or personal philosophy will inevitably play a crucial role in the therapeutic process. Therapists who are engaged in cross-cultural counselling have to be constantly aware of their underlying personal philosophy and how this influences their way of conducting therapy. None of us can claim that we are practising in an unbiased, culture-free, non-racist way, but we need to monitor our assumptions closely and be aware of the different ways the social world can have an impact on one's experience; for example, what it might mean to be brought up by an extended family in comparison to a nuclear family.

Leila and I engaged in an exploration in order to establish her subjective relationship to her culture as well as the nature of the attachment to the new cultural milieu. This is a process that requires time and much emotional upheaval. One culture can not be replaced by another. A person needs to go through the process of knowing what it is that they feel they have lost for their culture and what elements were meaningful from the new culture. Leila's dread of returning home was linked to her profound internal changes; after 8 years she had taken on a new culture, new norms and a new relationship, and what emerged towards the end was a very difficult parental relationship which she did not wish to repeat. This was also linked to the reason she had been sent to boarding school.

Exploration of the Whole Mind–Body–Culture Relationship

Cross-cultural counselling can only take place effectively if there is room for the relationships to be explored between mind, body and culture. It is important to validate the experience of ethnic groups. Often there is a feeling that anything different is "dysfunctional" or backward. The deviation from the norm gives rise to prejudices and stereotypes of people from a different race, culture, etc. These feelings can be perpetuated if the person's experience is not validated in the new culture. Attempts to understand other cultures have to be made from the position of "epoche" (Spinelli, 1989) or stepping back from our own prejudices and stereotypes. The existential therapist works with the person's feelings and behaviours within the four modes of relating; that is the *Mitwelt* or "social world", the *Eigenwelt* or "personal world", the *Umwelt* or "physical world" and the *Überwelt* or the person's "spirituality". It may be helpful here to refer to the concept of "ontological insecurity" which was first introduced by Laing (1987). This relates to fears of interactions with others and even oneself. In moving and trying to adjust to another culture, a person goes through many splits of the self and there are certain fears: that of engulfment, implosion and petrification. Engulfment is the fear of being taken over by something superior and alien, in this case by a new culture. Implosion is the emptiness an individual fears within her self. It is similar to engulfment, but it describes an internal sense of danger that something might take over and get into oneself, almost "get under one's skin". Petrification is the fear of turning into stone, an extreme form of depersonalisation.

It is a long process to support the individual to regain a sense of self when they have changed cultural context. I often hear comments like "A part of me has been left behind", "My heart does not belong here", "The wish to be returned home to be buried", "Feeling incomplete", "Something's missing" from people who have moved from their country of origin, which convey how divided the body or the person feels in the new environment. It is in a way of form of implosion, where there is something missing, but at the same time if the relationship to the body was not a secure one in the first place, it can feel that a part of the body has been left in the home country. This is because the body may be so linked to the cultural context and defined in relation to the socio-cultural context. When that context changes in a rather abrupt manner, the person can often feel a part of themselves being left behind. It may then take a long time to feel an integrated individual again and to redefine oneself as a whole in a new setting. This is particularly pertinent in a war situation, which may be so abrupt and traumatic that there is no time to process all the changes and implications for one's identity. For Leila, the body became a preoccupation when she had to go home, cover herself up, whilst in London she could dress quite differently and people, especially men, related to her differently.

Feelings of powerlessness to influence others in the social world also add to the withdrawal and may create very insular cultural groups. The feeling of being an outsider are also reinforced by the majority culture that may experience other ethnic groups as "foreign bodies", "aliens", that are powerful and engulfing, and it becomes safer to keep them at bay. This can alienate different cultural groups further.

Leila tried to adjust by creating a "false self" (Laing, 1987), where she changed her name, speaking another language all the time. She was rather surprised when I asked her how she preferred to be called. She told me to call her by her Arab name, but quickly added that I might not be able to pronounce it, so I might as well call her what everyone else does. She then asked me whether Zack was my whole name. I replied that perhaps she was wondering whether I also had a longer unpronounceable name and she was letting me know how difficult it was for others to understand her and her culture, starting from not being able to get her name right. She nodded, saying how strange it had become to be called by her whole name. Asking clients about names is an effective way of getting very emotional information about their views of themselves, familiar and cultural transmission.

People react differently to cultural moves; some reject the new culture completely and perceive it as inaccurate and try to make a minimal attachment to it, for example by only learning the language in order to get a job; or they reject their own culture and view the new culture as the ideal place which will offer them good things; or there is a struggle to integrate different elements from both cultures and live biculturally; or there is a complete rejection of both cultures. These patterns are paths that individuals choose, but one individual may alternate views at different times, and in fact most people change views according to the environment they are in. This is a way of dealing with conflicting values/ideas and traditions that had never been questioned before. Leila certainly demonstrated a fluctuation, trying to define herself according to her Arab context (especially after a holiday), because there was a fear of losing a part of herself through engulfment from the new culture. Leila would idealise Britain for a while and talk about how much freedom she could have if she was allowed to stay here. She would then find her new-found freedom rather frightening because she realised that she had changed in many ways in the 8 years of being away from her family. She wondered how she would fit in again and dreaded the return home. The pressure from her mother felt like implosion (Laing, 1987). All this had felt indigestible for her and she found herself unable to be with others or eat. Interestingly, cultural food and eating is generally a very powerful way of maintaining contact with one's mother culture. Leila's ambivalence towards her own culture was evident by the fact that she "could not take it in". What was to be taken instead, however, was also creating conflict in her. Leila did not feel that either avenue, going home or staying in Britain, would leave her with a place where she could be herself, or the opposite of what Laing called petrification. There was a threat that either her mother's pressure (which increased when she realised Leila's hesitations about returning home) would invade her, or the new culture would do so.

She often wondered what my views were on relationships and she assumed that the fact that I was working in London and not returning to my country meant that I must have some freedom. Without going into my own reasons for my travels, it felt appropriate to use our relationship and her ideas about me to explore her feelings. Clearly this was an area that could not be explored with her family, and I also had to be careful not to characterise them as the ones that did not understand while I became the sympathetic ear. Indeed, in the beginning her parents and myself were placed at opposite ends. It was important for me to hold on to these opposing views which represented her internal conflict. When there is a conflict between two cultures, often the therapist can rush the client to reach a resolution within one framework because it is so difficult to hold onto two. This was something I struggled with greatly, as I identified with her feelings of frustration as a woman who had restrictions in her Arab culture and yet had spent her adolescence in a different cultural frame-work. However, often this is exactly the goal of the counselling, that more than one culture can be retained alongside one another, sometimes in close connection and at other times in conflict.

Leila managed some integration of her experience, although the therapy came to an end when she was told she had to return back home. Towards the end of the therapy she had put on some weight, she decided to break off her relationship and ended up going back. I had a letter from her 6 months later in which she told me she had found going back very difficult, but at the same time she could no longer imagine herself living on her own in London.

CONCLUSION

In this paper an existential approach for working with cross-cultural issues, and how it was used in the case of a cross-cultural counselling relationship have been explored. This particular way of working has been chosen because it delves deep into fundamental questions of human existence, uncovering and questioning basic values, ideas and beliefs, rather than using any methods to alter any of them. It explores the client's experience in terms of all of the possible areas for connection of the person to the world; that is, physical, emotional, personal/intimate, social or spiritual.

This chapter highlights cross-cultural work, but it does not in any way imply that Leila only presented these. In fact, cultural concerns are usually linked with many other issues, and in Leila's case there was concern over the relationship with her mother in particular. The challenge of old values can also occur when people are faced with a crisis in their lives, such as when a close person dies. In Leila's case, the ending of her course triggered memories of other beginnings and endings in her life and questioned whether she was ready to face them. She was forced to look at her individual and cultural values in a way that she may not have done if she had never left her country of birth and reassess how her attachment to her family and country of birth had changed.

If a client can bear to examine their frame from a different perspective, or if the counsellor can bear to look at another frame, then this communication can be made and be effective and fruitful. Leila wanted to search beyond the cultural context of her early upbringing and she could only manage this if her culture was validated. Through the therapeutic process, she psychologically left her culture and almost re-entered it from a different, fresh perspective. She knew of the limitations she would face going back to her country as a woman, but psychologically she was helped to understand her feelings and why she had experienced so much distress at the end of her studies. As Sartre said, "Each man must invent his own values, and he exists authentically insofar as he strives to realise values that are really his own" (Macquarrie, p. 207, 1972). This follows the assumption, stated earlier, that we are changing beings, always in flux and therefore always faced with freedom, choice and responsibility, although these are within human limitations.

DISCUSSION WITH THE EDITOR

SIMON: I'm interested that you draw on Bowlby—not a theorist I would normally associate with the existential approach. I wonder if you have found other such writers whose theories may be useful to existential therapists, either as regards cross-cultural therapy or with other client groups?

ZACK: In relation to Bowlby, the reason I refer to his work is to highlight the whole notion of the *relationship* between the individual and their context. Bowlby's contribution can be viewed as parallel to cross-cultural work because he describes how secure an individual is when they have a satisfactory relationship with a mother or the "secure base"; in other words, a base which is familiar, predictable, reliable and safe. I am extending the notion of "attachment" in this chapter to refer to the relationship one has with one's culture, be it with (a) the physical environment, or (b) the more abstract element of one's culture. An example of the former is one's attachment to the familiar places in the country one is residing in, which evoke certain levels of security, such as sitting by a particular river or lake, watching a particular sky, etc. An example of the more abstract cultural elements is perhaps the way people of one's own culture think and relate to each other, which may be culture-specific.

I do not believe there is one "correct" theoretical approach to apply to cross-cultural clients, or indeed to any client. I draw on both existential theory and psychoanalytic theory because in cross-cultural work one needs to draw on more than one theory, particularly taking into account the fact that both theories are primarily embedded in Western culture. Therefore, using more than one way of thinking can provide a more holistic picture. The exercise itself is cross-cultural, as one has to try and keep more than one perspective in mind; this is indeed what is needed in working with someone else's perspective or world-view, especially if the two parties come from different cultures. The existential approach helps one to reach the breadth of social experience and the psychoanalytic approach is useful (and both approaches should be seen as a guide, not prescriptive in any way) when dealing with what I called earlier the more "internal", deeply buried conflicts that a client may not necessarily be aware of, even when they have made the decision to seek counselling.

SIMON: I have a certain amount of difficulty with the whole notion of cross-cultural therapy, viewed existentially. I don't think I'm just playing devil's advocate here: I have found it a positive advantage when clients come from a markedly different background to my own and have very different experiences, although, of course, we will always share some basic experience of what it is to be human. The more clients appear to be similar to me, the more I find I have to bracket my own prejudices and assumptions. So I guess that, given a shared language, the more puzzling I find the client, the more I can be open and naive.

ZACK: I agree that at times it can be creative to work with someone from another culture. However, one needs to look into certain elements first in order to understand the client's needs and whether it will be useful to work with someone who may have a completely different world-view. If the client had a choice of which therapist they seek, then it will be interesting to see whether they would go to someone of the same culture or not. For some clients, the most important element may be that the counsellor is of the same gender or political/sexual/religious orientation (amongst others). There are clients who will want to move away from their culture and explore something new (for example your own case; see Chapter 6) and sample new patterns of life. These clients are most likely to choose a counsellor from another culture and gain from the experience. Others may find this too frightening and may wish not only to mingle with those from another culture, but to retreat further into their own. These clients usually will not remain in counselling with someone from another culture. As stated earlier, it can of course be a creative relationship and a challenge when a client who does not think they will be understood finds that the counsellor has addressed cross-cultural/racism issues.

SIMON: How do you think an existential approach compares with, say, a psychodynamic approach in terms of its relevance to clients from non-European cultures? I ask this because it's my impression that many people from African cultures find an emphasis on early childhood experiences strange and sometimes invasive or even meaningless.

ZACK: My general belief is that early experiences have a great impact on later, adult emotional development. However, this is not the whole story of a human being's emotional development, as later experiences will also inevitably shape one's philosophy about one's relationships and view of the world. With any client it is important to pitch the exploration to where the client is at; for example, (to do with their parenting), the counsellor needs to explore it at that level, but if the person has had to move to another culture, or if they are refugees, then for the counsellor to address early relationships would be not only completely wrong but also insulting to the client, who had absolutely no control of socio-political circumstances. In the latter case, exploration may focus on "external" issues, such as the relationship to the client's culture, religion, the loss of the homeland, etc., but once again the key to sound counselling is that the dialogue will be determined by the client.

SIMON: You talk about "true" and "false" selves and although I know Laing uses these terms (he probably derived them from Winnicott), without wishing to be dogmatic, they are not really existential terms. For Heidegger, there is no such thing as a "self", only being-in-the-world, a constant process of relating to the world into which we are thrown. For Sartre, the attempt to create an enduring self is analogous to "bad faith", since it involves a movement away from openness to the world. I wonder what your feelings are about this, and whether you think we need to introduce these terms into our approach—although I think to do so would do violence to the logic of existential–phenomenological therapy.

ZACK: I agree that there is no rigid "self" and one only needs to take into account how we change during the process of counselling. It is of course a self which is in flux; however, at the same time there is continuity in the basic essence of a person, whether we call it "self", "personality" or "temperament". We may see a person after many years and recognise a gesture, an expression, a way of thinking, which makes us realise it is still the same human being. I refer to the idea of "true" and "false" self, the former being the experience of being congruent on the inside to the outside persona, and the latter when the person outside is not being congruent to what one feels inside, often not knowing what it *is* that one feels inside. I think many people from ethnic minorities have learnt, when trying to "fit in" to a new culture, to behave with a sense of "false self" to protect themselves from prejudice.

BIBLIOGRAPHY

Bowlby, J. (1982). *Attachment*. New York: Basic Books.

Eleftheriadou, Z. (1994). *Transcultural Counselling*. London: Central Book Publishing.

Laing, R.D. (1987). *The Divided Self*. Harmondsworth: Penguin.

Macquarrie, J. (1972). *Existentialism: an Introduction, Guide and Assessment*. Harmondsworth: Penguin.

Spinelli, E. (1989). *The Interpreted World: an Introduction to Phenomenological Psychology*. London: Sage.

van Deurzen-Smith, E. (1988). *Existential Counselling in Practice*. London: Sage.

6

AN INNOCENT ABROAD? AN EXAMPLE OF BRIEF STUDENT COUNSELLING

Simon du Plock
Regent's College, London, UK

INTRODUCTION

From 1991 to 1994 I held a post which included among other duties responsibility for coordinating the student counselling service of a college of higher education in Central London. Alongside home students, the college recruited widely in Europe and North America and specialized in offering 1-year or 1-semester experience abroad for liberal arts students. Louise, as I shall call her, was one such, spending a semester in London taking courses in English, history and psychology before returning to the States for her final year of study for a BA degree. She had initially seemed to her lecturers to be a model student, diligent and enthusiastic and consequently achieving high grades. Her performance had, in their opinion, deteriorated rapidly over the past few weeks. She had regularly missed classes and when she did attend was silent and withdrawn. She had finally asked to speak to her psychology tutor in private and had tearfully confided, ''I can't cope any more—everything has gone wrong somehow'', and further stated that she was afraid she would fail her final exams, which were only a month away, and would have to return home in disgrace. The tutor suggested that she might find

Case Studies in Existential Psychotherapy and Counselling. Edited by S. du Plock
© 1997 John Wiley & Sons Ltd

it helpful to talk to a student counsellor and she readily agreed to make an appointment.

THE CLIENT

She appeared in my office a few days later at exactly the time we had agreed on the 'phone. In response to my usual question, "Perhaps you would like to tell me what brings you here to see me today?", she immediately launched into a blow-by-blow account of the way in which she felt she had been swindled out of the deposit which she had made at the beginning of the semester on a house-share. It seemed that her three housemates had stated that a returnable deposit of £250 was a requirement for securing a place in the house, but now denied all knowledge of any such payment. She was stunned but resolute. In her own words, "They can't get away with it, I won't let them. What can you do about it—can you take them to court for me?"

Clearly she felt cheated and wanted a remedy. She fixed me with an angry stare and demanded to know what action I would take. While I was obviously not in a position to offer her a "quick fix" of some sort and certainly could not engage to remedy her financial troubles, I was also aware of the urgency of the situation, having had a fleeting conversation in the corridor the previous day with her psychology tutor. Such frame deviations are almost inescapable in this particular milieu, and in this instance I was glad I had not refused to listen to the anxieties of the tutor for an erstwhile high-achiever. Hearing now her story first-hand I felt my curiosity aroused: it seemed unlikely that the dramatic change in Louise's behaviour at college was due solely to her anger at being swindled out of an amount of money which, as she readily volunteered very early in our session, was "next to nothing" to her. She had presented the problem in a pragmatic way and yet I sensed a much greater hurt than that which she verbalized, if for no other reason than that this difficulty over her deposit did not appear of a magnitude to account for her change of attitude towards her studies. It is not unusual for students, particularly undergraduates, to misunderstand the role of the counsellor and to believe it to encompass considerably more than it actually does, but this seemed unlikely to be the case with Louise, a bright student with some knowledge of pyschology—albeit at an introductory level—and who had come to see me having reported emotional problems to her tutor. I must admit I was intrigued by her.

On first impressions Louise did not seem to be a candidate for the existential counselling which I practise. The existential approach is generally contra-indicated for those who:

. . . do not want to examine their assumptions and who would rather not explore the foundation of human existence. People who specifically just want to relieve a particular symptom should be referred on

(van Deurzen-Smith, 1995, p. 10)

On the other hand, there was an interesting discrepancy between Louise's stated aim in coming to see me (what might be called the presenting problem), and the major life events—leaving the parental home, travelling abroad, constructing her own life—which had precipitated our meeting. What I perceived from the vantage point of my own value system as a lack of congruence troubled me, as I recalled van Deurzen's advice that this approach:

. . . is particularly suitable for people who feel alienated from the current expectations of society or for those who are in search of looking to clarify their personal ideology . . . The approach is relevant to people living in a foreign culture, class or race . . . it also works well with people who are confronting particular upheavals in their lives.

(van Deurzen-Smith, 1995, p. 10)

Louise and I had met barely 10 minutes before, but already everything she had related for me with alienation, meaninglessness and upheaval. True, she presented a concrete problem, but it was entirely in keeping with the existential approach to see this as just one manifestation of a particular attitude towards the world.

The urgency of this situation seemed to present an opportunity as much as a difficulty for working with Louise existentially: the very attitude which she demonstrated in demanding an immediate solution might, paradoxically, be turned to advantage in encouraging her to take a more thorough look at the way she was in the world, given her wish to "get back on track" for the rapidly approaching exams. If she could understand that a quick fix would not deliver these exam passes, she might very well feel motivated to take the plunge and explore more fully. In any case if I were to refer her on to a cognitively-oriented colleague the inevitable delays would leave little, if any, time for the work to begin. After a few moments' consideration, I decided to take a chance and offer her the opportunity to work with me on the understanding that I was a therapist and not a solicitor or an advice worker.

"I can't offer you a solution to this problem in a legal sense, because that's not what I'm trained to do. You might want to think about telephoning the CAB to check this out further. But it seems to me that this whole experience has left you feeling upset and frustrated and I wonder if it might be helpful to you to talk about this with me".

At this point I briefly sketched in the way which I work, saying that as an existential therapist I tend to be concerned with the ways in which clients make sense of their lives and the meanings which they place on their experience, rather than attempt to fit them into models of health and illness. This attempt to communicate my approach and method of working (I have only mentioned the briefest outline here) sees quite crucial to me for the shape of the relationship which may ensue. It is humbling then to be brought up short by the client, as happened with Louise, when she cut through my explanation to ask what "CAB" meant. Had I thought, I would have realized that she was unlikely to have heard of this British institution. I explained what the Citizens' Advice Bureau was and then asked her if she felt she would like to talk to me about her situation. She seemed somewhat nonplussed on hearing that I had no powers which enabled me to force her housemates to return her money, but then quickly acknowledged that, of course, she "knew that really". But then what, she asked, was the point of talking about how fed up she was? I suggested that perhaps it might help her decide what to do if she were able to talk to someone who, up to now, did not know the details and might be able to offer a fresh perspective. After looking down for a few moments with a confused expression she agreed that it might be worth trying. Still staying with problem-solving language, she said that she had "nothing to lose" and that maybe I would "understand the mess better" than she did and be able to tell her what she should do to extricate herself from it.

I can still vividly recollect my initial impression of Louise. She was of average height and build with a great deal of very blond hair. She wore a polo-necked jumper under a pale pink shirt, pearls and designer jeans—altogether the ubiquitous preppy image the majority of the female American students on campus seemed to sport. I recall an impression of self-confidence, and also of frustration imparted by her direct, assertive manner and nervous, fidgety hand movements. I had to work quite hard from the first few minutes of the session not to pigeon hole her as a type, even the type which her appearance seemed to suggest she wished to be identified with. I see little to be gained from wrapping up my own tendency to categorize clients in terms of counter-transference, and it seems far more authentic to own that I had a dislike of the overly-enthusiastic, carefully groomed identikit image which seemed to be the hallmark of many of the students I saw on campus. Using a technical term for this dislike is evading the issue. While I was not particularly proud of my attitude, the fact that I was aware of the dangers it involves and did not pretend an immediate empathy made, for me at least, and continues to make in similar circumstances, something more real about any ensuing relationship. And from the point of existential paradox my ruminations on my ideal client tell me a great deal about my own strengths and weaknesses as a therapist.

Returning to Louise, having begun to talk she began to give vent to her feelings about being rejected by her housemates, her confusion about this, her fears of not meeting her parents' expectations academically, and her sense of having all her assumptions about the world thrown up in the air. She now felt she had nowhere to go and no one to turn to. If she quit her studies and returned home early, she would feel (for the first time in her life) that she had disappointed her parents by failing to live up to their idealised image of her. If she tacitly agreed not to mention the deposit again she would confirm for herself the label bestowed on her by her housemates of "rich bitch", which she found unacceptable. In fact the loss of the money would be no real hardship, but what it represented meant a great deal. As she expressed her plight, I received the impression that she felt herself to be the "innocent abroad" who had fallen victim to deceitful, unscrupulous people of a type who simply did not exist back in her home town. The confident image had fallen away to reveal the heroine of an old-fashioned melodrama!

It seemed important, having travelled so far in so short a space of time, to provide an opportunity for Louise to present the situation from her own perspective before attempting to re-introduce the elements of choice and responsibility which had become obfuscated. We all present ourselves as hapless victims of circumstances from time to time when we are at a loss as to how to conduct our lives, but to point out the self-deception which this entails too quickly will simply alienate clients and lead them to clutch their own particular hurts even more closely to themselves. The early existential philosophers, Søren Kierkegaard and Frederick Nietzsche, understood this well: their ironic aphorisms do not directly challenge the reader's way of being in the world; they unsettle readers and entice them to discover what is true for themselves, rather than what is held to be true for the crowd. Where the client feels overwhelmed, the existential therapist:

> . . . does not counter or challenge the client but neither does she agree or condone. She simply assists the client in the examination of her attitude in all its implications and she will therefore often . . . come to the conclusion that it is no wonder that the client feels as she does. At the same time she will help the client to translate that feeling into a concrete understanding of what is wrong with or missing from the situation. Her attitude will invariably indicate that a greater insight into what is expressed by the client will help her

find ways of altering her experience of the situation. The counsellor guides the client in the direction of such increased insight by dialectic questioning in the spirit of a philosophical investigation.

(van Deurzen-Smith, 1988, p. 34)

We are apt to think of culture shock as occurring between East and West or between those of different races. Although there is still much talk of a "common heritage" and a "special relationship" with regard to British–American relations, differences of work ethic and moral and social codes should not be underestimated, particularly as they are experienced by young people who have not travelled widely. In a sense, Louise felt herself "thrown" into her situation in London, rather as Heidegger (1967), in *Being and Time*, talks of the "thrown-ness" of human beings at the beginning of their lives. The crucial distinction between these two understandings of "thrown-ness" is, of course, that Louise had played an active part in creating her situation even though this fact was now hidden from her in her account of it.

Unable to secure accommodation on campus, she had found a room in a shared house by placing an advert in a local newspaper. While her fellow sharers had seemed friendly enough at their first meeting, she reported that she did not understand the lives which they seemed to lead. In fact, she saw little of them. One—a young man of around her own age—was, she assumed, unemployed. Certainly he never seemed to go to work. But although he rarely went out, he avoided the household chores. The other two—a man and a woman—seemed to be in a sexual relationship although, as Louise pointed out, she was sure they were not married or even engaged.

Louise felt that she had been tricked and lied to by these strange people and that her trust had been abused. The whole experience had been a bitter disappointment to her as she had expected this first taste of communal living to be an opportunity to make friends. She was aware that she had missed such an opportunity previously having, unusually for an American student, continued to live in the parental home after starting at university. As the only child of wealthy professionals in Florida, she had been used to a relatively luxurious lifestyle in which clothes shopping with her mother and parties around the pool featured large. She had never experienced any difficulty with academic work and told me that she had felt herself liked and popular. She expected on graduating to take up a well-paid white-collar post in America, if possible in Florida, in order to be within driving distance of her parents.

My sense of her was that to be anything less than happy and positive about life was not an option for her, and to admit to feeling depressed was quite alien to her way of thinking about herself. It was as though she observed herself experiencing difficulty and depression and did not know how to make sense of either. It seemed to her that she had suddenly found herself alone in a world of which she could make no sense, since her usual ways of operating in the world now failed to provide her with the social acceptance she was accustomed to. In fact what she thought of as her customary openness and friendliness made her an object of derision for her housemates. Her reply to my wondering how she was feeling at the moment, given all that she had related, surprised me somewhat and helped to strengthen the therapeutic relationship. She told me that she felt just like *Daisy Miller*, the heroine of Henry James' novella of the same name, which had been the set text for English classes. She asked, with an expression which suggested that she hardly expected that I should, whether I knew the book. I was able to respond quite truthfully that I did indeed. In fact I had read it some years before but did recall it as a moral tale of a type James developed and embroidered throughout his career. The important point about *Daisy Miller*, or at least that which I had taken from the tale, was that she is ignorant and therefore culpable and not simply naive in her attempts, as a young American, to get the most out of her visit to Europe. Paradoxically, for me at least, in telling me of her identification with such a fictional character, Louise set me to wonder whether she was not a more complex person than my prejudice had first suggested.

Did she bring up *Daisy Miller* simply as an example of an American woman trounced by European deviousness, or did she understand that James wished her to represent a rounded character with both naturalness and concealed intentions? It was important, of course, not to assume that my reading of *Daisy Miller* corresponded to that of the client. Indeed, I could be sure that our readings would not be identical. Given more time it might have been interesting to have explored this with the client further, always bearing in mind that the direction of therapy should be dictated by the needs of the client rather than the idle curiosity or wish to be seen as knowledgeable or well-read of the therapist. Nevertheless, the client's reference to *Daisy Miller*, and my confirmation that I had read the book, did provide some common ground between us and seemed to facilitate a greater degree of therapeutic alliance.

Perhaps, having established this much shared experience, Louise felt more confident in our relationship. Certainly she became more animated and spoke more quickly. Her housemates, she explained, apparently expected her to clean and to keep the fridge stocked with food. When she complained that they ate her food and did not pay her for it they told her she was "a spoilt rich bitch" and should stop wingeing. It came as a very great shock to her to realise that these people did not want to get to know her, and she found the label they put on her felt like an indictment of all she stood for—being a student, being American and affluent.

Things had finally reached crisis point a week before she came to see me, when she had mentioned to her housemates that she would be returning to America at the end of her semester, now only a few weeks away, and would, of course, expect the return of her deposit. To her amazement they denied all knowledge of any deposit and said she had fabricated a story to get money out of them. If she persisted with this story, they said that they would throw her out.

Louise and I had almost reached the end of the 50-minute therapeutic hour. While I occasionally continue for up to a further 10 minutes with clients when this feels appropriate, I have always been careful not to extend a session beyond this time. In this case I was aware that Louise had opened up and talked about herself to an extent that had seemed unlikely in the first few minutes of the session. There was a danger, I felt, that she might feel that she had exposed herself only to have it suggested that she return in a week. Her need to reach some clarity about her situation was pressing and her examinations, assuming she would be willing to return for weekly sessions, would give us only three more opportunities to meet. Besides, I sensed that her wish for quick results, if not addressed, would simply lead her to reject the idea of further meetings. She might easily argue that they would be a distraction from any revision she was able to undertake.

Although the pattern which sessions follow varies considerably with each client, I generally use the initial meeting with a new client to discuss what has brought them to see me and what their hopes and fears about working with me are, and then go on to discuss with them the contract that I feel I am able to offer if I feel that we can work together. I had been distracted to some extent by the amount of information Louise had presented and the urgency of her tone, but I now proceeded to raise the possibility of further meetings. As I had feared, she responded with a downcast expression, saying, "I'm not sure when I'm around, I'm going to the States in four weeks and I have exams and all—leastways if I take them".

The contrast between our animated discussion and this withdrawal was great and she appeared to shrink down into her chair—to become, literally, depressed before my eyes. I decided to depart from my usual methods and said, "OK, I would like to suggest, given all the difficulties of organising another appointment, that we have double time today and continue for a further 50 minutes. How does that sound to you?" Louise rallied immediately and her lost, abandoned expression vanished.

It seemed that my innovation might be a success. At the same time I had some anxieties. Was this ethical? Was it seductive? I was aware that I had departed from my usual way of working, which would have meant attempting to focus on our relationship and on what it felt like to the client to want a particular sort of interaction. On a more prosaic level, would one of us or both of us now begin to flag? In fact, the therapeutic alliance seemed strengthened by my willingness to make further time available to her. She expressed appreciation and I had the sense that this was the first time in months that she had felt really listened to and engaged with.

I pointed out what I felt to be something of a tension—that she had felt moved to leave her comfortable, secure existence in Florida and begin studies in a foreign city, living with people very different from herself. This suggested to me a certain flexibility and openness which had been hidden in her anxiety to be neither the "rich bitch" nor a victim.

The "rich bitch" label had stung her deeply, as she feared that there might possibly be some element of truth in it. She said it was as though her housemates had seen through her, had judged her, and had dismissed her as being of no consequence. That she felt their judgement so strongly and could not throw it off puzzled her and angered her because she felt she had not really been seen and that there was more to her than this. While she certainly felt their judgement of her, I fed back to her that I had been very aware of her judgement of them as shifty, lazy and lacking in initiative. Might it not be, I wondered, that they felt attacked in their turn by her, and that their wish to swindle her financially might be their way of getting even—of hitting her in the financial area where the greatest disparity between them was to be found. Louise looked startled by my reading of events and began to list all the ways over the past months in which she had helped them out by stocking up the fridge, even paying more than her fair share of household bills. And she had always taken care not to draw attention to this, in case it was out of line. But, I countered, how would she feel if the tables were turned and someone was doing all this for her, without ever being asked to, and then pointedly didn't draw attention to it? Her reaction to these words constituted one of those "Ahah" moments in therapy which are always so exciting and satisfying—"I would feel patronized". Louise looked dumbstruck as she spoke these words and then said, "So I really am the rich bitch after all?" Certainly, I agreed, neither side in all of this had really "seen" the other. For whatever reason, no meeting of real people had taken place, only a confirmation of a stereotype on the side of her housemates and a sense of being rejected and used on hers.

This new understanding of events was significant too with regard to the meaning each side attributed to the deposit. Louise had agreed earlier that the money *per se* was not important to her, what was important was the feeling that she had been taken advantage of. Now she saw that the message she had been giving her housemates was that she was quite willing to be used in this way. Her behaviour in relation to household expenses gave her a role and reinforced the image that she had plenty of money and could afford things the others could not. She had by her own agency been set up for their petty revenge—after all, if money was not as important to her as it was to them, why *not* relieve her of some of the stuff?

How, I asked her, did the picture I was describing fit with her own experience of herself? She had, she said, chosen to present an image of wealth to her housemates, thinking that by doing so she could get their approval and friendship. But this had been an inauthentic move on her part and had only succeeded in alienating them from her. Now that she could see this, she felt strong again and pitied them their petty revenge on her. She would, she said, "rise above it". "And maybe also learn from it?" I ventured, for this whole episode seemed to me to be a gift to her insofar as it enabled her to see herself in a new, perhaps more mature, active light than she had before. She still clung to the idea that it had almost been a "disaster' and that she had nearly been a "victim". It seemed important to enable her to understand that this "disaster", while being an uncomfortable experience, was also a valuable one. I sensed, too, that it was an experience which, whilst she might not fully realise it, she had actively sought. Not to choose is, in itself, to make a choice to be passive, to accept what others give you. But Louise had made a number of quite definite choices: she had chosen to place an advert for a house-share rather than live on campus, she had chosen the wording of this advert and, in due course, had chosen to move into the house where she had had the experiences she had recounted to me, even though her initial feelings about her decision to move there had been mixed.

One way into this might be to go back to the reason for her time in London. She had said that she came to London to improve her education: what, I asked her, did she think "education" was? Posed this question, she began immediately to talk about a process of certification, a fairly obvious route with a number of hurdles along the way in the shape of written examinations—a steady conveyor belt, in other words, to a well-paid professional career. But this, I pointed out, was a conveyor belt with bumps and jumps which were there for her to experience and which were sometimes unpredictable and could not be planned for. So, I asked, how about the idea of education as experience, what could she learn from *her* experience, what could she choose to take from it?

Once her agency in events became clearer, Louise was able to take a certain amount of pride in her adventurousness. She began to appreciate that what she had been describing in wholly negative terms had, in fact, constituted a tremendously important rite of passage for her from dependent "good girl" to capable "angry adult". At the same time she also saw that her lack of care in making arrangements about accommodation had "set her up" for this experience—she had thrown herself into an experience of which she felt a lack, but had done so incautiously. In appreciating more fully the reasons for events in which she had been an agent, not merely a victim, she began also to appreciate herself and relinquish the feelings of depression which had accompanied her muddled thinking. This movement in her perspective on life seemed to a great extent to have come about because I was willing to attempt to understand her personal world view and, in the spirit of exploration, seek out what made the world meaningful to her. This attempt to "tune into' the way of "being in the world" of the client seems to me to be the fundamental distinction between existential psychotherapy and the multitude of other therapies, which variously medicalise or otherwise pathologise often quite basic problems of living which are experienced in different ways by all of us at certain points in our lives, or which seek to free the client's capacity for transcendence or self-actualization and, in so doing, quite often pay too little attention to the ways in which clients relate to others in the world.

While the focus of existential therapy is the clarification of the client's way of being in the world and the way in which they create meaning, rather than solving a particular "problem" or finding a "cure" for some "dysfunctional" behaviour, I cannot claim to have been completely disinterested in hearing from Louise's psychology tutor a week later that she was now working hard for her exams, appeared cheerful and seemed far more engaged in classroom dynamics. Perhaps more significantly, when the tutor asked her how she had found the counselling, she responded that she felt better and that *she* had been able to clear some things up as a result of the session. I did not, of course, solicit this information, neither did I make any comment on what the tutor seemed eager to tell me. There is always a danger when summarizing a therapy, that the therapist will appear to be either foolish because they have overemphasised their misunderstandings of the client, while showing the client to discover (or rediscover) some innate wisdom which they had temporarily mislaid, or that the therapist will appear as a magician/thaumaturge who provides major new insights for the client in the space of a few brilliant interpretations. I do not wish to fall into either of these traps here: existential therapy is neither about patronizing the distressed client nor about the therapist's expert performance, but is rather concerned with the relationship between two people who together seek clarity on an issue of particular concern to the one temporarily termed the "client".

I feel the emphasis on relationship was particularly relevant in my work with Louise. Rather than simply function as a technician, I had sought to tune into Louise's way of being in the world and found myself relinquishing the stereotype I had at first had to work hard to bracket as I came to appreciate her as another human being. As Buber (1937) wrote, such "I–thou" meetings are enriching experiences for both parties. I was changed too.

It is not possible, of course, to know anything of the long-term effects of our meeting and there were no further sessions. My subjective experience was that of dramatic change in Louise, as though some block or barrier to movement had been lifted: even her body language on leaving the session appeared more fluid and open than had been the case at the outset. Given more time, I would have liked to know more about her relationship with her parents and about her plans for the future, but even if the change I observed should be short-lived it seemed to me that Louise had had a positive experience of therapy to take away with her and do with it what she would.

DISCUSSION WITH ZACK ELEFTHERIADOU

ZACK: I can see that you had to explore Louise's "thrown-ness"—as she did choose to come to the UK, live where she lived, etc. . . . The reasons for such choices are well hidden, but people leave one country or place with hopes of what they will leave behind and what they will find in the new one.

SIMON: Well there seem to be two kinds of "thrown-ness" in play here: on the one hand there is the thrown-ness which Heidegger (1962) and a number of other writers since Heidegger talk about. This is a radical notion about what it is to be human—that is, to find oneself born into a particular culture and family network, to have certain physical characteristics and genetic makeup, to be male or female, to age and die. We can't exercise choice over these but, and this is crucial, we can choose our reaction to them.

And, for Louise, there is her sense of finding herself almost inexplicably "thrown" into a different culture, but with the difference, of course, that she has chosen to be in a new place. The interesting thing is the way she makes sense of this experience, the degree to which she is open to it or, alternatively, denies her responsibility and also denies the value of this new experience and takes refuge—as Louise initially did—in the role of victim.

ZACK: Cross-cultural adjustment/culture shock includes the realisation that you no longer have a familiar frame. Your frame is no longer understood/liked/accepted, etc. . . . so it brings into question how much do others (the "host" community) have to do?

SIMON: Yes—and I also think the extent to which Louise felt her identity to be threatened by the reactions of the people she was house-sharing with draws our attention to the whole idea which is prevalent in the existential literature, particularly in the work of the Scottish psychiatrist

R.D. Laing, of ontological insecurity, the essential insecurity of the human condition.

I had a sense—and of course it can be no more on the basis of one session—that Louise's sense of self was very much connected to her ideas of family and being a dutiful daughter. This was quite rigid but also quite fragile, as her response to challenge indicated. I would have liked to have heard more about her experience of her family had we had further sessions.

Ontological security was linked by Laing to schizophrenia, but this anxiety about our existence is present in all of us. I don't think Louise was in danger of becoming mad, but I do think that, perhaps for the first time in her existence, she was suddenly in touch with insecurity. Getting her money back might have enabled her to evade this insecurity, but she recognised the value of this insecurity, however uncomfortable it was, when she began to work in the therapeutic session.

ZACK: Perhaps not only did her house-sharers hold onto the stereotype of her, but she also maintained it; as the "self" boundary became too unclear or unsafe and rejected by others she needed something more rigid to hold onto and hence present to others.

SIMON: I think that is true—we can probably all think of times when we have actively embraced a stereotype because its very narrowness seemed to offer some sense of certainty about who we are. I had a client who took on the mantle of evil black sheep of a very troubled family because that seemed to be all that was on offer, the role that the rest of the family had decided my client must have if he were to be part of the family system at all. In the face of annihilation most of us will accept any role or label that is available, even if it turns out, as in the case of my client, to be profoundly damaging. In this example, given a choice between being an annihilator or being annihilated, my client chose the former identity. But in the final analysis, if we seek to deal with our ontological insecurity by signing up to any very rigid notion of "self" (even a notion which at first appears very positive) we invariably limit our ability to be open to what life brings and reduce our ability to engage creatively with it.

REFERENCES

Buber, M. (1937). *I and Thou* (transl. R.G. Smith). Edinburgh: T & T Clark.
Heidegger, M. (1962). *Being and Time* (transl. J. Macquarrie and E.S. Robinson). New York: Harper & Row.
van Deurzen-Smith, E. (1988). *Existential Counselling in Practice*. London: Sage.
van Deurzen-Smith, E. (1995). *Existential Therapy*. London: Society for Existential Analysis.

7

THE INVISIBLE SCAR—
PSYCHOTHERAPY WITH A
HEAD-INJURED CLIENT

Alessandra Lemma
University College London, London, UK

INTRODUCTION

My aim in this chapter is to highlight the existential and psychodynamic aspects of recovery from a head injury. I consider these two perspectives to be complementary. Many of the challenges facing individuals who have sustained a head injury concern fundamental existential issues, in particular the question of the meaning of life following a life-threatening accident and the subsequent limitations imposed on the individual's functioning as a result of the injuries sustained. The manner in which such existential issues are experienced and managed by the individual will, in turn, reflect their own personal psychodynamics.

WORKING EXISTENTIALLY

Working existentially means different things to different people. My proposal to work both existentially and psychodynamically may even sound contradictory to some, but this may simply reflect the variety of interpretations of the very notion of "working existentially". For me,

Case Studies in Existential Psychotherapy and Counselling. Edited by S. du Plock
© 1997 John Wiley & Sons Ltd

working existentially is primarily about an *attitude* to therapeutic work which strives to give primacy to the client's story and the meaning they attribute to their experiences, as opposed to the constructions that I, as therapist, may place on the material presented to me in a session on the basis of my own experiences and prejudices. The psychoanalytic interpretations that I make inevitably reflect my understanding of what I hear, which is filtered through a theoretical framework I have found very useful. They are nonetheless presented to the client as mere possibilities and never as certainties. In this respect what I refer to as an existential attitude tempers the excesses of a rather unhelpful "psychoanalytic attitude", which tends to place the therapist not only beyond the reality-testing of the client, but which also grants greater explanatory power to the therapist's, as opposed to the client's, version of what both parties are ostensibly struggling to understand.

Working existentially also involves being open to *all* of a person's experiences and not simply those that are deemed important by the therapist on account of their theoretical allegiances. In the case I report here, the client's present concerns and his difficulty in managing his life were not reduced to the consequences of early experiences and unresolved conflicts. Rather, they were understood as arising in the context of a traumatic life event—a motorbike accident—which profoundly affected his existence. That this person's early experiences may have in some way shaped his responses to this event or resonated with the loss suffered by him, was neither excluded as an area of potential exploration nor was it rendered the focus of the work. On the contrary, it was approached as reflecting *as important* an area of exploration as any other which the client chose to focus on.

Finally an existential perspective helps to focus attention on the person's dynamic interaction with the world. This of course includes the relationship between client and therapist, who jointly co-create a very unique space where personal meanings can be safely explored. This relationship is one in which *both* partners are prone to the projections, distortions, prejudices and misunderstandings which can and frequently do occur in all relationships. The therapeutic relationship is, however, one where such interpersonal dynamics are made explicit and are explored. In this respect psychoanalytic ideas allow us to more fully appreciate the vicissitudes of human interaction. However, an existential perspective helps to remind us of the essential mutuality of this relationship.

THE CONSEQUENCES OF HEAD INJURY

Working with people who have sustained a head injury requires at least some rudimentary understanding of the nature of such injuries, as this helps the therapist to appreciate some of the behaviours typically displayed following head injuries. To begin with, it is important to see the brain as a dynamic and interactive system which allows for the complex range of activities we all engage in. It is the interactive complexity of the brain which explains why injuries to it can and do produce a wide range of deficits and symptoms. In an open head injury there is direct exposure of the brain tissue to the environment. In a closed head injury, as in the case reported here, there is no such contact, no visible scar on the surface of the head. As a general rule, more diffuse impairment results from closed head injuries. Many head injured clients display behavioural sequelae that render them apathetic, irritable, confused, impulsive and "childish". Lability or instability of emotional responses may be observed. Crying spells may occur without any obvious triggers. Periods of so-called manic excitement may alternate with periods of depression.

Cognitive impairments reflect more general limitations on higher-level, complex processes such as attention, concentration, perceptual speed, learning and memory. Such cognitive processes, while on one level a physiological reality, are also of course personal. As Sacks (1995) suggests, it is not just a case that we construct or interpret the world, but that it is our very own, unique world. Following a head injury, the "cognitive self", which is involved in our construction of the world, may crumble along with the damage to cognitive functions, thereby altering the very identity of the individual and the way they interpret and experience the world.

The critical question regarding the nature of the cognitive deficits typically observed following a head injury is the extent to which they reflect actual organic brain damage or are the consequence of psychological problems, such as depression or anxiety resulting from the psychic trauma of the injury. It seems likely that in many cases the observable pattern is the result of a complex interaction between the two.

CASE STUDY

Martin is a 31 year-old man who sustained a severe closed head injury following a motorbike accident when he was 26 years old, which has left him with both physical and cognitive deficits which have considerable consequences for his day-to-day functioning. He is a rather frail looking man with short brown hair. He walks slowly and has an unsteady gait as, since the accident, Martin has suffered from physical disabilities which affect his balance.

Martin's cognitive deficits are significant, yet subtle, and in many respects on first meeting him he comes across as an intelligent man with whom one can readily converse. People who have sustained injuries similar to Martin's show cognitive strengths and practical skills which they are nonetheless unable to integrate appropriately into ongoing behaviour but which create a deceptive veneer of coping which masks significant losses. Indeed, from being someone who ran his own small printing business, was involved in the performance arts and who had by all accounts an extremely promising career ahead of him, Martin now has to rely on a helper to assist him with everyday tasks such as cooking and gets very easily overwhelmed and frustrated if faced with too much information. He finds it difficult to take on more than one task at a time. Martin also frequently misunderstands what others say to him unless they speak slowly and give him plenty of time to process the information. These problems arise because Martin has suffered a severe impairment of his information-processing capacity, concentration and mental speed, so that he has difficulty in taking in either written or spoken information. His non-verbal memory has also been impaired. Although there is no significant decline in his verbal memory, in practice he does have a verbal memory problem because of the attentional limitations imposed by his slowed processing capacity, that is, his difficulty in taking in information. Such cognitive deficits affect his ability to "think on his feet".

Martin is prone to emotional outbursts, which are experienced by him as very frightening. These are characterised by what Martin experiences as uncontrollable anger and frustration, crying and shouting. In the sessions he would at times pace furiously up and down the consulting room, speaking at the top of his voice in the midst of tears. Although such outbursts are a not uncommon consequence of severe head injury, they are by no means haphazard or meaningless and occur often in response to external or internal pressures which are experienced as too overwhelming by the individual. At such times Martin feels "like a child"—and this also reflected my experience of him in the sessions. The consequences of the accident, in many respects, signified for Martin a return to the first chaos of infancy when he was no longer an infant and, more significantly, knowing that he once possessed knowledge and abilities at their fullest. While the process of relearning that clients often speak of following such injuries may be likened to the challenges facing a newborn baby, the analogy is misleading because these are adults who can still remember their lifetime's worth of experiences, even if some of their former abilities and potential may have become lost to them as a result of a head injury.

I first met Martin two-and-a-half years after his accident. He was referred to me with a diagnosis of "post-traumatic stress disorder", which the defence lawyers in his compensation case were arguing would account for his cognitive deficits. At the time he reported difficulties in sleeping, memory difficulties, tearfulness and labile mood, all of which are very common symptoms following a head injury and the psychological adjustment this necessitates. He was clearly distressed by the changes to his life and in his perception of himself which followed the motor-bike accident. In addition, he reported anxiety dreams involving road traffic accidents and expressed more general death anxiety. He did not, however, report any avoidance of stimuli associated with the accident. He displayed a diminished interest in life generally but did not express any suicidal ideation.

In this chapter I should like to focus on two particular aspects of my work with Martin, namely the nature of his relationship with other people, including myself at times, which was characterised by envy of their healthy, functioning brain, as well as the existential challenges he was confronted with in the course of his adaptation to the damage to his brain—damage which affected not just his physical being but the totality of his being.

The Damaged Self

The first few months of therapy were taken up by Martin's recounting of the accident and of his life since. He went into great detail as if he felt that I would otherwise not understand just how difficult his life was now— and indeed I could not really know and it was important to acknowledge this. He arrived for the sessions filofax in hand and would flip through it, day by day, to ensure that nothing that had happened, and which he now meticulously recorded, would be missed out. Since his memory began to fail him Martin had relied on his filofax to prompt him and he felt lost without it, as if his memory was contained in its pages. His need to share with me the minutiae of his days reflected how I also functioned as an auxiliary memory for him—as someone who recorded and stored his life story. Although his memory loss could be understood as a direct conse- quence of the injury, it seemed to me that Martin was essentially strug- gling with loss in a much broader sense and hence he was preoccupied with recording and so safeguarding his experiences.

Martin expressed considerable anxiety about seeing me, as he felt very mistrustful of professionals. He had had a very bad experience whilst an in-patient. A very strong theme which emerged in these first months, and which became a central feature of our work, was his perception of profes- sionals as in some way damaged. They were variously described by him as "incompetent", "stupid", as "not speaking English properly" or just as "sad" people whom he felt behaved as though *they* were head injured. It did appear, by his own account, that he had encountered a number of unhelpful professionals who had been acting on behalf of the defence as part of his ongoing litigation, and whose aim was to disprove or play down the extent of his injuries. Clearly this anger and disappointment needed to be accepted by me and appreciated as a reflection of his very real experience of being misunderstood and not respected by these professionals, for they appeared to have denied his loss. However, the persistence of his denigratory attitude even towards those professionals who had acted favourably on his behalf led me to a somewhat different understanding of this highly critical attitude, especially with respect to other people's intellectual abilities.

Throughout the therapy Martin referred to his now diminished IQ score: from a premorbid IQ which placed him the superior IQ range, Martin now scored in the average range. This represented a significant loss which was very meaningful for him. He had always prided himself on his communication skills, having been very good at school at writing, and he had hoped to publish in the future. In view of this his sometimes harsh criticisms on other people's use of English were unsurprising. In addition, he had to receive a great deal of speech therapy following the accident. His emphasis on other people's poor grasp of the English language seemed to reflect his own experience of how difficult communication had become, in terms of both his own struggle to comprehend others as well as in his attempts to convey to others his experiences in a manner that was meaningful to him. In a more general sense, Martin's onslaughts on professionals highlighted his apparent strong need to denigrate others as a result of his own envy of what he perceived to be healthy and intact. This process reflected his own struggle to come to terms with the damage to his brain and the loss this entailed, and hence with his altered existence.

The anger that Martin expressed towards the other professionals was also aimed at me. However, my attempts to point this out to him were met by denial. Over time I began to appreciate just how important it was for Martin to maintain an idealised view of me. He frequently commented on how well qualified I was and the fact that I was foreign seemed to be especially important to him. His world had been shattered and "damaged" by the accident and I felt that he was now terrified of also losing me in this wreckage. In order to hold on to this image of me as a good person he could only acknowledge his hostility when it was directed at others. The two main recipients of his projections appeared to be another head injured person he had befriended, who was in fact much more disabled than himself, and his carer, who was on the receiving end of some very virulent attacks by Martin. However, he was reluctant to consider the possibility that these hostile feelings might be partly the result of projections of his damaged sense of self onto others.

My anticipated fall from grace was not, however, very far away, as by the time the first year of therapy was almost upon us Martin began to show the first signs of more overt criticism towards me. He started to challenge the boundaries of the therapeutic relationship, referring to my "silly" rules. He thought I needed these and he would simply comply with my rules to humour me. His tone on such occasions could be rather contemptuous. Around this time I had also been asked to write a report on his psychological functioning for the Court. Although Martin was extremely grateful to me for the report, saying he had been very relieved to read that I had in fact understood his predicament well, he returned the copy of the report having made several corrections to my grammar. This was a regular feature of his response to all reports written about him. However, in this session he became very anxious, concerned that I might not be able to make the appropriate corrections to the report as my writing might not be up to standard for the Court. This proved to be an important turning point in the therapy. Although I acknowledged that it was quite possible that I had made some mistakes in my report I also invited him to consider why this possibility elicited such anxiety in him. This exploration led us to a joint understanding that he had come to experience me at that point, like himself, as in some way damaged and unable to express myself properly. This aroused anxiety in him as he then feared he no longer had available to him a healthy and competent thera- pist with whom he could identify. For the first time he expressed his anxiety that I might leave him. These fears were also linked to his sense that his own mother had found his brain-damaged state so distressing and unbearable that she could not take care of him. His mother, who was divorced from his father, had in fact, seemingly suddenly, decided to remarry and move abroad shortly after Martin's accident, while he was still an in-patient in a rehabilitation ward.

For a client to accept that which cannot be changed in their mental capacities it becomes important for the therapist to explore the extent of the abilities and potential that may still exist within them. In the course of my work with Martin it was thus essential to be mindful of the interplay between the state in which his disabilities were predominant and the state when a more perceptive and less damaged self was predominant. In particular, it was important to appreciate how his disabilities could be exaggerated for defensive purposes (Stokes & Sinason, 1992). I will high- light this process by focusing on one particular session.

Eight weeks after my report was submitted, Martin was reassessed by an eminent neuropsychologist who identified quite clear brain damage. Mar- tin brought this report to one of our sessions. He sat down and looked at me exasperated and said: "I cannot believe these people—this is a top neuropsychologist and he just cannot construct grammatical sentences". He read out several parts of the report, repeatedly stopping and expressing his criticisms of the grammar, saying that he did not really understand what the psychologist meant. Personally, I could not detect any such mistakes but I was aware of Martin's increasing agitation. He eventually got up to come and sit closer to me as he wanted to show me the report and commented again that this man was "so stupid". Martin turned the pages to the report's conclusion, which stated in no uncertain terms that he was brain-damaged and would be left with permanent impairments. As I read this quite definitive statement about him I too was incensed but for different reasons: it seemed so crude and I was aware of a need in me to soften the blow as though, like Martin, I also found the truth unpalatable. Yet Martin's focus was on the bad grammatical construction of the sentence. He made no reference to its content. It seemed as though he simply could not allow himself to process the sentence's very painful meaning. Perhaps he was hoping that if he could manipulate the report's grammatical structure he might also be able to change its message.

Martin asked me, still in his rather contemptuous tone, if I could understand what the psychologist was saying, and whether I could explain to him the meaning of a few sentences. I replied that reading the report had made him feel very confused and stupid as he felt he could not understand it. I added that it was perhaps less painful to act "stupid" because then at least he could protect himself from the report's painful message, because it reminded him so clearly that there was something wrong with his brain, something which neither the psychologist nor I could put right. I added that I felt he was actually asking me to make the painful links for him. I understood his attacks on the psychologist's grammar as reflecting his own attacks on his capacity to link words and make sense so as to preclude arriving at a meaning that was too painful to bear.

The Ebb and Flow of Acceptance

Adjustment following head injury makes many demands on the individual. One may liken the process to that of mourning, as the person has to adapt to the limitations imposed by the damage to the brain. The work with Martin taught me, however, that acceptance of such damage and the loss this implies at many levels is not a once-and-for-all process. Over the two-and-a-half years that I worked with Martin, he fluctuated from a position of acceptance and reconstruction of that which he could not change to one of withdrawal into a rather defensive stance, where the injuries he sustained had virtually elevated him to a higher plane.

In the early stages of therapy Martin would tell me that he felt the experiences he had undergone since the accident had radically transformed him. He now felt that nothing really mattered so that he was now able to just live one day at a time and was no longer bothered by the mundane issues which he observed his friends struggling with. Moreover, he felt that the process of relearning which he was undergoing was offering him a fresh perspective on life—one which he felt was precluded to those who had not undergone such a traumatic life event.

Life-threatening experiences do have the potential to alter our perspective on life and its meaning. The experience of an accident which leaves invisible yet indelible scars can give a person an enhanced appreciation of human vulnerability. Indeed, Bennett (1987) argues that the experience of a head injury may leave the person with a greater respect for life's fragility. Martin was very articulate on this point, revealing at times an enviable calm and acceptance of his own mortality. At times he also expressed his strong desire to live and to enjoy life in spite of his disabilities and was able to translate this into action. The end result could be great excitement about his strengths.

In some of the literature on head injury the so-called euphoria or manic excitement observed following accidents are understood as defensive measures against loss. This was how Martin's own "euphoria" had been interpreted in one of the reports written about him by another psychologist. While at times this applied to Martin, it was not invariably so. Indeed, it was important to share with him his genuine excitement simply about being alive and having survived a very serious accident, rather than pathologising his response to this traumatic event. Similarly, his altered perspective on life which he shared with me was not mere denial of his loss; rather, it reflected the process of adaptation to the world and the meaning he now attributed to his life from this new position.

During our sessions Martin would often engage in quite long philosophical discussions about the meaninglessness of existence. The changes in interpersonal, vocational and recreational activities which had followed the accident had depleted life of its meaning for Martin. That which he had once enjoyed, such as reading and going to the theatre, now acted as a sore reminder of the loss of his own talents and his promising career. The importance of work or a vocation in lending structure and meaning to our lives cannot be overstated. We only have to anticipate our own reaction to having our chosen vocation, one in which we are fully engaged, cruelly and suddenly snatched away by an accident we were powerless to prevent, and we will catch a glimpse of what Martin has had to face up to. I was, however, repeatedly impressed by his willingness to accept his limitations and the changes to his life circumstances while struggling to assume responsibility for the choices that were still open to him. At the same time I was also reminded of just how difficult it can be to assume responsibility for oneself and consequently of how tempting it was for Martin to hide behind his disabilities, giving himself over to the bitter twists of what he at times simply saw as his "fate".

The quality of Martin's philosophical explorations, however, differed over the course of the therapy and our joint understanding of such nuances became very important. At times, often following a painful confrontation with his limitations, the way Martin spoke about such matters was characterised by a particular quality which I felt belied a rather omnipotent attitude, as though he had moved beyond mere mortal concerns. On such occasions he appeared to idealise his "post-accident state" (as he called it) as a defensive measure against the experience of his significant loss. At other times his monologues also served the purpose of keeping me at bay, of shutting me out. If I tried to intervene he would frequently ignore my attempt to speak. When I managed to find a space and I would just reflect on how difficult it seemed to hear what I had to say he would at first appear to consider what I had said but would soon dismiss it in what I experienced as a rather contemptuous manner. He could easily make me feel totally impotent, as I suspect he often also felt as his experience of his capacity to control his environment had been curtailed by his injuries.

Reconstructing the Self

As biological organisms we seem to carry within us a sense of the whole. Sinason (1992) suggests that the intactness of our bodies and our minds confirms this sense of wholeness. However, following a severe head injury a part of us is no longer whole but is damaged irretrievably. The organic damage to the brain needs to be understood as affecting both the person's physical and non-physical being. Even if the individual can compensate for some of the cognitive losses which may follow such injuries, as Martin certainly has, the subjective experience for him was nonetheless that some part of him had been damaged and lost. Any loss of cognitive functions is therefore a threat to the sense of an integrated identity (Miller, 1993). Although the emphasis in current thinking is on the question of loss or preservation of identity following a head injury, the more interesting question, as Sacks (1995) suggests, is about an "adaptation or transmutation" of identity. The work of therapy is to facilitate such an adaptation or, if you like, to help the person to accept their "facticity" (Sartre, 1956) while helping them to assume responsibility for the freedom which exists within the limitations of their existential situation.

In psychotherapeutic work with people with organic brain damage we can appreciate the relevance of the concept of facticity. Human possibilities are always set in a framework of facticity. Freedom can never be absolute for it is always hedged and limited in so many ways. An organic problem and the person's consequent disabilities serve to illustrate this existential "truth". However, as we can see in Martin's story, a range of choice has been and is possible, and it is precisely this degree of choice that Martin fought so hard both to safeguard and to run away from. The existential paradox which was so central to my work with Martin is one which has a familiar ambiguity: on the one hand I am projected into the world; on the other I make my own project in it. Living with this paradox introduced a creative tension into Martin's life and enriched my understanding of, and respect for, human resilience.

CONCLUSION

This chapter has focused on psychotherapeutic work with people with a head injury. The existential implications of such an injury are far-reaching as, depending on the extent of the damage, the person will need to adapt to quite different capabilities and degrees of autonomous functioning. Such changes are accompanied by a very painful re-evaluation of one's life and its meaning as well as of one's own identity. The organic damage and the psychic damage are inseparable. To facilitate the process of re-evaluation it is essential to work in the here-and-now as the client construes his/her experiences. The disability may, however, at times itself be used defensively to retreat from a painful exploration of the loss which has taken place, as well as from the freedom and responsibility that remain open to the person. Throughout these explorations it is helpful to be mindful of the very complex dynamics that may develop between client and therapist. The therapist, while needing to be experienced by the client as strong enough to contain their despair and hopelessness, may well also be potentially experienced as the object of envy because of their perceived health.

DISCUSSION WITH THE EDITOR

SIMON: This is, I think, an immensely important account of client work for a number of reasons, not least because it suggests the direction existential therapy might take in the UK. It is clear to me that you value both the existential and the psychodynamic ways of working, and I imagine that in your work as a clinical psychologist in the NHS, of the two the psychodynamic is the approach which you are expected to employ. I wonder to what extent you find your colleagues open to existential ideas and whether you feel that clinical psychology in general might benefit from taking on board some aspects of existential psychotherapy.

Alessandra: Generally speaking, existential psychotherapy is not an approach that most clinical psychologists would be familiar with. The emphasis on evidence-based practice means that, in the main, it is those approaches which have been shown to be effective that are the ones of choice. Having said this, I also think that most sensible practitioners, especially those working with people suffering from long-term, chronic mental health problems, would be especially alert to the existential issues that their clients struggle with. Indeed a very recent paper deals specifically with the question of the clinical relevance and the predictive power of the "meaning in life" construct, suggesting that it is related to the outcome of psychotherapy (Debats, 1996). It seems to me that in addition to the varied intrapsychic and interpersonal conflicts that clients present with in therapy, they are invariably concerned with understanding their personal existence. This concern is more explicit when people have suffered a trauma and are trying to make sense of why this event happened to them. It is easy to reduce such existential concerns to the level of a manifestation of some underlying psychodynamic conflict, but in my opinion this reductionistic approach misses the very core of the individual and precludes the articulation of their philosophy of life. However, it seems to me that the individual ways in which we negotiate what life throws our way cannot be accounted for without recourse to our individual developmental histories. My bias here is towards a psychoanalytic model and I do think that a major weakness of the existential model is that it does not articulate a developmental theory.

Simon: Even as I expressed the idea that some of the existential approach might be useful in your work I was aware that there are some difficulties here. For example, how much of the existential–phenomenological perspective do you subscribe to and what of it do you abdure?

Alessndra: As I already mentioned in my chapter, the existential approach for me is not about technique but about an *attitude* towards clients. This attitude can be defined in relation to the basic phenomenological tenets of enquiry, namely the importance of bracketing our assumptions as far as possible; treating all material as being potentially relevant rather than giving priority, say, to sexuality, because our theoretical model focuses on that aspect of experience; and finally, monitoring our tendency to fit what the client says into our preferred theoretical model so as to allow for an understanding of the client's story (Spinelli, 1989). I am reminded here of a colleague's report in a psychoanalytic supervision group of her work with a 7-year-old girl. After giving the girl an over-elaborate interpretation of the meaning of her play, the little girl turned round and said indignantly, "That's *your* story, not mine"!

SIMON: How compatible do you find the existential and psychodynamic approaches to be? I know a number of practitioners would say that they are so radically different as to be mutually exclusive. It seems to me that very many therapists are unhappy with the distant, blank screen of the psychoanalytic and, to a lesser extent, the psychodynamic approach, and that they are attracted by a sort of misconception of the existential approach—that it is all about warmth, empathy and equality. These people then set about applying some of this to their original approach— "existentializing" it, as it were—but do not take on board the underlying philosophy. So people can shuttle back and forth between two images of therapy, both superficial and largely erroneous . . .

ALESSANDRA: To the extent that I see working existentially as being primarily about an attitude which encompasses a concern, and sympathy, with the need to make sense of one's existence, I do not experience working psychodynamically as being incompatible. For example, my own belief in an unconscious realm of experience is but an assumption which helps me to make sense of my personal and professional experiences. We are always guided by certain interpretative constructs. What is dangerous is to forget their status as such and succumb to the tendency to reify. If we can manage to stand back sufficiently from the investment we have made in one particular way of seeing the world, we can pre-empt the abuses that can arise within any theoretical framework and associated therapeutic approach.

REFERENCES

Bennett, T. (1987). Neuropsychological counselling of the adult with a minor head injury. *Cognitive Rehabilitation*, 5(1): 10–16.

Debats, D. (1996). Meaning in life: clinical relevance and predictive power. *British Journal of Clinical Psychology*, 35, 503–516.

Miller, L. (1993). *Psychotherapy of the Brain-injured Patient*. New York: W.W. Norton.

Sacks, O. (1995). *An Anthropologist on Mars*. London: Picador.

Sartre, J.P. (1956). *Being and Nothingness*. New York: Washington Square Press.

Stokes, J. & Sinason, V. (1992) Secondary mental handicap as a defence. In A. Waitman & S. Conboy-Hill (eds), *Psychotherapy and Mental Handicap*. London: Sage.

Sinason, V. (1992). *Mental Handicap and the Human Condition*. London: FAB.

Spinelli, E. (1989). *The Interpreted World*. London: Sage.

8

WHO AM I, IF I AM NOT A MOTHER?

Harriett Goldenberg
Regent's College, London, UK

INTRODUCTION

Infertility can be seen to raise fundamental questions about the meaning of one's existence, often leading to a struggle of "how" to be-in-the-world as a childless person.

A diagnosis of infertility can shake the individuals' understanding of who they are and what their existence is about. Many find they have to redefine themselves, their place in the world, and the meaning and shape of their lives—to scrap whatever blueprint they thought they were following, and think afresh. It is as though the anchors have been taken away.

The struggle with nature, with one's body and reproductive capacity is often a protracted, humiliating and painful one, striking at the core of one's sense of womanhood or manhood. Studies have shown that for men in particular, "fertility" and "virility" are experienced as closely linked, while "emptiness" can be a powerful metaphor for a woman.

Among the many losses of which the infertile often speak is the loss of control. Infertility unfolds gradually, painfully slowly. First they discover they cannot have a child when they choose. Then possibly, they cannot have a child "naturally", so they find themselves relinquishing control of the most intimate aspects of their lives and relationships to medical science. The sense of loss of potency goes far beyond biological

Case Studies in Existential Psychotherapy and Counselling. Edited by S. du Plock
© 1997 John Wiley & Sons Ltd

dysfunction to a sense of loss of power over their own lives and bodies. In many instances they only ultimately regain any sense of control by finding the will to say "enough", bringing the process of medical intervention to a close. They are then left with the even more daunting challenge of how to be with this new unwelcome "given"—of infertility and possible childlessness.

How to "be-in-the-world" is often the most difficult area for the childless, as they feel themselves involuntarily marginalised. They have become part of a new minority—one they did not choose. As such, they can feel a strong sense of isolation and alienation from family, friends and what they perceive as mainstream society. This sense of isolation and alienation can be felt as a separation from the core and rhythm of life, sometimes to the point where the infertile can doubt the reality of their own existence.

They must look afresh at the life cycle. Many childless individuals speak of not feeling "adult", of feeling "stuck", that they feel they are observers of life. And yet at the same time as not feeling grown-up, they may be acutely conscious of their mortality. In a sense, a part of them has died already. Their lives will end and they will leave nothing of themselves, or so it seems. Their struggle is often to find new reasons and new ways to live.

The existental–phenomenological approach seems very well suited to working with this client group, as it should already be apparent that infertility can pose fundamental existential questions.

In order to help individuals come to terms with their situation I have to help them gain a very full understanding of the particularity of "how it is" for them. The openness of the phenomenological approach, being receptive and alert as the process unfolds, while attempting to "bracket" my own assumptions and views, allows me to explore, together with my client, what infertility uniquely and distinctly means for him/her, and to be alongside him/her as this understanding unfolds. As part of this process, it is my job to help my client stand outside of her/himself so as to be able to reflect upon her/his own attitudes, views and ways of being—to question and clarify.

Infertility throws up complex questions about the individual's relationship with his/her body. The existential approach, viewing all experience as encompassing both body and mind, can be very useful when working with a client who is struggling to accept and reintegrate their body into their sense of self.

It is an underlying tenet of the existential approach that we cannot choose the "givens" of our lives (in this instance infertility), but rather we can choose our response to those "givens". The existential approach then goes on to provide a forum in which the sense of responsibility and anxiety to which this ability to choose leads can be openly addressed.

Infertility is a very personal experience, but also throws into question the individual's relation with the rest of the world. The existential approach acknowledges the centrality of the relational aspect of life. It also puts great emphasis on the relationship of therapist and client. The ability and willingness of the therapist to truly be a partner, fully engaged in the therapeutic enterprise, can play a crucial part in combating the sense of isolation so deeply felt by many infertile people. I believe strongly in Buber's notion of "the Between", that we (therapist and client) can go beyond our separate experiences and "meet" in some new place we have created together, and that such "meetings" are potentially powerful moments of healing.

Rather than focusing on the search to find explanation, existential–phenomenological thinking boldly addresses the uncertainty and ambiguity of life, and encourages an authentic way of living that accepts and recognizes the anxiety that this "not knowing" engenders. Such a theoretical framework is ideal for the infertile, as relinquishing the path they had envisaged and struggled with the uncertain shape of their future is perhaps the major challenge they face.

THE CASE

Sophie came to me when she was 30 specifically, as she said, "for infertility counselling". She walked into my consulting room stylishly dressed, seeming poised and confident. She met my glance straight on with big, lively blue eyes, and very quickly began to pour out the story of the past few years. She needed no prompting.

She began by telling me that she had already started infertility treatment, in fact had just had her first failed attempt at IVF (*in vitro* fertilization) which had been preceded by 2 years of drug treatment. It seemed that these were things she wanted me to know. She spoke gently, with a matter-of-fact tone. I listened.

She went on to tell me that she was a New Zealander, and had come to this country 9 years earlier to study. She'd met someone, married and stayed. She described herself as very happy in her relationship—in fact, considering herself to be nice-looking, well-educated and with a very comfortable life, she was staggered by the enormous pain she felt about her infertility.

There had been other tragedies in her life—she had had an ectopic pregnancy at the age of 21; a year later she and her boyfriend (husband-to-be) had been in a very serious car accident; 9 days after the accident her partner's mother had died of cancer. It had been a horrendous time, but she had coped really well with these events; in fact those around her had been enormously impressed by her strength and optimism and she had discovered an inner reserve that she felt glad to know about. I sensed her pride, but also perhaps a fear about whether this "inner strength" was holding up.

Then her voice dropped and she looked away from me as she spoke about how she had failed at her attempt at a career—"That was the first time I had ever failed at anything". She had struggled to recover from this blow, and to rethink the direction of her life. She described many tortured, tearful nights lying beside her husband, who seemed helpless and sometimes simply unaware ("That hurt a lot . . ."). In fact, she was still in the midst of this struggle; and the idea of having children had arisen as part of the solution. She said that she'd always wanted children but probably wouldn't have started trying when she did, if her working life had come together. This was her way of trying to make things okay, of trying to get back on track; to use time well.

"Then this—another brick wall. This is unbearable!" Her small, delicate shape heaved with the pain. We sat together quietly for some time.

I was struck by the force of her feelings, and although numerous questions were on the tip of my tongue about her relationship with her husband, and about the power and impact of all the other blows she'd already spoken of, it seemed inappropriate to pursue these areas now. She was consumed by her immediate pain. I remained quiet.

A few minutes later she said, "I don't know what's going to become of me; I'm so scared!"

"I guess it rocks you to the core, not knowing what's ahead of you, and whether you will be able to have children. It seems bigger than anything else you've faced in your life."

She nodded and sighed. "It seems too big to bear. I just don't have a picture. I try and look ahead and I get so scared!"

"Maybe we can try and face that fear together?"

As that first session drew to a close, we spent some time discussing practicalities, and chose to work on an open-ended basis, beginning the next week.

Over the following 3 years I came to recognise the cycle she went through, as she proceeded with four more attempts at IVF. She would build herself up, finding hope and optimism, seeping into the depths of despair, shame and hopelessness after each failure, then quickly picking herself up and beginning again.

During this period I watched her ride an emotional roller-coaster. Most of what I felt I could offer was simply to be alongside her as her mood and perspective fluctuated week to week. I would take my cue as she walked in the door.

Sometimes she would be focused on the detail of the medical process she was going through, and how those around her were responding to her pain and preoccupation. The hardest time for her was the two-week waiting period to see whether the embryos had implanted. Each time she tried a slightly different strategy. After the third failure she told me, "Do you know what I did? I laid in bed and I fantasised, and I remember actually saying to myself—it's okay, have your dream. It's not going to hurt any more because you've dreamt now. Enjoy it while you can. And I did . . . It was so lovely; I could almost feel myself holding a tiny baby close to me. It was so peaceful and warm. It was bliss . . . Then I went to the loo yesterday morning and there was the blood . . . again. I was stunned. It gets worse and worse." She began to cry. "One of the most awful bits is telling Jamie. It's like until I say the words, it's not entirely real, but then there's my pain and his, and the dream is completely over."

"Your life is not the dream."

"What life? I feel like I'm floating in outer space somewhere. I feel so unconnected. How will I be connected? Sometimes I wonder if I'm really here. You know, two nights before I got married my sister had a big party for us. I remember sitting on the steps with my best friend, and seeing everything ahead of me. It felt like I was stepping onto a ladder. You know . . . you get married, have kids, grow old and die. But now I don't know where I am. If you come off the ladder, then what?"

"I guess that's an enormous question that we have to spend some time with—what it might mean to come off the ladder you had envisaged—if you can find another path."

A few weeks later she began by posing questions. "What sort of life am I supposed to have? What's wrong with me?"

"I wonder who you are addressing when you ask those questions?"

"That's just it," she sobbed, "I don't know. I don't know the answers. I don't know where the hell to find the answers. This hurts so much, and it goes on and on, and I don't know . . ." She hesitated.

"How to make it stop?"

"Exactly. What if it doesn't work out? What if I don't get pregnant? Is it going to hurt forever?" She cried and cried.

"That seems like a terrifying prospect."

"There are no words . . . and what's even more terrifying is that I can't see anything else."

"I wonder about that. I wonder what it would mean to consider other possibilities."

After a few minutes, she responded quietly.

"I do, you know. I sort of think about adoption. Jamie is already talking about it. I can't do it. I think about Jamie and me. Physically we're very much alike. Everyone in my family really looks like each other. Jamie's nice looking, and smart and funny. If we adopted a baby it wouldn't be us—it would be someone else."

"It would be someone else."

"That hurts so much. I want my baby. I want to get pregnant, to get fat, to breastfeed. What the fuck is my body for!"

"It's as though your body is separate from you in some way."

"It feels like that—it's out of my control. I wish . . ."

"You wish?"

"I wish my body wasn't me! It disgusts me, this so-called body, and I'm angry and confused. Why do I have to face this? I want to have a normal life."

"I wonder what you mean by that—a normal life?"

"Normal, you know, like everyone else. I don't want to be different. It's all well and good being 'special' in some ways, but this isn't special. This is deficient! I remember after the car accident. At one point we weren't sure if my arm would heal properly. A houseman came to talk to me, and started discussing the different ways I might do things if I didn't have full use of my arm. I just looked at him, and said, 'Thanks but no thanks. I don't want to be innovative. I just want to do things the way I want to do things'. I know I'm very stubborn."

"But I guess the idea of having to consider other possibilities is very, very frightening for you. Maybe we have to try and understand that better."

"It is absolutely terrifying for me. Gives me a head-ache actually. I don't know if I'm brave enough to do this."

She got to the point where she didn't want to tell the other women at the clinic how many attempts she'd had.

I see the fear in their eyes. I don't want to make it harder for them."

"You feel concerned for them?" I queried.

"I never thought I would get to this place, being on my fourth attempt. It's unbelievable. My worst nightmare come true. I do feel concerned for them—those other women. I know how hard it is to hold onto hope. I don't want to rain on their parade . . . but that's not all. I can't bear the pity. No one has ever felt sorry for me before; in fact, all my life people have envied me." The tears poured down her face.

"But now?"

"Now I feel sorry for me. Now I feel like I have nothing. I'm cursed with a body that doesn't work. It's not going to happen is it? I'm never going to have a baby." The words hung in the air.

"I wonder how it feels to utter those words that you have never said before?"

"I guess you must have been thinking them for ages. I've been thinking them for ages . . . or I guess I've been thinking 'what if', but now it's starting to seem like the most likely thing. I remember when it finally struck me that I couldn't have a baby without help. We'd been having treatment for a long time already, and I knew the facts, but suddenly one day in the doctor's office it struck me in a different way. It was almost as if I had never heard his words before, 'You cannot have a baby naturally', even though I had heard them, even said them myself many times before. He hasn't said we should stop trying. He hasn't even hinted, but we will have to stop sometime, and somehow I just don't think we're going to have a happy ending."

Much of the time during this phase was spent in silence. Sometimes there simply were no words for the pain she felt. The silence we shared seemed fuller, and hopefully more respectful than any words could be.

One day she came in looking very tearful.

"I don't want to talk."

"I guess maybe there aren't words for what you are feeling now; simply enormous feeling." We sat together silently, the stillness punctuated by tears and sighs. I sensed we met in that silence. A little while later . . .

"Thank-you."

"Thank-you?"

"This goes on and on. There's nothing to say about it anymore, but here at least, I don't feel alone with it. Here I can just be."

"Maybe that's quite crucial, figuring out how to just allow yourself to be, to be who you are without a child."

Ten days later after her fifth attempt had failed, she came in and announced, with a glazed look in her eyes, "Well, that's it. I have had enough. We've decided to stop. It's finished."

We sat together quietly for a time, and then I said, "I wonder if you're not thinking, 'I'm finished' . . . I guess a certain vision of you life is finished."

"No, I am not finished. I know I can't just give up. In some ways I would really love to. But, I also sort of feel relieved in a way. Infertility treatment has been the main thing in my life for so long. I don't know how to do this—but I have to figure it out."

"Maybe we can begin to do that together, to see how to shape a different sort of future."

We had clearly reached a very important time. Sophie had fought very hard for the child and the life she wanted. She felt enormous fear and anger about not achieving it, and now she was saying that she was about to move into that blank space she had so dreaded.

Then for the first time a note of defiance seemed to creep in. She began a session some weeks later by saying:

"I've been doing a lot of thinking. It is a huge tragedy that I can't have kids—I know that probably sounds melodramatic but anyway—I'm not going to have my own child and, as it stands at the moment, it seems unlikely that I will adopt. But enough is enough. I realize I've got to the point where I have allowed myself to be defined by this. It's almost become my mantra, 'I can't have children—there's no place for me—I'm not really here.' "

"So it's almost as if there is only one way to live?"

"Yes, I realize now that it's sort of part of my stubbornness."

"I wonder about that stubbornness you describe."

"I don't know how to do this. It's very scarey, but it seems I haven't really got a choice . . ."

"Maybe in fact you are making a choice."

"Yeah . . . I guess so, in a way. It's my way to try and make sense of things, give them meaning, and I can't figure out the meaning in this, and that is so hard for me to take on board."

"So perhaps taking on board the mystery—what seems inexplicable is very important."

"I think I have to let go of this struggle to figure it all out—the why—I have to try and figure out how to be now . . . with what is . . . I would love to be as daring as I dream of—it's very, very scarey—all this 'unchartered waters' stuff, but somehow it seems there's a bit of me that is also really excited and curious to see what lies ahead of me."

Her eyes were sparkling, not with tears as they so often had been, but it seemed to me with a tentative sense of anticipation, even daring. I felt a huge sense of awe. We smiled at each other, and shared her sense of triumph and strength.

It was clear that our work was drawing to a close. We carried on for another 6 months, by which time she had begun a new course of study and was contemplating moving. In our final session she said,

"I never thought I would get here. I feel so much lighter. I know there will be times when it will hurt like hell, but all in all my life is turning out to be quite an adventure . . . Now I don't know what to say. What's happened here has been so important. I guess it saved my life."

To which I responded, "I guess you've started a new sort of life."

COMMENT

To accompany someone on such a journey as Sophie's was a huge privilege. The process was very challenging for both Sophie and me. Over a

4-year period she went from a determination to have certainty and the life she envisaged, to relinquishing her search for answers and accepting uncertainty and the unknown, courageously and with similar determination. I believe the fact that we stayed with questions of meaning throughout our work played an important part in enabling this transition.

There were times when it was very tough for me to remain alongside Sophie in the depth of her struggle but, as became apparent, what I could provide and what she desperately needed was a partner in that process. Working in an existential–phenomenological way, in which the therapist addresses the phenomena as they appear, made it possible for me to be guided by her pace and to be alongside her as different aspects of her experience became important for her.

It is obviously impossible to convey all that went on between us. One aspect which perhaps I have not focused on in my case description is those instances where I allowed myself to be visibly touched by Sophie's pain. I believe that there are times when it is totally appropriate, in fact very valuable to the client, as part of genuine engagement on the part of the therapist, to allow oneself to be "real" in such a way. It proved to be the case for Sophie.

Finally, I believe that working in an existential–phenomenological way made it possible for us to address issues of meaning (and meaninglessness), being-in-the-world, choice and anxiety fully and openly. There were times of discourse and times of shared silence.

DISCUSSION WITH THE EDITOR

SIMON: I'm very struck in your chapter by the paradox that it is when Sophie lets got of her image of how she thinks she should be that she begins to get a sense of living, of choosing herself again. This seems to bear out the idea central to existential philosophy that an existential crisis, however painful, is also an opportunity for change and growth. While it's terribly hard for Sophie to discover she is infertile, it does push her to consider what else she might be, how she might construct a life. How often have we met people, socially or in therapy, who say they live for their children, and sensed a kind of desperation—a need for the children to live the life they were afraid to engage with, a kind of living by proxy?

HARRIETT: I agree with you, Simon, that what Sophie experienced would be described as an existential crisis, very much so, in fact. Working with this client group, I am always working with people at a crossroads; if they have treatment and are successful, they are embarking on a dramatically new phase of their lives—if unsuccessful, they are then often thrown into a struggle with existence, as illustrated by Sophie's struggle.

Looking at Sophie's experience, there's the relevance of what in existential terms we speak of as "sedimented" or fixed ideas or attitudes, either about the nature of our own existence or of how life in general should be. You could say that much of Sophie's struggle and pain revolved around the fact that she had very fixed views of how her life should be; i.e. that she must be a mother. Her case also demonstrates the fact that individuals cling to these fixed ideas because to relinquish them, and be faced with a blank piece of paper, so to speak, evokes enormous anxiety and apprehension. This sort of anxiety about the uncertainty and fluidity of life is part of what is described as existential angst.

SIMON: Looking at childlessness from a slightly different angle, I am aware that the majority of gay men are in the interesting position of being fertile but face great difficulties in fathering children. Of course it might be argued that there is a far greater element of choice here, but I nevertheless wonder if your own work offers some valuable insights for therapy with this group too. I have found in my work with gay men that a number have talked about a feeling of "incompleteness' which comes somewhere between the "fertility/virility" link made by men and the "emptiness" experienced by women which you talk about.

HARRIETT: Yes, I certainly think that the insights gained from this sort of work have further applications. To start off with, it's useful to separate out the issues of "fertility" and "childlessness". They are two distinct dimensions. In a study I carried out in 1990, it seemed that the issue of "childlessness" was in fact the more crucial. It would seem reasonable to assume that the opportunity (or lack of) to parent is important to many. In fact I led a workshop 2 years ago, at a Jewish Women's Conference about childlessness. It was attended by infertile women, single women, single men, and a gay man in a relationship—all of whose lives were deeply affected by the issue.

To respond to your comment further, research and instinct suggest that you are correct in emphasising the role that "choice" plays in this issue. There are, of course, people who choose not to have children, and it has been found that the two groups (those that are voluntarily childless, and those who aren't) have little in common. Both have lifestyles different from mainstream society, but I have used the term "involuntarily marginal" to describe the social situation of those who want to have children but are unable to. Again, the fact of finding yourself in a situation that you do not want, of being different in a way you did not choose, seems to lead to enormous emotional struggle and turmoil. The linked issues of difference and choice are relevant not only here, but to gay men and lesbians, to immigrants, to minority groups in general.

SIMON: Your belief in Buber's notion of "the Between" seems to be
illustrated by your work with Sophie. Can you say a little more about
it, the qualities of the therapist which can help facilitate it and the
implications for the therapy if it doesn't occur?

HARRIETT: Martin Buber's concept of "the Between" is a complex one
that I have discussed in some detail recently in a paper I co-authored
(Goldenberg & Isaacson, 1996). Briefly, "for Buber, 'the Between' is a
realm which is neither objective nor subjective nor the sum of the two"
(Wood, 1969, p. 41). It is about going beyond one's isolated experience
and demonstrating a willingness to "meet' with other people. I believe
strongly that the "meeting" of client and therapist in "the Between"
forms a powerful part of the therapeutic process. The demand made
upon the therapist is that he/she demonstrate a willingness to really
move towards the other, to take what is known as an "I/Thou stance"
towards the client. It is an onerous demand, but I believe possible.
Often "the Between" is reached during times of silence, as demonstrated by my work with Sophie. To allow the client to be "with" an
other and to be quiet, to be caught up with their thoughts or feelings,
but to not feel alone with them—I believe this is something rare and
healing that we can sometimes offer to our clients.

SIMON: I'm not sure whether you have always worked existentially . . . I
wonder whether you have drawn in the past on other ways of working
and how they compare, particularly with regard to working with
infertility.

HARRIETT: Interesting question—I have not always described myself as
existential, in fact in the beginning I was not entirely sure how to
describe my orientation. At first I thought I lent towards the humanistic approach, but only briefly. Very quickly I felt that it was one-sided
and incomplete. It offered me little when faced with issues such as
hopelessness and finality. It was inadequate for my work with infertility which, as it happens, was my first client group. In retrospect, I
guess you could say that I landed in at the deep end, working with
fundamental existential issues and dilemmas.

REFERENCES

Buber, M. (1958). *I and Thou*. Edinburgh: T. and T. Clark.
Buber, M. (1965). *Between Man and Man*. New York: Macmillan.
Frankl, V. (1946). *Man's Search for Meaning*. London: Hodder and Stoughton.
Goldenberg, H. & Isaacson, Z. (1996). Between persons: the narrow ridge where I
    and Thou meet. *Journal of the Society for Existential Analysis*, **7**, 118–30.
Macquarrie, J. (1972). *Existentialism*. Harmondsworth: Penguin.
Spinelli, E. (1994). *Demystifying Therapy*. London: Constable.
Wood, R.E. (1969). *Martin Buber's Ontology*. Evanston: Northwestern University Press.

9

THE CLIMBER—DREAMING AND ITS THERAPEUTIC VALUE

Lucia Moja-Strasser
Regent's College, London, UK

INTRODUCTION

Michael is a single man in his late 30s, who experiences difficulties in sustaining long-term intimate relationships with women.

We have been working together for over 2 years. In the early stages of the therapy Michael seldom presented dreams. However, he often considered it worthwhile to mention that he could not remember a whole dream but just snippets, which he himself considered as meaningless anyway and not worth spending time in understanding. Nevertheless he swiftly learned that his dreaming states communicated to him something about himself that was of importance, of which he was not aware in his waking life.

This case study will demonstrate how an existential–phenomenological investigation of dreams can throw light on the individual's existence and give a more complete picture of how the dreamer experiences his being-in-the-world. The dreaming state, like waking life, is inextricably inter-twined with aspects of human existence, and both reveal how the individual connects to the meaning of whatever she/he encounters.

It is inconceivable to talk of dream analysis without mentioning Freud's view on dream interpretation, even if only very briefly, as an existential analysis builds on this model to some extent.

Case Studies in Existential Psychotherapy and Counselling. Edited by S. du Plock
© 1997 John Wiley & Sons Ltd

FREUD'S DREAM THEORY

Although he was not the first person who believed that dreams were meaningful, Freud was the first to develop a complete psychotherapeutic theory of dreams and provide a means through which one can gain an understanding of dreams. For Freud, dreams, parapraxes and neurotic symptoms are meaningful mental phenomena. This raises the question: how can we assign a meaning to a dream? In order to answer this question we have first to clarify what dreams represented for Freud.

In *The Interpretation of Dreams* (1900/1976) he argues that like day-dreams and hallucinations, dreams are a form of thought and also a form of memory. What we remember in our dreams is beyond the reach of the waking memory. The type of memories that Freud refers to are the forgotten infantile experiences or wishes that remain to some extent active in the daily life of an individual. When the person is freed from the conscious preoccupations of daily life, during sleep, these wishes or memories become accessible to the dream. In his *New Introductory Lectures to Psycho-Analysis* (1933), Freud claims that dreams illustrate this aspect of the human mind's activity. All dreams are attempted wish-fulfilments.

One of Freud's justifications of the unconscious mind is that the truth of what the person feels or thinks is revealed in their "unguarded moments", hence the dream. Thus, for Freud dreams are "the royal road to a knowledge of the unconscious" (1976, p. 647). In Freud's view the meaning of a dream can be accessed only through the help of interpretation. An interpretation (Deutung) is just an hypothesis about the meaning of a dream. To interpret a dream is not like decoding a message but requires from the analyst an in-depth knowledge of the dreamer. When we look at dreams from a Freudian perspective we always deal with two distinct aspects of the dream: the manifest dream (the dream as remembered) and the latent dream (the wish, other desires and associations that the dream reveals).

In order for the unconscious wish to become the dream, it goes through various distortions and transformations which are called the dream-work. Dream interpretation is the reverse journey to that of the dream work in that it moves from the dream phenomena, by free associating to each element of the dream, to the latent content of the dream (the wish).

Although the dream phenomena are the starting point of any dream interpretation, the attitude of a Freudian analyst to the dream phenomena is not entirely a phenomenological one. That is, there is no attention given to what the dream appears to mean. The dream phenomena stand for something else, the unconscious wish. The instigator of the dream is the unconscious wish which is linked to the meaning of the dream. The analyst is able to interpret and give meaning to the dream using the dreamer's free associations in conjunction with his own knowledge of symbols.

In stating that dreams have meaning, Freud's theory is consistent with a phenomenological approach. However, unlike phenomenological theory, Freud's approach invokes the notion of an unconscious mental system. Only by accepting this standpoint can we adhere to this way of working with dreams.

EXISTENTIAL–PHENOMENOLOGICAL APPROACH TO DREAM ANALYSIS

My way of working with clients is informed by existential philosophy and Heidegger's phenomenology. There are a number of assumptions that I adhere to and that colour my attitude towards the world, myself and others.

First of all, to exist as a human is to exist always in a particular world, never in isolation. We exist and define ourselves through the relationships we have with people and things. Heidegger refers to a human being as *Dasein*, which means being-in-the-world, thus indicating that a human being is not a substantial self but a relationship. Our lives have meaning through these interactions: "Dasein only 'has' meaning so far as the disclosedness of being-in-the-world can be 'filled in' by the entities discoverable in that disclosedness" (Heidegger, 1962, p. 151). We are a flexible, dynamic openness which is the ability to disclose the world and ourselves. By being constantly attuned to the world there is a mutual shaping or moulding that goes on. Intrinsic in being human is finding oneself always in a mood (state of mind) or moving from one mood to another. In this sense, mood is a general attitude towards the world that is at the ontological level. Our world relations move between two poles: either out of ourselves towards connecting to others in order to make contact and create meaning, or towards oneself—away from the others, seeking surrender, abandonment or letting go.

An existential–phenomenological approach to dreams focuses on an individual's expression of their world relations as they appear in the dream. As there is no single agreed model for doing so I shall now present my own understanding of phenomenological work with dreams. In general I see my work with clients as a sort of creative exploration, and similar to other forms of art it never repeats itself. However, what my clients consequently get in therapy is my own individual style. This is unique as well as being influenced by a number of thinkers and practitioners.

Working with dreams from an existential–phenomenological perspective does not refer to a single explanatory model. Dreams are not seen as the result of some magical "dream-work" that needs to be re-traced. The phenomena of the dream stand for what they are and they do not "symbolise" something else. We exist as much in our waking lives as we do in our dreaming states, they are different aspects of the same existence.

Dreams usually are an expression of the dreamer's current existential position, and in this respect they can be an invaluable asset as they give the dreamer a message about their way of being-in-the-world. "Designing one's dreams as blueprints for reality is the beginning of a life which brings fulfilment" (van Deurzen-Smith, 1988, p. 173).

As in waking life, in dreams we exist always within a world with which we interact constantly. We do not have dreams, "we are our dreaming state, in that we exist in the ways of our dreamed behaviour toward the world as much as in our waking behaviour" (Boss, 1963, p. 261). Working with dreams from an existential–phenomenological perspective is in many respects simpler than Freud's approach to dream analysis. This does not mean that it is easier.

Throughout the investigation of a dream, as a therapist one has to be constantly aware that this is the dreamer's search and not one's own. The client is the one who assigns meaning to the dream. The role of the therapist in this exploration is just to be a co-explorer, an interested and sensitive companion who follows the lead of the dreamer.

After listening to the dream it is useful to ask the dreamer to put the dream in the present tense and re-count it in this way, maybe several times. This procedure takes the dreamer back into the experience and mood of the dream, as if it was happening just then. The dreamer is able to reconnect with all the dream images. At this point all the various elements of the dream can be explored further, by clarifying assumptions and pointing out contradictions or paradoxes.

The next step is that of systematically examining the four different levels of existence as they appear in the dream. These are the physical, social, psychological and spiritual dimensions. These different levels represent the context or the possibilities within which we experience our world relations. They are basic dimensions of our existence and, as all aspects of existence are relational, it is helpful to explore how the dreamer relates on all the different levels and to which aspects he/she might be open or closed.

Emotions are always present on each dimension of our existence and they illustrate how we are attuned or how we find ourselves in-the-world. The emotions that clients always express in a dream reveal where they find themselves on the territory of living. It shows how open and flexible they are to the paradoxes that are present on every level of existence. By exploring the different elements of the dream, the dreamer will be confronted with assumptions, values and beliefs. By clarifying and exploring these further, a better understanding of the client's worldview can be achieved.

In order to bring into focus the most essential images and elements of the dream, it is important to ask the dreamer to sum up the dream into one sentence.

As the dream unfolds so does the meaning of the dream, which comes out of the connections made by the dreamer with the various elements of the dream. Once the meaning is established, the dreamer can be asked to see what connections can be made with his/her day-to-day experience. In every dream there is an existential message which expresses how the dreamer relates past, present or future projects. A description of a specific client of mine will illustrate the above points.

CASE STUDY
Referral and Contract

Michael is a self-referred client. He is in his late 30s. His reason for coming to therapy is that he experiences difficulty in sleeping due to some disturbing thoughts that wake him up early in the morning. Also he is concerned that at his age he is not able to have a long-term relationship. He has given a great deal of thought to these issues but has not succeeded in finding a solution on his own. In the past he had been in analysis for a while and had found this a waste of time. What he aims to achieve in therapy is to get a clearer understanding of what is "wrong" with him, what makes him so different from other people of his age.

Michael is an attractive-looking man. He has brown curly hair and blue eyes. His smile is charming and he uses it often to cover up painful experiences. He is highly intelligent and very articulate. Michael is cynical, particularly about himself. He has a dry sense of humour. Initially he gives the impression of being a fairly confident, happy, outgoing person. He spends a lot of time worrying about a lot of things. Michael has a number of close friends and seems to be getting on well with his colleagues at work. His parents play a marginal role in his life. He had never experienced the loss of any significant other. However, he is dreading the idea of his parents getting old and possibly dying soon. Michael is Jewish but does not practise his religion.

At the first session we agree on an open-ended contract, meeting once a week. After six months this contract is renewed as Michael requests to see me twice a week. We continue to meet on this basis.

It is interesting to note that an early stage of therapy Michael mentioned that he can never remember his dreams. He recalls only one dream which is a recurring one and which he first had as a child.

BIOGRAPHICAL DETAILS OF CLIENT

Michael is the second child born into a Jewish family. He has an older sister who is married and who has children of her own. Michael feels warmly towards his mother, whom he describes as being loving, gentle and caring. His relationship with his father is tenuous; Michael always finds it difficult to communicate with him. At present he is seeing his parents infrequently. The relationship with them seems to have become quite formal; he is unable to discuss with them many matters that are of significance to him. However, he remembers his childhood as a happy one. In his late teens he felt particularly supported by his parents when he had a nervous breakdown, as a result of which he became completely dependent on them. At that time he was labelled as mentally ill, having had a psychotic episode. This lasted for a number of months, which he describes as living hell. He used to have obsessive thoughts and no control over them. He lived with the terror of becoming possessed by the devil.

There were two different conflicts that he had to cope with in those days. One was not knowing whether it was really possible to become possessed by the devil or whether it was just his own fantasy. The other conflict was that he had a short time during which he was unable to sleep because of his fear of becoming mad and because of thoughts that were racing in his head. On the one hand he wanted to sleep, on the other hand he feared that if he fell asleep the devil would take over. In his effort to make me understand what he was talking about he compared his experience to that of watching a horror film, where you want to stop watching but at the same time are glued to the screen (he has never watched a horror movie again). He went on to explain that this whole experience was not just an ordinary fear but that it was more like an indefinable and very fundamental terror that touched and shook his whole being. In his own words, he defined existential anxiety. Every time he is unable to sleep he fears that this experience will come back and because of that he takes sleeping pills, particularly when he travels away from home. He was under medication consisting of antidepressants, antipsychotic drugs and sleeping pills for about 3 years.

Looking back at this stage, he evaluates it as having changed his life drastically. First of all he had to stop college and, as mentioned earlier, became completely dependent on his parents. He feared being on his own. He remembers being able to share with his mother all these horrible thoughts as they came into his head and found this extremely helpful. He felt that without the drugs he could not have survived.

Michael had great difficulty in letting go of the label of being mentally ill and he tried to convince me of the rightness of this label. Over time he was able to gain some clarity and understanding of the so-called "psychotic episode'. For about 9 months prior to this, he had been work-ing in a psychiatric hospital, where he had been receiving limited super-vision or support. This had some bearing on the subsequent events.

When exploring with him the way in which he felt that the "psychotic episode" has affected his life, he acknowledged that as an immediate result he became less intellectual than previously. By this he mean that for a while he had to stop reading, as any new idea became a threat for him. He had so many ideas in his head that he found it difficult to cope with them. Michael became interested in more basic things, such as just to be able to regain "mundane consciousness" and not to be chased by all these "paranoias". This was all that mattered—all he wanted. He also remarked that this whole experience has deadened his feelings. His responses to situations had changed—he became a sort of "cold fish". He was not touched by other people's physical pain. When one of his colleagues who was seriously ill had broken her ribs through coughing, this had left Michael completely cold.

To some extent he lived with some sort of "obsessive" thoughts, on and off, ever since he had his nervous breakdown. Before he finally got a job that felt to him was satisfying and gave him a sense of self-worth, he used to be woken up in the early hours of the morning by thoughts that were self-torturing. He basically blamed himself for not being good enough.

Once he got his present job, which happened some years ago, the "self-torture" shifted, to blaming himself for not having a long-term relationship. This would occur whenever he happened to be between relationships. He was very clear about what makes it so important for him to have a long-term relationship. When asked what is "long-term" he defined it as 2–3 years. Not to be in a long-term relationship makes him feel uncomfortable and sad. He feels like a freak, and also it gives him a sense of having failed as a human being. He compares himself to other people of his age, most of them in relationships with families. At the same time he realises that not to fail by having a long-term relation-ship does not equal success. Many of his married friends stay in those relationships whilst being extremely unhappy.

Michael has been living in shared accommodation since he left home in his 20s. He resents having to share with other people and complains of having his personal space invaded by others. After a year in therapy he decided to buy himself a flat and finally have his own space. When all the negotiations for purchasing the flat started, Michael became extremely anxious at the thought of living on his own. After almost a year of living in his flat, he seems to enjoy his own company and is pleased to have his own niche.

His hobby is climbing. At times when he is climbing, he feels in his element, at one with nature and happy to be alive. For him to climb is to be in control and to be able to face difficulties. Very recently Michael attempted again a very difficult climb, which he had had to give up once before. This time he succeeded and he was very proud of it (even more so because not long before on the same climb a very famous climber had died—and a wreath was placed where he fell). But Michael said that he would not take the risk of climbing without a rope.

Since he has been in therapy with me, which is for almost 3 years, he has had three different girlfriends. The first relationship lasted for about 5 months, the last two for a year each. Michael's present relationship is very rocky. He lives with the conflict of wanting to end it and at the same time not wanting to lose the good things about this relationship. Joyce, his present girlfriend, is an extremely nice person, very intelligent and sensitive and extremely tolerant with Michael. They have very similar tastes and Joyce is able to respect and give the space that Michael requires.

To my surprise, one day he became interested in presenting the only dream he had ever remembered. He was amazed to discover a significance in this dream which before had seemed completely devoid of any meaning. After this, he would often bring just snippets of a dream until slowly he became able to remember a whole dream. It was obvious that he very much enjoyed working on his own dreams. He described his dreams as all being surrealistic and absurd.

The salient issue, prior to the dreams I am about to present, was that he lived with the ambiguity of either ending his present relationship and living with the guilt of having hurt such a nice, loving person as Joyce, or staying in the relationship and having to feel suffocated because some of his basic needs were not met. The dreams that I will present were brought in two sessions within 1 week.

3 SHORT DREAMS

Dream 1

> I am driving a car and you are driving behind me. I am driving on a very busy road. The road is ugly and there are lots of cars on it.

When he recounts the dream the second time, he reports it as if I am no longer driving behind him but just monitoring his driving. When we begin the work on the dream. Michael says that being in the car means being in control. At the same time he has no idea of where he is going. For Michael the car is like his life—he is in charge of it without having a sense of direction. The busy road is just annoying and unpleasant by its ugliness, but nothing can be done about that. Having me behind him and monitoring his driving makes him feel perplexed, uncertain and uneasy. He is perplexed just to see me behind him, uncertain if this is part of therapy. Unease is the general mood which is connected with him being observed by me.

It seems to me that Michael is not willing to delve any deeper into the meaning of the different elements of the dream at this point and he sums up the dream as follows: "I am driving a car being observed by Lucia and feeling uneasy and uncertain". However, Michael is much more interested in making connections between the dream (without fully exhausting all the elements) and his everyday life. For him, this dream is about his experience and the process of therapy.

He does not seem to understand how therapy works, if it does, because he does not have a yardstick. By "yardstick" he means something that one could compare it to. But then the question that arises is, whose yardstick would this be? After some thought, he concludes that it would be better to use himself as a yardstick and to keep in mind that therapy, most of all, is a process. Often he feels that being in therapy is fake and that he is malingering.

He sees me in the dream as he sees me in therapy: neutral and cool. By neutral he means that I am with him and observing his process without "leaping in" prematurely. He says that he supposes that this is what he needs, because half of the time he doesn't believe what he is saying and he needs me to be critical and sceptical. He sees me as somebody who observes his struggle and who does not take charge, and helps him, in this way, to overcome it. It seems that his dilemma in relation to the dream is whether I should be the driver or whether I should leave him in sole charge of his vehicle. By seeing me as "cool" he means that I do not pretend to know what he is experiencing and remain at a distance from his experience. It is interesting that he also connects the dream to his experience of becoming mentally ill at the age of 18. This was for him a very confusing, emotional time, of which he could not make sense in those days. Often after that breakdown he went through periodic difficulties and crises. In therapy he is slowly gaining some understanding of this experience and is able to make sense of his mental world, which involves containing the anxiety and uncertainty that goes with it. This has happened over a long period of time in which small aspects of "that life" have become clearer.

Examining the four different levels of existence shows that the *physical world* is present in the form of the car and the road, which are both man-made environments. The physical world is taken over by people. It is notable that the road is experienced as unpleasant and ugly. On the *social level* by implication, people are there driving their cars, but they are anonymous and he does not know them and is not interested in knowing them. I am also present, but he is uncertain whether I am just behind him, monitoring him, or somewhere else. The relationship between us is that of him being passively observed and monitored by me. On the *psychological level* he feels on his own, being observed and maybe judged, having to perform and conform. He is not only conforming but he would like to have the standard more clearly defined. As for the *spiritual level*, it appears that he has the project of learning to drive his car better. In spite of the ugliness of the environment, the annoyance of other people's presence and his loneliness, it also looks as though he craves guidance in pursuing this project.

Obviously there is a lot more that could have been further explored from this dream had there been more time for this in therapy.

Dream 2

> I see this magical mountain landscape. There is something weird and surreal about it. I know that my parents are there but I do not take much notice of them. They take a different route. I am taking a short cut by climbing up the rock. The cliff is very steep and I am climbing without a rope. Whilst I am climbing I feel the texture of the rock, which has something delicious about it. The texture is rounded, grey-white and silver in colour. I get to the top of the mountain but actually it does not look like the top; indeed, I find myself on the lowland. There is a country lane, a street where lots of people are passing. Somewhere there is also a fair.

Michael describes the general mood of the dream as being one of excitement and at the same time one of dread. In the dream there is daylight but he describes it as a dull day. Finding himself on the mountain is very exhilarating. The presence of his parents in the dream has little significance for Michael. They just happen to be there and are walking around the mountain. He isn't sure, but he thinks that they were supposed to meet at the summit. By taking a short cut and climbing up the cliff, ironically Michael arrives where he started from, at the base of the mountain.

Questioned as to what it is like to climb on his own and without a rope, his response is that it is exciting but also scary: "Going against gravity, the ground can embrace you at any time". When I asked him, "So what if the ground should embrace you?", he smiles and mutters, "I don't want to think about it". When I point out to him that obviously he does not want to use the word death, he swiftly changes the subject. The texture of the rocks evokes in Michael delicious feelings that he used to have about many things when he was a child, e.g. listening to fairy tales. Touching the rocks—their roundness and smoothness, in spite of their coldness—is very sensual.

I ask him what it is like to take a short cut. "Well," he says, "short cuts don't take you anywhere. If anything they take you back where you started from". I ask him what the top of the mountain signifies. "Well, it is some expectation, some kind of reward for having climbed up." I suggest that it must be very disappointing to see that you arrive, after all that effort, back where you started from. Michael says that arriving at the "top" of the mountain he finds himself walking on a country lane where he sees a lot of people walking around and being quite jolly. He doesn't know anybody and he feels quite lonely. There is also a fair somewhere. In spite of this absurd ending, the dream is not unpleasant.

He sums up the dream as follows: "I am climbing up this mountain and I arrive at the top, but actually I find myself at the base". As in the previous dream he sees a connection between the dream and his experience of therapy. He is having difficulty in understanding the process of therapy. It appears that this present dream is about some effort he is putting in, in order to get somewhere where he thinks he will be rewarded. However, he finds himself back where he started.

I point out to him that I have often heard him question to what extent therapy is of use to him. It is astounding to me that despite all the work and the risks he has taken here, he is still doubting its worth. At this moment I allow my own doubts about the benefits that he gets from therapy to overshadow what actually his experience of therapy might be. My interpretation is taking into account only the result of this climb, which is arriving at the bottom again, and seems to lessen the importance of everything that has taken place before, such as him enjoying the scenery, feeling exhilarated and challenged by the climbing. Also, the presence of people in the dream and the fair that takes place somewhere implies that there is a possibility for relating as well as for having fun.

It becomes obvious to Michael, through looking at this dream, that indeed he has some expectations and wants to see very obvious results from therapy and, as it transpired in the previous dream, he also wants to have clearly defined standards.

Examining the four dimensions of his existence as presented in this dream, it appears that in the *physical world*, the natural environment is beautiful and stimulating and he copes with it well. He finds his way through the natural world with ease. Climbing and the physical contact with rocks gives Michael a sense of oneness with the elements of the natural world. He feels free and in control of his life. The fact that he is climbing without a rope, and running into danger by doing so, adds some thrill to this activity. It shows his confidence in his ability to survive. On the *social dimension*, the first presence is that of his parents. He pushes them into the background by abandoning them and by taking the short cut. Other people are present in the dream and Michael experiences their presence more as if they are part of the scenery. They are just passers-by; complete strangers with whom he has no contact at all. He doesn't aspire to go towards the fun fair—a place where he could be together with others. He ignores others. On the *psychological dimension*, he enjoys being on his own with nature, in fact so much that he pushes other people away. He is at ease with himself and in complete control of his life. His power to concentrate intensely on the task in hand, like climbing, eliminates everything that could interfere with his task. On the *spiritual dimension* he is pursuing some sort of achievement which is attainable to him, although it appears in a different light when it has been achieved. The intention in the dream is to take a short cut in order to get quickly to the top of the mountain. Michael is clearly determined to expose himself to some risk, only to realise eventually that he has got back to where he started from. He recognises areas where he fails and he sees that there is room for improvement. This is relevant in his relationship with his parents. They matter to him but he rather opts for being on his own, even to the extent of taking a risk that puts his life in danger.

Dream 3

> I am part of a project. There are other people involved in it but they are just bystanders. A man is in outer space and he is attached to a rope, something more like a cable. I am aware that this cable is extremely tenuous and that it could snap at any moment. I also know that if the cable snaps, he will be floating in outer space and he will be lost for ever.

Recounting the dream, certain new elements are introduced:

> I am part of a project and we put this man into space (beyond the atmosphere) and the only connection is this cable, which is very tenuous and extremely thin in some parts. I am very *worried* that at any time this cable will break and the man will be drifting in space forever . . . The *horror* of it.

First of all, emotions are much more clearly described in this second version. Michael obviously is very worried and feels responsible for the man who is in outer space. He is worried because this man can be lost at any moment and he feels responsible because he, together with the others, have put him in outer space. Being worried and responsible makes him aware also that he cannot save the man, because just touching the cord could break it.

I note that Michael is part of this project together with others, but he does not know the other people—there is no connection with them; they are just around. He says that his sense of responsibility is not diminished at all by the presence of the others because he, and only he, is responsible for the man in outer space. Whilst he is aware of the presence of others, he does not share with them the sense of responsibility but rather carries the burden on his own.

Questioned as to how the man could stay alive if he was beyond the atmosphere, Michael says that he gets air through the cable. I point out that it was interesting how he sometimes used the word rope (as in climbing) and at other times, the word cable. The cable, paradoxically, is the connection to both life and death. As a life-line it provides the person with oxygen, but at the same time, because it is very tenuous and thin, it could break at any time and consequently the man would be drifting forever. For Michael, outer space refers to infinity, beyond the atmosphere. It is all empty and cold, as in a science fiction film. The man in space is unknown to Michael.

When I question Michael whether he thinks that the man could live in outer space, he says that this is only possible through the cable that supplies air for him. Nevertheless, I point out to Michael that his worry and horror is about the cable snapping, because of which the man would drift in space for ever. Although Michael's worry is clearly about the snapping of the cable he does not face up to the immediate consequence of asphyxiation. His concern is for this aimless floating about rather than the concrete consequences—which is death. When Michael talks about the cable rupturing he does not face up to the fact that the man will die of asphyxiation.

In summing up this dream, Michael says, "Oh God, Oh God, this cable might break at any time and this man will be lost for ever, and I am very worried".

He easily connects the dream with one of his own projects on which he is working at the time. This could become a great success or it could also become a disaster. Similarly, as in the dream, there are other colleagues who are involved in this project but who do not play an important role in it. It is entirely Michael's project, as is the responsibility that goes with it.

Examining the different aspects of his existence as it appears in the dream, it seems that the *physical dimension* is represented by the space that is occupied, the ground on which Michael and the people find themselves. It is there implicitly but it is anonymous: one could say it is taken for granted. Another aspect of the physical world is the outer space, an environment which is spacious and wide open, which Michael has no experience of but that he describes as being cold, empty and infinite. One needs to use one's imagination to get a sense of that. It can be linked with his climbing experience, which is also about heights and open space. There is a juxtaposition of two environments: the outer space and the ground. The rope connects the two and is the spatial foreground in the dream.

The rope or cable that connects the man in the outer space with the earth is an aspect of a man-made environment and can be looked at in two different ways. One is as that which supplies air for the person out there, keeping him alive. The other is that it is merely something that keeps him attached. Much of the physical environment is a hostile one. The outer space cannot sustain human life.

On the *social level* he finds himself in the company of other people who share in his project. They are unknown to Michael. They are anonymous entities. Nevertheless, they are in the dream without Michael having a relationship with them. They are passive, faceless and inactive, rather more like observers or props than human beings. However, he relates to them indirectly. The only other person present in the dream is the man in outer space, who is also unknown to Michael. Michael is in charge of his life. This man is also passive, dependent on others and out of control. Michael is relating to a person that is out of control and needs to be looked after. It is interesting to note that Michael relates to this man in outer space, with whom he is connected by this rope and who is at a great distance from him, whilst he is not relating to those that are near him and with whom he is sharing the task in hand, the project. If the rope snaps there is the threat of losing the man and consequently all connections might be lost and with it all possibilities of relating. In spite of the presence of other people in the dream, Michael seems essentially alone with his responsibility.

On the *psychological dimension* Michael is burdened with an immense sense of responsibility for the man in the outer space. He is solely responsible for this person. Michael can fail, and failure is imminent loss of human life. This also implies failure of staying connected to another person. When he talks about his dream he often says "I know", "I am aware", which illustrates a strong sense of self-awareness, self-consciousness, reflectivity and a strong awareness of personal responsibility. This worries him, which indicates that he takes his responsibility seriously but fears being overwhelmed by it. There is a bit of a sense of inadequacy here.

On the *spiritual dimension* his project is an unattainable one, which is keeping this man alive through a cable that provides air. Michael has put this man into space, which is a rather omnipotent act, considering that the others in the dream have no significant role other than as bystanders. Although this project is an ambitious one, his preoccupation is with the fragility of human relations and the fragility of human life. One can identify the values he places on responsibility and adequacy. There is a lack of basic care between Michael and the people involved in the project. The failure of the project is blamed on failure of the equipment. He is not actively responsible. Although he is responsible he cannot take the responsibility. It is a fated universe in which he can not help but fail.

Having this very ambitious project he overlooks the consequences of this, which is that of bringing the man back to earth. This becomes an impossible task when he realises that the very attempt of trying to save the man could actually bring about catastrophe by snapping the rope and losing the man for ever. The word "death" is not mentioned by Michael when talking about the man in outer space; it was implied, though, by referring to it as "he will be drifting in outer space for ever".

The exploration of the dream does not end in that session. There is an epilogue to it.

Epilogue

At the very next session Michael announces that he has ended the relationship with his girlfriend. He is very upset about losing her and extremely guilty for believing that he could damage this woman by his decision to end the relationship. His guilt is coupled with a great sense of responsibility for her well-being. He experiences mixed feelings about having ended the relationship. He feels that for all the obvious reasons, which are beyond the scope of the present case study, he could not continue this relationship, whilst regretting this.

As we are exploring the various emotions that he is struggling with, Michael suddenly says, "I think that the dream I presented in the last session was a premonition dream". What he is saying is that the dream represents his desire to hang on to the relationship (by the rope or cable), an ambivalent attempt which is doomed to fail. He recognises that he is actually the man in outer space and that the cable which is so tenuous has now snapped.

We explore together his great sense of responsibility towards his girlfriend. He is facing his own destructive potential towards another person. The other side of this is that he believes that he is so powerful as to be in charge of the other's well-being. Considering this, it is not surprising that he feels so responsible. His expectations in the relationship are extremely high and if they are not met he has difficulty in maintaining a relationship where he loves the person and leaves the responsibility for their own survival. Instead he takes over and expects to be in control.

If we consider this dream as being a premonition, then this can be used as a good example of how present preoccupations in waking life can appear in our dreams and enable us to reflect on them. Whilst he had considered ending the relationship in waking life he had not had the courage to act on it. In his dream Michael knows that he is fighting for a lost cause and it is just a question of time admitting this to himself.

CONCLUSION

Working with Michael on these dreams is an illustration of how I understand using the existential–phenomenological framework in clarifying and elucidating a journey in the search for truth. In these dreams Michael is confronted with the difficulty that he experiences in relating to people, a difficulty which often makes him feel isolated and alone. It also makes him realise how much he is instrumental in that. As waking and dreaming life are an expression and part of the same existence, that of being-in-the-world, they are highlighting aspects of Michael's existence that have not been focused on before and thus bring them into awareness with more poignancy.

In Michael's case, through the dreams he gets a clearer understanding of his position with regard to certain existential issues, in particular those connected to his attitude to others. It makes him recognise the unlived possibilities that are there for him, that he has not yet actualised. Michael has also to admit to himself that he is not yet able to see what is qualitatively essential in an intimate relationship, the bottom line being what is he willing to give in order to get.

By allowing the dream phenomena to unfold, and by examining his relationship to those phenomena, he is able to face his existential condition with all its limitations and in particular how he is attuned to and responds to the phenomena that reveal themselves. Consequently, we were able to look and understand all those phenomena in terms of their current essential significance. Exploring the different levels of existence and elaborating on each aspect of the dream, through the associations and connections Michael was making, provided him with more information about what in the external world he is, or is not, able to resonate with.

In all three dreams, Michael is on his own. The presence of others is incidental. Even the presence of his parents is not particularly significant. People in his dreams are more part of the scenery than epitomising a relationship of any sort. The only relationship that seems to have some significance is that in the first dream, between him and me. This he experiences as passively being observed and monitored by me.

Exploring these three dreams gives one a clear picture of Michael's worldview—how he sees himself in the world and how he relates on the different dimensions of his existence.

DISCUSSION WITH THE EDITOR

SIMON: I was interested to see, so clearly expressed, the distinction between a psychoanalytic and an existential–phenomenological approach to dreams. You say that your own method is unique to you, but I wonder if it is true to say that existential therapists, in general, do work in this way?

LUCIA: Well, I think your question is much more complex than you intend it to be. Before I answer it let me just make one correction. I do not remember ever having said that I am using a "method". This would go very much against my understanding of the existential approach. I would like to highlight, however, what you seem to imply in your question, that there might be a "method" that in general existential therapists adhere to. I would argue very much against that! A "method" is just a way of *doing* something. According to my understanding of the existential approach, the emphasis is on "being with" the client, rather than doing something *unto* the client, which would exclude the use of a particular method. For the argument's sake, let's say that you are correct in your assumption. If you are correct, it means that my way of working with clients cannot be unique, yet I believe it is.

The uniqueness consists first of all in the particular alliance that I have with my client, which is paramount; secondly, in the attitude of openness and respect that I have for my client's reality. This attitude is phenomenological to the extent that it remains at the level of description, with no attempt to fit that reality into any diagnostic framework. This also means listening to the explicit, as well as the implicit, level of my client's discourse.

The quality of engagement that I have with any client includes that of not being judgemental, but not as a moral ideal—more in the spirit of helping them to see where they find themselves situationally, and enable them to re-formulate their past through the present. All this is in order to be able to use this new awareness in making more informed choices for the future.

As I bring into this interaction my world and my whole being, this adds another element of uniqueness. You might say that most existential therapists will agree with this, but if you do believe in the uniqueness of each individual and each encounter, the outcome is also going to be unique.

The attraction and specialness of the existential approach for me is that there is no model and no assumption of how to work with the clients. It does not prescribe some particular method, but requires that however one works, one must be in accord with existential–phenomenological philosophy.

SIMON: I often wonder whether dreams do represent existential messages. Quite often they seem to me to be just so much dross—at best a process of sorting and tidying of associations prompted by events of the day. I'm interested when clients make a point of recounting dream material, and so I suppose I accept that they will decide when something is important, but do you think there is always an existential message, just as Freud believed them to invariably be symbolic?

LUCIA: Dreams are what you make of them. All depends on how you relate their message and the meaning you attach to them.

Now, answering your question: first of all to my knowledge Freud did not think that all dreams are symbolic. For Freud, symbol interpretation is a small part of dream interpretation and must be used cautiously.

Yes, I do believe that all dreams potentially have an existential message, but for those who might use symbolism as a means through which they can reach to the meaning of a dream, the analyst has the key of the symbolic meaning, which invariably is the same for each person. From my perspective, the existential message is arrived at by the dreamer, which is the result of their exploration of the meaning of each element of the dream. I am part of that exploration but, as I said earlier, I am only a co-explorer and always following the lead of the client on that journey.

The meaning of the dream is not there from the beginning but it does emerge from the interaction of the client with the elements of the dream. Dreams have no intrinsic meaning; however, pragmatically one can always find meaning in dreams, although this may in the end be meaning that we simply attribute to them.

SIMON: You quote from van Deurzen-Smith (1988), 'Designing one's dreams as blueprints for reality is the beginning of a life which brings fulfilment'. This appears to raise the exciting prospect of dreams as something we can influence and use as a means of discovering solutions—or at least new perspectives on—our problems of living. Have I understood this correctly, and if so how would this work?

LUCIA: There is an intangible quality to dreams; however, I do not believe that they give solutions to our problems in living. Having said that, it all depends what the dreamer makes of the dream, and if they believe that the dream's message can be seen as a "solution" for a particular problem, then that is so for them.

The way in which I understand this quote is: we *are* as much ourselves in our dream as we are in our working life. If we accept that dreams are our own work and not a "thing" that happens to us from somewhere, i.e. the work of an unconscious, and if we are able to distil their message or messages, these can become a map for the dreamer's original project.

BIBLIOGRAPHY

Boss, M. (1957). *The Analysis of Dreams*. London: Rider.

Boss, M. (1963). *Psychoanalysis and Daseinsanalysis* (translated by L.B. Lefebre from *Psychoanalyse & Daseinsanalytik*, 1957. Bern: Huber). New York: Basic Books.

Boss, M. (1977). *I Dreamt Last Night* . . . New York: Gardner.

Boss, M. & Kenny, B. (1987). Phenomenological or daseinsanalytic approach. In J.L. Fosshage & C.A. Loew (eds), *Dream Interpretation—a Comparative Study*. New York: PMA.

Condrau, G. (1991). Professor Medard Boss (translated by Anthony Stadlen). *Journal of the Society for Existential Analysis*, **2**, 60–61.

Freud, S. (1990/1976). *The Interpretation of Dreams*, vol. 4. General Editor: Angela Richards (1976). Harmondsworth: Penguin.

Freud, S. (1933). Revision of the theory of dreams. In A. Richards (ed.), *New Introductory Lectures on Psychoanalysis*, vol. 2. Harmondsworth: Penguin.

Heidegger, M. (1962). *Being and Time*. Oxford: Blackwell.

Spinelli, E. (1989). *The Interpreted World*. London: Sage.

van Deurzen-Smith, E. (1988). *Existential Counselling in Practice*. London: Sage.

10

UNHAPPY SUCCESS—A MID-LIFE CRISIS: THE CASE OF JANET M

Arthur L. Jonathan
Regent's College, London, UK

INTRODUCTION

People tend to assume that there are two categories of clients seeking counselling: on the one hand the weak and disadvantaged and on the other hand the wealthy with time to spare. This case suggests something very different. It is about someone who has "made good" from comparatively poor beginnings; someone who is almost totally immersed in her work and has little time for leisure pursuits; someone who cannot comprehend why, given that she has riches, success and power, she is not happy. Janet M is a highly successful woman, just entering mid-life. She appears to have everything one could wish for and yet is desperately unhappy. She is discomfited with her life and often feels "lost" and alone, even though she has dozens of friends and acquaintances who appear to like and admire her. She is very good, in fact excellent, at her job and her skills and prowess are widely acclaimed—and yet she feels strangely unfulfilled and disappointed in the midst of her success. She is aware that she is actually overachieving in one or more sectors of her life, but subjectively she experiences a sense of failure or underachievement in other sectors. She cannot make sense of what she is experiencing: she reckons

Case Studies in Existential Psychotherapy and Counselling. Edited by S. du Plock
© 1997 John Wiley & Sons Ltd

that she should be feeling satisfied, happy and fulfilled, but she feels none of these things. She has come to therapy, she says, for a reappraisal of her whole life. She wants to find out what it is all about.

THE CASE

When she first came to see me, Janet M looked every bit the successful businesswoman: she was exquisitely turned out in a well-tailored business suit, she spoke in well-modulated tones, her bearing was one which exuded confidence and when she shook my hand her grip was firm. It was only when she sat down and began to talk earnestly and initially hesitatingly that it soon became apparent that she was sorely troubled. She was, she said unhappy and dissatisfied with her life, but couldn't understand why, as she had everything which she guessed most people would say were the essential ingredients for a happy life. She needed, she said, to make some sense of it all. It was June 1992 and Janet M had just turned 38 years of age. Some 14 years earlier, armed with a first class honours degree in computer science, she had come down to London from Birmingham. Bill, her childhood sweetheart whom she had married during her final year at university, had come down to London with her. His job was also involved with computers and he had arranged a transfer to the London branch of his firm. Janet M had taken a job with a large firm in the City of London and had immediately felt that she had entered a crazy world where a very few were earning a lot of money, whilst most were earning comparatively little. Janet M was a very bright young woman whose abilities were soon recognised, acknowledged and rewarded, so that she very quickly rose through the ranks, achieving a high status in the firm within a very short time. After two moves to even more highly-paid and higher-level jobs, Janet M started her own computer software company. This became so successful that she now employed over 100 people and her own personal income was of the magnitude of the salaries of the top 2% of the highest paid in the country.

Following several moments of mutual silence, Janet M looked at me for a while before saying: "You must think it strange that I want to see someone like you when really I have everything in life most people would dream about!" My response was to say nothing and just wait for her to go on. "I should be happy, but I'm not, and I can't understand why."

Our session yielded the following information: Janet M's problem had started from the time she began to be successful and to earn vast sums of money. She had many friends and acquaintances, people who all seemed to like and admire her, and yet she often felt alone and lonely. She was very good at her job and yet she felt discomfited and unfulfilled. She and Bill had begun to grow apart and he had devoted more and more of his spare time to the pursuit of his hobby, sky-diving. Eighteen months ago Bill had gone on a sky-diving weekend in France. He had been killed when his parachute failed to open. Janet M was quite dry-eyed when she was talking about Bill's fatal accident.

"I'm not looking for a bereavement counsellor," she informed me. "I want to look at myself, at my whole life. I want to find out what it is all about." Would I be prepared to work with her, she wanted to know. I replied that I was. The remainder of the session was devoted to clarification of practical and "frame" issues, such as time, cost and frequency of sessions. We would meet once a week.

I was a bit surprised, in the light of what she'd said about bereavement therapy in our first session together, that in the following few weeks the main focus of our dialogue, set by Janet M, was her late husband Bill. She and Bill had grown up together, in fact they had lived but a few streets apart, their families were friends, they had gone to the same school and they had become sweethearts at a very young age. It had always been expected that they would marry when they were old enough and this they duly did, when she was in her final year at university. At first their marriage had seemed idyllic, but things started to go wrong between them after they had come down to London. Bill seemed to lack drive and to have no ambition. He was quite content to "cruise along", as she described it, at the same level and more or less in the same job. So, it soon became obvious, he was not as successful as she. She was advancing whilst he appeared to be standing still. "That's when we grew further and further apart," she said, in a matter-of-fact way. In the end they were sleeping in separate rooms and hardly communicated at all. I wondered what Bill had said about all this. She replied that although he was the sort of person who never said a lot about anything and would rather keep his feelings to himself, he had at odd times blamed her work, her ambition, her new friends and her new social circle. He felt left out and discarded.

Janet M's whole demeanour then suddenly changed. She was no longer exuding an air of calm and composure, in fact the very opposite seemed to be occurring. She was fidgeting in her seat, there were beads of perspiration on her forehead and I noticed that her hands were clasped so tightly together that it looked as if all the blood had drained from her fingers, they were so deathly white. All the signs pointed to someone who was sorely troubled. She opened her mouth to speak several times, but no sounds emerged. My first reaction was to say something, perhaps to remark on what I was observing with regard to her body language, but in the end I decided to say nothing. I felt that just being there with her, in a totally engaged manner, paying full attention to her, was sufficient. We sat, looking at each other, for what seemed like an eternity but what was in reality a very short time. When Janet M started to speak, the words seemed to rush out after each other.

"It's about Bill," she said, "about his death. I'm not sure. I don't know what happened. I think I know what happened, but I'm not sure." This was followed by a short silence.

"What is it you're unsure about, Janet?" I ventured.

"It's the parachute not opening," she said. "Why didn't the parachute open? It's very strange, isn't it, about the parachute not opening?"

"What are you saying, Janet?" I asked. "Are you saying that it wasn't an accident?"

She was again silent for a while and then said, in very calm, clear, deliberate tones, "Yes, that is what I'm saying. I believe that Bill deliberately did not pull the rip cord. I think he killed himself."

She was full of guilt and remorse, she said. I pressed her to talk about this. What was the guilt and remorse about? She had some difficulty in putting this into words, but what eventually became clearer was that it wasn't so much the fact of his death, but more about the way she felt about it and, of course, about Bill as well. In the months and weeks before his death, she had found herself beginning to despise Bill and to feel ashamed of him. Her feeling was that he seemed to be locked in a certain social class into which he'd been born and from which he didn't appear to want to escape, whereas she was socially upwardly mobile. It was almost as though there were a class difference between them. He seemed to be becoming somewhat of an impediment in her rise to the top. She had been surprised at her reaction to his death, and it was this that was causing her to feel a strong sense of guilt. Her reaction had been one of relief. She had felt almost pleased that he was now out of the way. She stated quite emphatically that she wasn't mourning and wasn't feeling sad but that she did feel guilt and remorse.

Janet M talked about another reaction to Bill's death that had quite surprised her: it was the realisation that she could now possibly make a good match with someone in the City. She actually found herself beginning to look around for a suitable partner. She had had an affair which had started while Bill was still alive, but this had proved to be very unsatisfactory. She had met Tom through her work. He was the head of an advertising agency which was promoting an advertising campaign for her company. As our discourse proceeded, it was becoming apparent to Janet M that somehow the question of her sense of power was a factor. With her rise in the City had come this realisation that she was a powerful person, and this feeling of power was a heady one and she found that she quite liked it. She was now beginning to realise that her sense of power was a strong factor in the breakdown of her marriage. Bill had been a weak character, with no drive and no ambition. His response to her rise to power was not to exert himself and try to go along with her, but rather to withdraw into himself and into his hobby. That was when she had started to despise Bill. That was also when, she now realised, she had become attracted to powerful men. She had become attracted to Tom, whom she thought was powerful. She had found that this was not so, not at least in his relationship with her. As the head of an advertising agency employed by her company, at that point Tom was also her paid employee and this made a difference. Tom was a married man with young children and Janet M was now wondering what he had been running away from by entering an intimate relationship with her.

Janet M and I talked about how her sense of power had driven her away from her husband and had actually alienated him, and how she had taken up with a man whom she found not to be as powerful as she had at first thought. She had been surprised to find that the man to whom she had been attracted turned out to be her inferior as well. If she had been a man, she conjectured, then she wondered whether she would see it all like this. Perhaps it would be different for a man. As a woman, she was starting to see how this sense of power stood in the way of closeness to other people and of closeness in what she called her "love" relationships. She felt now that it was her power that alienated her from others, so that she had no real friends, and that even alienated her from her family in Birmingham. She wondered about her relationship with Tom. There had been a complete sexual role reversal: she had sought him out, rather than the other way around: she had become the hunter. She was left with a doubt about whether she'd actually been manipulative and even guilty of using him and so abusing her superior power over him.

In the next few sessions, Janet M returned to the question of why she was not happy and fulfilled, in spite of success related to money, status and power. Power, she had come to see, did not bring happiness in its wake. She wanted to take a good look at her life, if I would bear with her, she said. She was clear about one thing: all focus in her life was solely on her career; there were no other categories of meaning. She spoke of an arid landscape, with the only peak being her career, everything else being flat. It was a very powerful image that she presented. She spoke about living in no-man's land; belonging neither here nor there. She realised that many values had been stripped from her life and the only values she could now recognise were values to do with success, something she could never have envisaged when young. She felt cut off from her past. Her success was something that she found difficult to even compare with what she had come from in Birmingham. Values, she felt, lay in comparison and now there *was* no comparison. She felt cut off from her past, from her roots, from all she learnt to value as a child growing up in Birmingham.

What also became apparent in our discourse was that Janet M was embarrassed by her success, by her status and by her money. In the midst of the hustle and bustle of her work, in spite of having many friends and acquaintances (all from the world of high finance) she often felt alone and in isolation. The problem, she had come to realise, was about values. She was not sure any more what her own value system was. What she was doing now, she thought, was searching for a personal value system. She was searching for meaning in her life. She recounted how she had once been convinced that financial rewards would supply this meaning, but she had found that they in fact created the opposite: a sense of having no particular meaning or purpose. She was reminded of feeling down at one time and going on a massive spending spree, including the purchase of a new car, and feeling a sense of great elation for a time. She also recalled how this had been followed closely by a sense of hopelessness and the slow realisation that money was not the panacea she had thought it would be.

Janet M started one of the sessions by saying that she had been agonising over her life and all the things we had been talking about. She had come to realise that somehow the question of choice was involved and this was a question which troubled her. What were her choices? What could she choose? Sometimes the huge scale of the responsibility she felt towards her job, her employees, her business associates and herself almost overwhelmed her. She had disturbing dreams, she said. Lately she had been waking up with a start, with startling questions buzzing through her head. How did I do this? How did I get into this position? How did all this happen?

What emerged in our work together in therapy was a very complex set of emotions, feelings, needs and desires. She had not told her parents, family and friends in Birmingham about her position in the City, or about her success or about what she was earning. "I daren't," she said.

"I daren't? What stops you?" I enquired.

"Look, it's not easy; it's not all that simple. I'm not even sure . . ."

There was a pause. Janet M looked at me and swallowed hard before speaking again. "I don't want to worry them. I'm afraid of worrying them. I don't want to crush them."

"You feel that telling them about your work, your success and your wealth would crush them?"

"Yes, I do. It's like I've let them down, as if I've gone against them."

She paused again, then added: "It's not what my parents would have wanted for me. They would have wanted me to be more like them and to be closer to them in my lifestyle".

"What do you think they would have wanted you to do?" I wondered.

"It's not what they would have wanted me to do, it's more to do with what they wouldn't want me to do. I was a rebel, you see. I went against them."

Janet went on to explain how she had rebelled and not done an Arts degree, which was what they had hoped she would do after she had insisted on going to university.

"They didn't really want me to go to university and that's the truth. They would have been very happy for me to take what they called an 'honest job' after my 'A' levels."

She went on to describe how her father was always saying how proud he was of the fact that he'd been an "honest, hardworking craftsman" all his working life and how her mother had enjoyed working in a shop. He and her mother had "lived well" and had brought up Janet M and her brother, Fred, in a comfortable, loving and secure home environment.

"Can you imagine what it was like when I announced that I was going to read computer science at university?"

"Yes, I think I can."

"At that time, it was something unheard of for a woman to do."

When she graduated with a first class honours degree, she had felt so proud and hoped they would feel the same way too.

"But they didn't, you know. Not really. They said they did and I think they wanted to mean it, to believe it; but they didn't really. I should have been feeling happy, but I felt so utterly miserable. I think that's why I decided to come to London: I couldn't stand living in Birmingham any more. I just had to get away. Yet as soon as I started working in London, I began to feel a sense of isolation; I began to feel that I had cut myself off from the family."

"Is there something there," I suggested, "about releasing yourself from having to account to others? Have you, in fact, created a secret universe where you're independent and autonomous and where you don't have to account to anyone?"

Janet M felt that this rang true. Yes, she had wanted to escape from her family and friends, from their low expectations of her, from what she called their "narrow and limited" view of life and its possibilities. Yes, she had wanted to "have a go" in London, to achieve more than she thought would have been possible in her home environment and yes, she had definitely wanted to "be her own person", to be independent and to fashion her life for herself. At the same time, she had not wanted to hurt them, or demean them in any way.

She paused for a while and, from the look on her face, it was quite apparent to me that she was struggling with some thoughts. I decided not to make any intervention and to wait until she was ready to talk again. When she did continue, it was in a very hesitant and earnest manner.

"I've just had some rather shocking thoughts going through my head," she said.

When she paused again and looked at me rather expectantly, I nodded my head and waited for her to continue.

"The first one was about chasing my dream, about wanting to be independent and wanting to be a success. The thought struck me that I've really been holding my parents at bay, at arm's length, by not sharing with them. It's true about my friends in Birmingham as well: I think I've been very superficial with them."

"Superficial . . ." I repeated.

'Yes, as if I've not let them into my life, my real life, I mean. Like I've been holding my friendships on a superficial basis."

"This seems to worry you a lot."

"Yes. I wish sometimes I could be more open with them."

"What prevents you?"

"As I've said before, I don't want to hurt them, both my parents and my friends. I don't want to lord it over them with my wealth, my position and my power. I feel a bit guilty, but at the same time I am pleased with what I've done, with what I've accomplished. So you see, I'm a bit ashamed to let my folks know about all this. But I'm also not ashamed about my success. In fact, I'm quite proud of it."

She lifted her head in what I took to be a defiant gesture and became quiet again for a while.

"You said earlier that you had some rather shocking thoughts going through your head. Were there more than the ones you've just been talking about?"

"Yes and this one's not so easy to talk about."

She paused for a while, then said:

"I had an awful thought about Bill. The thought occurred to me that I might have, in some way, got rid of him."

". . . got rid of him . . ." I echoed her words.

"Yes, it's awful, but in some senses it's true. I grew further and further away from him and, in a way just as I did to my parents, I cut him off from my life concerning my work, my success and so on. I kept him out of a big bit of my life. I couldn't share that with him."

"Couldn't?"

"Well, okay, I wouldn't. And that's what makes me feel badly about it. I was really mad at Bill, for not having any ambition and for being content to stay just where he was. As I became more and more successful, so I came to see that Bill reminded me more and more of what I'd left behind in Birmingham, of all that I'd tried to escape from."

She had pushed him away, held him at arms length and she now realised how hurtful this must have been for him. The session ended on this rather sombre note.

From the very start of the next session, it was obvious that Janet M had been going over all the things we had been talking about the week before: indeed she said as much. Much of the session was spent in exploring her understanding of, and feelings about, all this. She worked on being able to hold and tolerate somewhat contradictory thoughts and feelings. Towards the end of the session, we returned to the analogy of her life within an arid landscape. As we looked at this again, what then became apparent was that, although she had created a sort of desert: she was in an oasis. Paradoxically, she was not totally racked with guilt, or loneliness or desolation. Although she was surrounded by the desert, her oasis was indeed her work, her success, her status, her power and control, and her autonomy and independence.

Janet M spent some time in the following sessions re-examining the sorts of interests she had had as a schoolgirl and as an adolescent. She began to acknowledge a desire, even a yearning, to recapture some of those values and interests.
"Maybe I can even strike a balance between them and what I am doing now?" she pondered.
She remembered that she had had a burning desire to teach. What had happened to that ambition, she wondered. In fact she hadn't thought about it for years. She'd almost completely forgotten about it, she said with a laugh. I encouraged her to explore that ambition further.
"Perhaps," she said, "I can find a way of using my computing business and training skills in some teaching capacity."
She left that session in a buoyant mood.

I realised that we were nearing the end of her therapy with me from the things she started to discuss in those latter sessions and the manner in which they were discussed. She embarked upon a consideration of how she wanted to spend the second part of her life. She had made lots of money; she had spent lots of money, she said matter-of-factly. Being in therapy had provided her with some distance and, therefore, a somewhat different perspective. She felt that she was now able to step back a pace, take stock, and even make some sense of what she was doing. She said she realised that, because of her changing perspective and focus, she had provided herself with greater opportunities to make choices in future, rather than to feel that her destiny was fixed and determined.
"My life is in my hands," she said with a broad grin. "I may even decide to make a change of career!"

She returned again and again to the idea of teaching and seemed to be enthused by the thought of it. She appeared more animated and alive when talking about this. She remembered that her family at one time had been quite keen for her to become a teacher. She was redefining the role she had originally rejected. She told me that she felt that, having travelled this distance, she had gained a certain insight and was now defining a teaching role in a new and dynamic way. She returned to the idea of combining her present occupation with some teaching role. Not necessarily schools, she said, but perhaps an educational consultancy, or something similar. She seemed to revel in the thought of combining both a challenge and doing something useful and worthwhile. Towards the end of the session, she told me that she felt she had got a lot out of therapy and was glad that she had come, but that she would really like to end therapy, if only for a time. We discussed this and agreed that she would come for one more session.

Janet M entered the room for her final session with me grinning from ear to ear. She could hardly wait to blurt out the news that she had been headhunted to direct some government project that would entail her working half-time. This arrangement had been negotiated and she was really pleased with the arrangement, as it would enable her to keep control of her own company, although she was thinking of promoting a senior employee to the position of General Manager, something, she said, she had already been contemplating for some time. Her whole manner was one of animation and elation. She felt chuffed, she said, because she had been headhunted and this meant that she was very highly regarded. "They wanted me and no one else," she said delightedly.

The rest of the session seemed to be completely taken up with Janet M talking about her plans for the future with regards to "this exciting challenge". When the session drew to a close, she thanked me warmly for "everything" and left.

DISCUSSION

When Janet M first came to see me, I estimated that we would be working together for quite a long time, but it didn't work out that way. In the end we had 32 sessions together. However, I chose to present this case as it fairly typically reflects the way I work. I describe myself as an existential/phenomenological therapist. What this means in practice is that I adopt a certain stance with regard to working with a client which encompasses a fundamental premise: accepting and working with whatever is presented by the client without, from the outset, seeking to impose upon the enterprise any preconceived theoretical or other assumptions concerning the meaning, understanding or import of the presented material. This requires the therapist to make the sorts of interventions which will facilitate the exploration and clarification of the meanings of the client's statements in terms of the client's own understanding and perception of them. My approach would therefore centre on the client's being-in-the-world, as expressed by the client's disclosure of their on-going relations with the world. It is the relational aspects of the client's existence that provide meaning for them at all levels of their existence and these need to be explored and clarified.

This entails my "being there" for the client in a very real sense: attending, listening, trying to hear what the client is saying and, above all, being non-judgemental and accepting of whatever stance the client maintains. This should provide the client with the experience of both being heard and of hearing themselves. This way of working with the client does make certain demands on me as the therapist, in that it challenges me to consider and confront the biases and assumptions that I bring to the encounter. If I fail to set aside, or "bracket", preconceived personal views, assumptions, biases and prejudices, this will certainly impede my ability to listen openly and respectfully to what the client is saying. The approach is essentially that of therapist and client working together in order to try to understand the inner and outer world of the client. What the approach should be doing is offering the client the means to examine, confront, clarify and reassess their understanding of life, including the problems they have encountered and the limits imposed upon the possibilities inherent in their being-in-the-world. It can be seen, therefore, that the interrelationship of therapist and client is a very important aspect of the therapeutic encounter, and the therapy is more concerned with the quality of the relationship than with the emphasising of set skills and techniques.

Unlike what occurs in working from other theoretical orientations, in this approach the client is not regarded as suffering from some pathological condition and there is therefore no notion of a "cure". By the same precept, a therapist working in this approach resists the temptation to change the client. Rather than trying to get the client to fit into some preconceived notion of what the therapist thinks they ought to be like, or into the sort of life the therapist thinks the client should be living, the therapist will provide the environment, the space, the time, the attention and the understanding for the client to take stock of their life and their way of being-in-the-world. Once the client has gained a fuller and, hopefully, clearer understanding, then the next step is up to them entirely. What the client wants to do is their decision and theirs alone. It is certainly not the therapist's.

This is clearly illustrated in the case of Janet M. At the end of the therapy she decided to accept the offer to manage and direct a government project, rather than perhaps go into some sort of teaching. Now this may not have been the resolution that I might have wanted for her, but it has to be recognised that in this form of therapy clients must in the end make their own choices. It is not for the therapist to direct what choices are to be made or to stipulate how people ought to live their lives. I am reminded of what brought her to therapy in the first place. Her value system had been shaken and she had come to therapy for a reappraisal of her whole life, a decision which appeared to have been prompted by the death of her husband. Her life on the face of it had seemed to be the epitome of what a self-made woman strives for. She had created success virtually out of nothing and had been deliberate, systematic and determined about things. She had made choices. On the face of it, she should have been happy, yet she found that she couldn't just freely accept and enjoy the rewards. There was always a sense of owing something to herself, a sense of discomfort accompanied by a feeling of guilt because of virtually cutting herself off from the value system embedded in her roots and in her upbringing. In the therapy she had become increasingly aware of the difference between being and doing, yet somehow failed in the end to link it in with her own existence, with her sense of value towards herself. In fact, what became apparent was that what she had achieved still felt detached from her own sense of self. It seemed as though she had a cut-off point. She had certainly reached a point of awareness but couldn't (or wouldn't) go further than that. That was where she was with her life. She had come to realise that she couldn't kid herself any more and that her job and her success were very important to her. She also couldn't kid herself that they were everything, even though that was the path she had chosen. In the end the need to be seen as a success by others overwhelmed her sense of her personal worth. That was the choice she made.

I named the study "Unhappy Success—a Mid-Life Crisis" but came to realise, in working with Janet M, that a mid-life crisis is only the expression of a conflict that has been there all the time. It has just been made more plain, and perhaps a little more clear-cut and easier to identify: it is not something new that has come along in the client's life. Perhaps a way of considering a mid-life crisis could be, not as something new, but rather an intensification of unresolved conflicts that have been present for years and years.

DISCUSSION WITH THE EDITOR

SIMON: Janet M seems to provide a good example of the way clients are often dissatisfied, feel something vital is missing from their lives, because they are living on one dimension. Do you find your clients come to you and talk about one aspect of their lives, such as their career, and that you need to encourage them to think in terms of all the other aspects of their way of being too?

ARTHUR: Yes, indeed, that was what I tried to do in working with Janet M. One of the assumptions embraced by the existential–phenomenological approach is that all issues in the client's life, whether of a problematic nature or not, reflect assumptions or world-views held by the client. My task as therapist would be to challenge such world-views, which would in effect mean challenging the assumptions and limitations inherent in these world-views held by the client. It is also clear that no effective challenge is possible unless the client's world-views have been sufficiently described and clarified. The concept of 'world views' was postulated by Binswanger (1968) as consisting of three dimensions: the *Umwelt* (physical dimension), the *Mitwelt* (social dimension), and the *Eigenwelt* (psychological dimension). Another dimension, the *Uberwelt* (spiritual dimension) has since been suggested by van Deurzen-Smith (1988).

The *Umwelt* has been described as the "natural world, with its physical, biological dimension" (van Deurzen-Smith, 1988, p. 69) and is the dimension wherein we relate to our environment. Spinelli (1989) explains that, although we are all limited by what he calls innate, biological variants, we nevertheless provide ourselves with unique meanings and interpretations of the physical world we inhabit. This physical dimension may be experienced as pleasurable, secure and essentially harmonious, or as anxiety-provoking due to perceived limitations, doubts, insecurities, even dangers. Janet M's attitudes to a wide range of variables within this physical dimension, when emerging in the therapy, were duly examined, considered and discussed with a view to clarifying her meanings, concerns and issues.

The *Mitwelt* dimension focuses on the way we relate to others. Herein are reflected our responses to, and the inferences we draw about, our race, class, gender, language, culture and the codes of our society. From this we are invariably led to develop a wide range of attitudes and values. Spinelli speaks of people feeling empowered or invalidated by their public-world interactions, which in turn may engender in them feelings of "acceptance or rejection, dominance or submission, conformity or rebellion" (Spinelli, 1989, p. 128). On this dimension, the public world may be perceived as loving and respectful or as hateful, disrespectful, uncaring or even dangerous. Once again, Janet M's stated perceptions of her dealings with her public world were accorded due attention and investigation and, hopefully, led to clearer understanding and clarification.

The *Eigenwelt* deals with the way we relate to ourselves and to significant others in our lives. It includes views about ourselves in terms of our character, our individuality, our self-acceptance or self-acceptance or self-rejection and the degree of self-confidence we possess. All of this is significant in the way we interpret our responses to, and interaction with, our family, our friends and our intimates. On this dimension, "People often search for a sense of identity, a feeling of being substantial and having a self" (van Deurzen-Smith, 1990, p. 5). As Janet M's views and perceptions emerged in the therapy, they were examined closely and carefully.

The *Uberwelt* "refers to a person's connection to the abstract and absolute aspect of living" (van Deurzen-Smith, 1988, p. 97), and thus involves our spiritual or ideological outlook on life and the beliefs we hold about being, about existence and about death. It has very much to do with our sense of meaning and purpose, or lack of it, in life. Janet M was encouraged to voice her attitudes and beliefs in this regard, which enabled them to be examined and assessed more carefully.

Working in this way with a client requires the therapist to attempt to enter, experience and interpret the "meaning world" of the client as the client experiences and interprets it. This requires the therapist to set aside or 'bracket' their own beliefs, assumptions, biases and prejudices. Only then will the therapist be able to challenge the assumptions, beliefs, limitations, biases and prejudices held by the client. These should become apparent, and the challenge thus be able to be made, through the perception of inconsistencies, gaps and even unstated assumptions in the client's meaning-system.

SIMON: And yet the main thing which Janet M leaves therapy having done is to decide on a change of career. It is an important development and I notice that she is now able to work fewer hours and may, therefore, have more flexibility in the future. Nevertheless, it seems that she uses therapy to make a relatively limited adjustment to her way-of-being in the workplace. Do you think there are wider implications from the therapy?

ARTHUR: It may appear that not much has changed, especially externally, but I have a sense of a lot happening beneath the surface, as it were. It may be that the work done in therapy may find expression in her life in different ways and at different times, especially as regards her world views. Towards the end of the therapy, Janet M herself had said that being in therapy had provided her with some distance and, therefore, a different perspective, that she was now able to step back a pace, take stock and even make some sense of what she was doing. She had also talked about providing herself with greater opportunities to make choices in future, rather than to feel that her destiny was fixed and determined. These seem to me to be rather significant "shifts".

SIMON: I'm very interested in your attitude to "mid-life crisis". As you
say, what seems to be happening is an intensification of unresolved
conflicts . . . in a way it seems that mid-life crisis need not necessarily
be thought of in terms of, for example, middle age, but that it is more
useful to think of it in terms of a shake-up in a person's particular way
of being-in-the-world, a particular "lifestyle" to use the jargon, so that
an individual may experience several such crises during their lifetime.
In fact, maybe they should if they are fully engaged with life.

ARTHUR: I'm sure you're right and that people do tend to experience
several such "crises" during their lifetime, and times such as childhood, adolescence, mid-life and retirement age spring to mind in this
regard. The term "mid-life crisis" appears to be a psychological thing,
and refers to a time which has no set boundaries, is not strictly defin-
able and yet is a time when concerns and issues appear to assume a
sudden importance and urgency. As I have stated elsewhere in this
study, I came to realise, in working with Janet M, that a so-called mid-
life crisis is only the expression of a conflict that has been there all the
time.

REFERENCES

Binswanger, L. (1968). *Being-in-the-World*. New York: Harper Torchbooks.
Spinelli, E. (1989). *The Interpreted World*. London: Sage.
van Deurzen-Smith, E. (1988). *Existential Counselling in Practice*. London: Sage.
van Deurzen-Smith, E. (1990). *Existential Therapy*. London: Society for Existential
Analysis.

11

DECIDING ABOUT DRINKING—AN EXISTENTIAL APPROACH TO ALCOHOL DEPENDENCE

Christopher Wurm
Private Practice, and National Centre for Education and Training on Addiction, Flinders University of South Australia

INTRODUCTION

Those of us who have contributed to the literature about models of drug dependence, have indulged in irrelevances. We have pursued an abstract scientific course rather than responding to existential needs. We have produced a psycho-bio-social model of drug dependence that excludes the essence of human existence – options, freedom to choose and the centrality of human values.

(Drew, 1990)

The use of alcohol is widespread, perhaps even an integral part of life in many industrialised nations and some traditional societies. Patterns of alcohol use vary significantly from culture to culture, and there also appear to be significant physical differences between individuals which

Case Studies in Existential Psychotherapy and Counselling. Edited by S. du Plock
© 1997 John Wiley & Sons Ltd

contribute to some people developing greater degrees of harm. Alcohol has a variety of effects and the pattern of drinking (which is largely determined by culture) influences the pattern of problems which may develop (Wurm, 1993). Some problems are related to regular, daily drinking, while others are due to sporadic drinking and the effects of intoxication. Dependence itself can bring extra problems. Physiological differences may also contribute greatly to the difficulty which some individuals have with making changes in their drinking pattern. None the less, problems related to alcohol and to other drugs are a particularly fruitful area for the application of existential concepts, particularly in considering how people decide their priorities.

Various models have been put forward to try to explain drug use and the problems which may arise. Pols & Henry-Edwards (1991) list five, starting with the moral model, leading to various applications of the medical model including Jellinek's "disease concept of alcoholism" and, more recently, the definition of the "alcohol dependence syndrome" by Edwards & Gross (1976). International collaboration under the auspices of the World Health Organisation led to a "Bio-psycho-social Model", which incorporates elements of social learning theory. Observations that levels of alcohol-related harm varied according to the total alcohol consumption among groups led to the "Population Consumption Model". This chapter will illustrate the application of the "Existential Model" and try to highlight the advantages of this approach.

Five Models of Drug Use
(after Pols & Henry-Edwards, 1991)

- The Moral Model—early Temperance movements, Alcoholics Anonymous (AA) and Narcotics Anonymous (NA).
- The Disease Model—Jellinek's disease concept of alcoholism, leading to the later definition of the alcohol dependence syndrome.
- The Social Learning Model—WHO Bio-psycho-social model.
- The Population Consumption Model—Ledermann hypothesis.
- The Existential Model—Fingarette, Frankl, Drew, Black.

Trying to define specific models is very difficult, as many strategies may contain elements of more than one model. Alcoholics Anonymous (AA) can be seen to have aspects in common with most of the above five models, but is not necessarily seen that way by its members. According to the 12 steps of AA, the person is "powerless over alcohol". In the original description of the alcohol dependence syndrome, there is an element of "loss of control". Bergmark & Oscarsson discussed this issue, saying "It is unclear, however, whether the experience is truly one of losing control rather than one of deciding not to exercise control" (Bergmark & Oscarsson, 1987). In Drew's words: "The simple fact that a person keeps on repeating the same hurtful behaviour does not mean that they have lost the power of choice, whether or not the behaviour involves the use of drugs" (Drew, 1986).

CASE STUDY

The Setting and the Therapist's Background

The theoretical basis for this case may differ from many of the other cases in this book, not so much due to any Australasian bias but due to a strong Austrian influence. While still an undergraduate medical student in Adelaide, I became very interested in the work of Professor Viktor Frankl and this interest grew as I read more of his work. There was virtually no mention of any of the humanist or existentialist psychotherapies in my undergraduate medical career, and a 3-month training position in a psychiatric hospital after I graduated was not much different. I reached the point where I was quite determined to learn more about Frankl's "Logotherapy and Existential Analysis" and ultimately 4 years later was accepted into a course at the "Institut für Logotherapie und andere Methoden der Psychotherapie" in Vienna. By this time I had chosen to pursue further training as a family physician, or "general practitioner" as they are known in Australia. Hence I divide my time now between general practice, psychotherapy and teaching. I work in a group general practice, providing primary care to people in the north-eastern suburbs of Adelaide, a city of approximately 1 million people, the capital of South Australia. I also work in private practice at two separate locations as a psychotherapist, seeing patients for 1 hour at a time, rather than the 10 or 15 minutes traditionally allocated for general practice appointments.

The Referral

It was one of my colleagues in the general practice setting who asked me to see Harold. I had actually seen him once before for a general practice consultation, but this time he made it clear to his doctor that he was having trouble sleeping and felt himself to be under considerable pressure with stresses at work, with his finances and in his marriage. After discussing the situation with his GP, he agreed to come to me for psychotherapy.

The referring doctor had already taken a fairly detailed history. He described Harold lying awake at night, thinking of work and drinking port. He would get up at 6 a.m. full of energy for work, but often had a feeling of "butterflies" in his stomach as he set off for work in the mornings. He denied feeling depressed and said that he had "lots to live for". He was married with two teenage children, and his wife also helped in the administration of his business.

He was born in a small country town in Tasmania and moved to South Australia at the age of 21. He has an elder sister and also a younger brother. When Harold was born his father was 68 years old. He remembers his childhood as being relatively happy, although his brother viewed it more negatively. Harold describes his father as having been authoritative and not one to show any feelings. When Harold was 21, his father was senile and bedridden, and died at the age of 89.

Beginning Psychotherapy

At his first psychotherapy session with me, I got Harold to outline more of his family background and his current work situation. He was the manager of a small car yard with six employees. His general health had been good apart from a back injury which led to a brief hospital admission 2 years earlier. His blood pressure was normal and he reported having a normal cholesterol level. Reviewing his general practice notes, it became apparent that he had presented 6 years earlier asking for a "health check". At that time his alcohol intake was noted as 7–8 pints of beer each night, and a blood test was done showing abnormally high levels of a liver enzyme, gamma-glutamyl transpeptidase (GGT). He did not return to the practice for another 2 years.

Elaborating on his concerns in his first psychotherapy interview, he said that he had only had two periods of holiday in the last 10 years, the most recent being a fortnight off 5 years ago. He felt a huge pressure to catch up lost ground after losing some money. Amidst these pressures, he had become troubled by insomnia. He would go for three or four nights without sleep and then "crash out". This pattern had been present for 2 years. He had been drinking 4 or 5 pints of low-alcohol beer mixed with stout, followed by 1–2 litres of port wine each night. This constituted an intake of 220–340 grams of alcohol daily, vastly in excess of safe drinking guidelines by either Australian or international standards. He acknowledged one drink-driving charge 20 years before, and had lost his driver's licence before he moved to Adelaide, but that was for speeding, rather than any alcohol-related offence.

He was aware that his whole lifestyle was reaching a point where he had to take action. He said, "My wife has run out of sympathy for what I am doing to myself". Although he felt guilty at not going back to work on the weekend, he did manage to get to a football match with his son. He found it difficult to find time to do things with his wife and children. On the other hand he described having a large circle of acquaintances whom he saw at the pub.

At the close of the first interview I asked him to have more blood tests done to review the physical impact of alcohol on his health, so that we could discuss together what steps he wanted to take. I explained to him that alcohol would interfere with his sleep, particularly the rapid eye movement phase. I mentioned that he might be able to sleep much better if he was able to bring his alcohol intake down to a safer level. He said that he was quite keen to do this. I mentioned that he may also experience some withdrawal symptoms and gave him a prescription for diazepam to take if he needed them to control withdrawal symptoms over the next 5 days. I emphasised that after that time, there would not be any significant level of physical withdrawal symptoms and that taking the diazepam longer than that would create the risk of him becoming dependent on them as well as on alcohol.

The Next Step

He returned a week later quite pleased with his progress. He mentioned that he had been doing his current job for 11 years, and that it had been very stressful for the last 10. In fact he related an incident 13 years ago when he came home from work and his wife tried to tell him about the bad day she had has with their two children, who were then aged 2 years and 6 months. He still remembers replying to her with, "Don't bother me with the details—I'm too busy".

He surprised me by saying he had just resolved a dispute over an account which he had put off paying. He felt quite relieved that the matter was now quite settled even though he felt he had been in the right.

During that first week he reported that he had slept well every night and had completely avoided alcohol for the first three nights, he took diazepam on four occasions when he noticed some anxiety, tremor and nausea. On the fourth night he reported going back to the pub and drinking some additional port wine when he got home. He was already drinking much less than usual in that week and told me that he had decided to make some changes to his drinking. He would limit his drinking at the pub to 3 pints of low-alcohol beer or half a bottle of red wine and set aside 2 days a week with no alcohol at all. Thursday and Friday nights were the nights he traditionally stayed late at the pub, and he decided to arrive at the pub later so that there would not be so much pressure to keep drinking. He was quite frank about the fact that time spent at the pub would inevitably involve drinking, and the easiest way to cut down on this was to arrive later, because after a few drinks he might find it difficult to follow through with the decision to leave earlier.

We finished that interview with an arrangement to meet again in 3 weeks after a follow-up blood test.

Progress

When he returned as arranged I was able to congratulate him on the fact that his liver function tests had in fact shown some improvement. He mentioned that he had tried to have some alcohol-free days, but this had proved difficult. Although he generally slept well, one night he had gone to bed feeling quite worried and did not sleep well. He felt that he had neglected his son. This was brought out only by a comment his son made to Harold's wife, saying, "Dad is grumpy and won't talk properly to me".

Harold had reduced his alcohol intake quite substantially and no longer drank any fortified wine. He still drank somewhat more than originally intended on the Thursday and Friday nights when he went to the pub. He did feel that he was handling things much better at work and he mentioned that he had given some advice to one of his staff who also drank too much and had urged that he go and see a doctor. Harold had also made plans to go on a fishing trip with six friends. This had been quite a tradition for the other men in the group, but Harold had never joined them. Fishing trips in Australia are often associated with consuming above-average amounts of alcohol. Harold knew that his friends were no exception to this rule. Even so, I felt that it was perhaps still a positive sign that he was prepared to take time off work and have some kind of holiday, even a risky one! I mentioned my concerns to him but wished him well and arranged to see him again 6 weeks later after a further blood test.

When he returned from his fishing trip, Harold was in a much better frame of mind despite having had problems with an ear infection. He reported feeling better about many aspects of his life. He had enjoyed spending some time with his wife, redecorating a living room. He still described feeling quite anxious at times in the workplace, but felt that his relationships at home were much better. He was surprised that this had happened without having to alter his life dramatically. Previously he often had a horrible tight feeling in his stomach which he no longer felt at home, and now only had to deal with at the workplace. His finances had improved, not least because he no longer spent $100.00 a week on alcohol. His sleep had improved dramatically, although he still had one night each week when he would stay awake "thinking about hundreds of unimportant things". Even on those nights, he was able to get back to sleep more easily than before.

During the fishing trip he had been the only one drinking light beer. Since coming back he had almost completely stopped going to the pub on week days. Port wine had also been almost eliminated for a month, although he did buy some 4 days earlier and had already finished half of the 2-litre container.

He was very pleased with the changes he had made in his life and told me that he wanted to come up with a new plan. The new plan was not to drink any port wine, stout or regular beer, and restrict himself only to low-alcohol beer. He still intended to drink 8—10 pints of beer on Fridays and Saturdays, and along with some smaller amounts during the week would still have been drinking at a hazardous level. He seemed a little disappointed that even this reduction in his drinking would still put him in the hazardous range, but said he would try that plan for 2 months and think about what to do afterwards. We agreed to review the situation later on, but did not set any fixed date. He did not make a further appointment, but I did catch up with him several months later and he reported that he had made further reductions in his drinking and that his life was going well. Two years later, he is in good general health and is still pleased with the changes he had made to his life.

What Actually Happened?

Altogether, I had seen Harold four times over a period of 3 months following his initial referral from his GP. The process involved eliciting from Harold a detailed description of the issues which concerned him, particularly, in the first instance, his problems with sleep. Once it became apparent that this was closely linked to the amount of alcohol he drank, I was keen to clarify what he saw as the role of alcohol in his life. Even as a young man, he had used alcohol regularly and at a high level. Although he now began to associate his alcohol intake with his tension at work, he tended to use the pub as a social outlet, but also a meeting place for many aspects of his life. He had commented at one stage that if he ever wanted to find a tradesman to help him with a particular job, he would simply think of the people he knew at the pub.

My role was to get him to firstly recognise what his actual pattern of drinking was and then to assess for himself what effects it was having. This required some objective information from me about the effect it was already having on his physical and psychological health. It was also necessary to indicate to him that his drinking was well in excess of guidelines put out by the National and Medical Health Research Council (NHMRC) of Australia (Pols & Hawks, 1991). However, it was much more effective to tell him about the abnormal results of his own blood tests, which showed damage to his liver. This constituted concrete evidence to him that there was already some harm being caused by his own drinking, as opposed to some potential harm according to an abstract set of guidelines which he might not see as having anything to do with him. Fortunately, I was also able to mention that I had read the report on which the NHMRC guidelines were based and that I knew the two authors through my involvement with the Australian Professional Society on Alcohol and Other Drugs (APSAD).

As we spoke, Harold reflected on the way he was living his live, and the choices he was making. He realised that the emphasis he placed on making up "lost ground" in terms of the business and his financial situation was conflicting with his wish to spend time with his children and care for his family. He was trying to provide for them, but in the process he was avoiding them. At the same time, he was under so much stress that he spent even more time away from them, drinking—either at the pub, or physically present but not engaging with them, because he was affected by alcohol. It was dramatic to see how determined and effective he became, once he saw how his strategies were backfiring.

Although Harold did not set out initially to abstain from alcohol, this is often the most attainable goal for people with alcohol dependence. Where a person has good social supports and the level of alcohol dependence is low, it may be possible to sustain a new pattern of drinking at a safer level. However, many people find that they gradually—or rapidly— return to the old pattern, despite clearly stating a preference for a reduction (Miller & Hester, 1986).

There is now much research which indicates that different types of patients may find one goal easier or safer than another (Mattick et al., 1993). An existential approach is still compatible with imparting this knowledge. This constitutes part of the objective assessment that they are entitled to from a health professional. In general the research shows that older, isolated individuals with a high level of alcohol dependence are less likely to achieve their goal if the treatment is aimed at "controlled drinking" rather than abstinence. However, the individual's own preference has been an even more important predictor of success in some of the studies reported. To immediately go along with patients' preferences without warning them that they may be more likely to succeed at abstinence deprives them of crucial information. This is not to say that they shouldn't even try, but such an attempt would certainly call for a clear

plan with good provisions for a fallback option. Knowing that their preferred option is made harder by the likely presence of withdrawal symptoms and sensations of craving gives persons a chance to state their level
of determination and to plan accordingly, but it also gives them the
chance to return without losing face if they do find that their drinking
escalates.

THEORETICAL BACKGROUND

The approach which I was using was based on a combination of my own
professional training and ideas gained from my general reading on the
field of alcohol and other drugs as well as my specific training in Logotherapy and Existential Analysis. Some of the most important writings in
helping me develop my approach are those by Drew, Miller, Black and
Frankl.

In describing this case, I have used the term "alcohol dependence",
because it is a clear term with a readily accessible definition and it is
relatively uncontroversial. The term "alcoholism" might have been regarded in the same way once, but it is no longer considered to be just a
clinical term, having acquired the stigma of an insult in many circles,
while losing its clarity of meaning.

People make decisions about how they will behave according to their
own hierarchy of values. This is referred to as "salience" in the original
description of the alcohol dependence syndrome (Edwards & Gross,
1976) and as "Progressive neglect of alternative pleasures or interests
because of alcohol use" in the Tenth Revision of the International Classifications of Diseases (ICD-10) (WHO, 1992).

W.R. Miller's "motivational interviewing" combines existential concepts with cognitive behaviour therapy (Miller, 1983). Key features are a
deliberate attempt to de-emphasise labelling and avoid self-fulfilling
prophesies, an emphasis on the client's own personal responsibility for
their behaviour and a "Socratic" style of questioning, intended to elicit
awareness in the patient rather than telling them what to do.

> This assignment of freedom of choice to the client (which of course
> the client has whether or not we assign it) leads to a more existential
> approach to counselling.
>
> (Miller, 1983)

The importance of this approach can be seen in its appeal to individuals
who are still ambivalent about making changes in their lives. This is
eloquently described by a client who published her perspective in a professional journal:

Before I ever had a drug problem, I, like many people, had an existential problem. The phrase: "There is no meaning in my life", dogged me constantly.

(Marsh, 1992)

Like Miller, she emphasises the value of eliciting from the client the features of drug use they most like and those which they most dislike.

THE SPIRITUAL DIMENSION

. . . an entire class of potentially important variables is being over-looked in current research and (to a lesser extent) practice in the area of addictive behaviours. These are *spiritual* variables. By "spiritual" I refer to transcendent processes that supersede ordinary material existence. This includes, but is not limited to, systems of religion . . . At our present state of understanding, we are account-ing for only a minority of variance in addictive behaviours and treatment outcomes through psychological, biological and social variables combined. That is, most of the variability in the onset, process and outcome of addictions remains unexplained at present, and we can ill afford to ignore any class of variables with potential explanatory power.

(Miller, 1990)

In spite of Miller's comments above, there are several research tools which can be used to examine constructs empirically. Probably the best known and most widely used is the Purpose in Life test (PIL) (Crumbaugh & Maholick, 1964). The Existenzskala, developed in Vienna, shows great promise but the English version is relatively un-tried (Orgler & Längle, 1990). Two other widely studied concepts that are relevant here are "anomie" and "locus of control". Dr William Black has written an excellent review of empirical research in this area, with a helpful summary of the underlying philosophical concepts (Black, 1991).

Drew (1991) objects to the "reductionism" in most current models of drug- and alcohol-related problems. Frankl also objects to reductionism, comparing it to nihilism (Frankl, 1978). Drew and Frankl both point out that it is necessary to consider a further dimension which adds to the scientific developments already made, and any additional discoveries that the scientific method may still bring. This specifically human dimen-sion is what Frankl calls the "noetic" or "spiritual" dimension (Frankl, 1967).

"Logotherapy" is the name given by Professor Viktor Frankl to the form of existential psychotherapy which he developed in the 1920s and 1930s. He also refers to his theoretical approach as "existential analysis", which may confuse some who associate that name with the later work of Medard Boss and Ludwig Binswanger. In his original works in German, Frankl used the term "Existenzanalyse", whereas Binswanger developed an approach which he called "Daseinsanalyse". Both terms have unfortunately come to be translated into English as "existential analysis" although they are quite distinctly different.

Frankl is best known as the author of *Man's Search for Meaning* (1984) and for becoming Professor of Psychiatry at the University of Vienna after spending much of World War II as a prisoner in concentration camps. Having outlined his philosophical approach and treatment strategies in *The Doctor and the Soul* (a translation of *Ärztliche Seelsorge*) (Frankl, 1973), he describes his wartime experiences in *Man's Search for Meaning* (Frankl, 1984), originally published anonymously as *Ein Psycholog erlebt das Konzentrationslager* (A Psychologist Experiences the Concentration Camp).

Some individuals prefer existential treatment approaches such as logotherapy because it fits their personal outlook. The counsellor may see logotherapy as particularly appropriate because of problems in the noetic dimension, e.g. existential frustration. Alternatively, alcohol dependence may have followed a separate primary disorder such as depression or panic disorder. "Dual diagnosis" is a quite common and significant issue in the area of problems relation to alcohol and other drugs.

Frankl's technique of "paradoxical intention" is sometimes particularly effective in phobias and OCD. Although it appears beguilingly simple, and appeals to behaviourists as well, paradoxical intention utilises the specifically human capacity for self-detachment (Frankl, 1967).

Drew states:

> The person must accept that he bears the primary responsibility for change in his situation. Although other people can assist the person in many ways, and even though the options open to a person may be limited by various unchangeable realities, each person continually makes choices between options. Persons with addictive behaviour have, by definition, given up the responsibility of making difficult choices. They tend to feel more externally determined than other people. They will need help to develop a strong sense of autonomy. They should not be allowed to excuse their behaviour because they "have an illness", or are underprivileged, or anything else.
>
> (Drew, 1986)

Recovery also involves a process of dereflexion (Froggio, 1988). The aim of treatment is not just to stay sober but to find more and more reasons for staying sober—more ways of making life more meaningful instead of resorting to intoxication and fleeing from reality.

Overcoming a drinking problem by no means guarantees a happy or meaningful life. I remember another man who had been to great lengths to get away from alcohol, including 2 months in a remote residential treatment programme. After discharge from there he returned home, tired and disappointed. Soon he was back drinking again. He said, "I stopped drinking, but my life didn't get better!" Making such a change creates the possibility for improvement and growth, but none of this is automatic. Removing one set of activities may make very good sense, but then it is necessary to take stock of how one wants to proceed with life. Perhaps a whole new set of values is called for—or possibly just the reinstatement of old values which were abandoned in the course of becoming alcohol-dependent.

Many people who develop dependence lose some of their traditional cultural attitudes and behaviours. Favazza talks about people from ethnic minorities in the USA who developed alcohol or heroin dependence and became so deeply involved in either the heroin or the alcohol sub-culture that their ethnic identity became secondary (Favazza, 1981).

Westermeyer (1981) described a phenomenon where people from different ethnic groups develop new attitudes and values along with their altered behaviour pattern as they develop drinking problems:

> Core ethnic values such as truthfulness and honesty—while still important to some extent—become secondary considerations relative to the value of obtaining and using alcohol. Other values are gradually eroded and replaced by new alcohol-centred values and behaviours.

Activities of obtaining alcohol and drinking it began to take priority over spending time with family and former friends and participating in sporting or other cultural activities.

> The aim of existential counselling is to clarify, reflect upon and understand life. Problems in living are confronted and life's possibilities and boundaries are explored . . . Clients are considered not to be ill but sick of life or clumsy at living . . . The assistance provided is aimed at finding direction in life by gaining insight into its working. The process is one of reflection on one's goals and intentions and on one's general attitude towards living. The focus is therefore on life itself, rather than on one's personality.
>
> (van Deurzen-Smith, 1988)

In conclusion, existential approaches offer great potential in both the clinical and research areas. Existential approaches are especially valuable in treatment, because they deal with issues which many patients recognise as central and because they help counter some of the self-fulfilling prophesies and therapeutic nihilism inherent in other treatments.

DISCUSSION WITH THE EDITOR

SIMON: Your way of working, the way you draw on existential concepts and Logotherapy when working with "alcohol dependence", seems very innovative to my way of thinking. Are you unique in working in this way, or do you know of others similarly attempting to employ an existential perspective of this type in general practice?

CHRISTOPHER: There was a time when it felt like I was unique working in this way, but I have since met many people, who have read some of Frankl's work and use it in their day-to-day consulting. Certainly Logotherapy is less well known in Australia than in other countries such as Austria, USA, Canada and Argentina. Since I first became interested in existential approaches to psychotherapy, I have had many pleasant surprises, and realised that I am not alone.

Perhaps the best example of how acceptable existential perspectives are in General Practice is this quotation from the widely acclaimed work by the Professor of Family Medicine at the University of Western Ontario:

> The majority of so-called mental illnesses encountered by family physicians, however, are existential crises, and these are problems of the human spirit rather than illnesses.
>
> (McWhinney, 1989)

SIMON: You talk about Frankl's Logotherapy in this case study and mention in passing problems in the noetic dimension, dereflexion and paradoxical intention—I wonder if you can briefly describe Logotherapy?

CHRISTOPHER: Logotherapy is an approach based on existentialism, developed by Professor Viktor Frankl, Emeritus Professor of Psychiatry and Neurology at the University of Vienna. This approach sees the main motivation in humans as a will to find meaning and purpose in their lives. The word "logotherapy" is derived from the Ancient Greek word "logos", which refers to meaning or spirit in the sense of an aim or objective.

Frankl refers to a specifically human dimension which he calls the "noetic" dimension, to complement the physical and psychological dimensions already described by previous models. Two features that characterise Frankl's noetic dimension are self-detachment and self-transcendence (Frankl, 1978). Self-detachment is probably best illustrated by humour, particularly the ability to laugh at oneself. It refers to the ability to observe oneself as from another perspective. This capacity is used in one of logotherapy's best known techniques, namely paradoxical intention. Paradoxical intention can be used for phobias and obsessive-compulsive disorder. It involves inviting selected clients to welcome the feared event, typically making it less daunting by exaggerations so dramatic as to make it clearly impossible, while also laughable.

Dereflexion is a specific therapeutic measure which aims to confront introspection and preoccupation with internal sensations by bringing out the capacity for self-transcendence. Having referred to these specific strategies, it is probably important to say that the essence of logotherapy is in the themes explored, rather than any techniques employed.

SIMON: I wonder if the context in which you work presents any particular problems. I was especially aware, for instance, that you are very definitely present as a medical practitioner, able to give information, advice and drugs. Also, you meet Harold (and I think you are accurate in calling him a "patient" rather than a "client") relatively few times and at intervals related to his blood tests . . . do you think this detracts at all from the existential injunction to "be with" rather than "to do things to/for" people who consult us?

CHRISTOPHER: Context is of course very important. I have found it very helpful to create a separate setting where I can see people for psychotherapy. This is not only geographically separate from the practice where I see people as a general practitioner, but it is a totally different kind of place. The changes include longer appointments, a much less clinical atmosphere—to the point of not having an examination couch or the characteristic sterile paraphernalia of a doctor's surgery. Although some quite productive psychotherapy can take place in the general practice setting, I find it much easier to keep the two roles very separate. Even though the appointments at my psychotherapy practice are for 1 hour, I also find it important to get patients to have their general practitioner continue to deal with their other health problems.

Certainly, sometimes it is hard to keep the two roles separate. This presents even more difficulty for those general practitioners who conduct psychotherapy at the same location within the same consulting times. There are situations where it is much more appropriate to be quite directive, such as recommending antibiotics for a case of tonsillitis or recommending a plaster cast for a broken bone. It is sometimes hard to resist the temptation to give very direct instructions when somebody appears to be endangering their health by their use of alcohol or tobacco. Certainly this also sometimes appears to produce quite dramatic changes in behaviour. But it is often very instructive for me to take note of what inspires patients to come seeking assistance in changing their lifestyle. Often people who have been advised to stop smoking seem to ignore the advice, and then present later on asking for help when the price of tobacco goes up.

SIMON: I think your emphasis on choice and your work to encourage Harold to accept some responsibility for his choice to drink is very much my own way of working with people who talk about addiction. I would agree with Bergmark & Oscarsson (1987) that this repetitive behaviour is about deciding not to exercise control. For me the most helpful thing is enabling the person to clarify the meaning of their behaviour to themselves . . . did the two of you discover what this was for Harold and how it had changed after 20 years, such that he entered therapy?

CHRISTOPHER: I think this is a very helpful question because it clarifies exactly what kind of meaning logotherapy is interested in. Although I would not overlook the usefulness of clarifying the meaning of a particular behaviour to the patient, this sounds less like an existential question than one that belongs in a psychodynamic approach. The particular emphasis in logotherapy is on what makes life meaningful for the individual, rather than what a particular behaviour or experience might represent or mean.

Trying to establish, especially in retrospect, the meaning of the drinking behaviour might make sense in attempting to look for a causal explanation of what started the process. It is not always necessary to go through this process, however. With Harold, it was possible to discuss the notion that he could make choices and live his life in a variety of ways, some of which would be more meaningful than others. He was then able to reflect on the choices he had been making, and the possibilities available to him in the future. I remember asking him what he liked about drinking, but not about what meaning it had for him. When we did talk about meaning, Harold was certainly clear that there were other things that would help make his life more meaningful in the future, and that they would not be possible unless he changed his drinking.

REFERENCES

Bergmark, A. & Oscarsson, L. (1987). The concept of control and alcoholism. *British Journal of Addiction*, **82**, 1203–12.
Black, W.A.M. (1991). An existential approach to self-control in the addictive behaviours. In N. Heather, W.M. Miller & J. Greeley (eds) *Self-control and the Addictive Behaviours.* Sydney: Pergamon.

Crumbaugh, J.C. & Maholick, L.T. (1964). An experimental study in existentialism: the psychometric approach to Frankl's concept of noogenic neurosis. *Journal of Clinical Psychology*, **20**, 200–207.

Drew, L.R.H. (1986). Beyond the disease concept of addiction. Drug use as a way of life leading to predicaments. *Journal of Drug Issues*, **16**, 263–74.

Drew, L.R.H. (1990). Facts we don't want to face. *Drug and Alcohol Review*, **9**, 207–10.

Drew, L.R.H. (1991). Morals, science and chance. *Drug and Alcohol Review*, **10**, 277–82.

Edwards, G. & Gross, M.M (1976). Alcohol dependence: provisional description of a clinical syndrome. *British Medical Journal*, **1**, 1058–61.

Favazza, A. (1981). Alcohol and special populations. *Journal of Studies on Alcohol*, Suppl. 9, 87–98.

Frankl, V.E. (1967). *Psychotherapy and Existentialism*. New York: Simon & Schuster (Touchstone).

Frankl, V.E. (1973). *The Doctor and the Soul* (translation of *Ärztliche Seelsorge*). New York: Vintage.

Frankl, V.E. (1978). *The Unheard Cry for Meaning*. New York: Simon & Schuster (Touchstone).

Frankl, V.E. (1984). *Man's Search for Meaning* (translation of *Ein Psycholog erlebt das Konzentrationslager*). New York: Simon & Schuster (Touchstone).

Froggio, G. (1988). Bemerkungen zum Einsatz der Logotherapie bei der Behandlung des Alkoholismus. In A. Längle (ed.), *Entscheidung zum Sein*, pp. 230–37. Munich: Piper.

Marsh, A. (1992). What makes treatment work? A client's perspective. *Drug and Alcohol Review*, **11**, 94–6.

McWhinney, I.R. (1989). *A Textbook of Family Medicine*, p. 68. New York: Oxford University Press.

Mattick, R.P., Baillie, A., Grenyer, B., Hall, W., Jarvis, T. & Webster, P. (eds) (1993). *An Outline for the Management of Alcohol Problems: Quality Assurance Project*. National Drug Strategy Monograph Series. Canberra: Australian Government Publishing Service.

Miller, W.R. (1983). Motivational interviewing with problem drinkers. *Behavioural Psychotherapy*, **11**, 147–72.

Miller, W.R. & Hester, R.K. (1986). Matching problem drinkers with optimal treatments. In W.R. Miller & N. Heather (eds), *Treating Addictive Behaviors: Processes of Change*. New York: Plenum.

Miller, W.R. (1990). Spirituality: the silent dimension in addiction research. The 1990 Leonard Ball Oration. *Drug and Alcohol Review*, **9**, 259–66.

Orgler, C. and Längle, A. (1990). *Existenzskala*. Vienna: Gesellschaft für Logotherapie und Existenzanalyse.

Pols, R. & Henry-Edwards, S. (1991). *Responses to Drug Problems in Australia*. Canberra: Australian Government Printing Service.

Pols, R. & Hawks, D. (1991). *Is There a Safe Level of Daily Consumption of Alcohol for Men and Women?* Canberra: Australian Government Printing Service.

van Deurzen-Smith, E. (1988). *Existential Counselling in Practice*. London: Sage.

Westermeyer, J. (1981). Research on treatment of drinking problems—importance of cultural factors. *Journal of Studies on Alcohol*, Suppl. 9, 44–59.

WHO (1992). *The ICD-10 Classification of Mental and Behavioural Disorders: Clinical Descriptions and Diagnostic Guidelines*. Geneva: World Health Organisation.

Wurm, C.S.E. (1993). *Reaching all the Right People: Sharing the Load between Primary Care and Specialised Services*. Beyond the Barriers, Parramatta: Drug and Alcohol Multicultural Education Centre.

12

WORKING WITH EXISTENTIAL GROUPS

Bo Jacobsen
*Centre for Human Science Research in Health and Ageing,
University of Copenhagen, Denmark*

INTRODUCTION

Working with existential problems in groups has its strengths and its weaknesses compared to working with individuals. The main weakness is the limited space and time it is possible to devote to each individual to disentangle their individual patterns of living. The main strength lies in the phenomenon of resonance and the possibility of comparing "similar" experiences: to discover that one is not alone with one's fear of decay and death, that some fellow human beings have a similar strong anxiety and horror may be a powerful growth-stimulating experience. And to discover that what you see as frightening another person sees as stimulating, may provoke much reflection and development on your part.

To work with individuals within a person-to-person framework is by far the most widespread form of existential therapy. However, scattered in the literature we find reports on working existentially with pairs (van Deurzen-Smith, 1988, pp. 92–6), groups (Yalom, 1980) and organisations (Tame, 1995). The application of the existential approach to entities that transcend the individual (i.e. pairs, families, groups, organisations) is an expanding field with many future challenges. The individual lives in a

Case Studies in Existential Psychotherapy and Counselling. Edited by S. du Plock
© 1997 John Wiley & Sons Ltd

social context. The problems of living and working together are of an existential nature, and people are becoming increasingly aware of this.

We may now want to ask whether the theoretical and conceptual base is the same in working with individuals and in working with groups (or pairs, families, and organisations). I believe that it is not. Individual work is based on a deeply penetrating, phenomenologically oriented understanding of the existential make-up of that unique individual (Cohn, 1994; van Deurzen-Smith, 1988; Spinelli, 1989). If we work with a group of eight individuals, we definitely have to understand them as eight individuals on this basis. But, in addition, we have to understand the interrelationships (what A means to B, what C thinks A means to B, etc.) as well as such collective phenomena as group emotion (Stimmung), group climate, group structure and the like.

A core problem here is: which kind of group theory (family theory, organisational theory, etc.) is suitable to combine with the existential–phenomenological base for understanding individual lives? Not all existing theories of group psychology are equally suitable.

If we consider, for example, the case of Paul and Pamela (van Deurzen-Smith, 1988, pp. 92–6), they appear as two individuals-under-development, each with his or her own, unique view on the other and on their relationship. Standard theories of the social psychology of dyads do not explain the ramifications between the two persons. The theory must be able to encompass the fact that different individuals in the "same" group may construe their worlds and their relationships in highly individual and personal ways. They may not at all live in the same world although, seen from the outside, they belong to the same pair, family, group or organisation. The theory of the collective entity in question must depict reality as socially and personally constructed, not as objectively existing out there. Otherwise the theory will not be able to fit in with an existential–phenomenological understanding of the individual.

The theories or conceptions which by far best meet this requirement are the so-called systemic theories and approaches, which are built upon the foundation that every individual in an organisation construes their world, their organisation and their life in a different way. The systemic theories are under development in general (Bateson, 1972; Maturana & Varela, 1987; Watzlawick, 1974), in relation to families (Palazolli et al., 1978), groups (Mills, 1967, pp. 19–23) and organisations (Campbell, 1989; Morgan, 1986).

The combination of an existential–phenomenological understanding of the individual and a systemic understanding of the group creates a powerful approach to human problems, sufferings and potentials in the global society of today.

In Denmark there have been a number of experiments with applying existential approaches to group work. Also, there has been a noticeable amount of individual counselling on an existential basis in relation to people with somatic illnesses (cancer, sclerosis, AIDS).[1] These two bases of experience—together with a strong phenomenological tradition in the training of psychologists—have led to certain priorities in the view of what constitutes existential therapy. The basic concept is in accordance with the position of Cohn (1994), but certain points are highlighted here:

1. Human suffering, including the physical pain which is so common among our somatic patients, is seen as something one has to learn to live with, to enter into a dialogue with. It is not something to "master" (cope with) or something to resign oneself to, as many cognitive and analytic therapists tend to think. It is a potential for development (Frankl, 1955).
2. The role of detailed, concrete phenomenological description is considered very important (Spinelli, 1989). To let the client describe in a very detailed fashion what they experience is very fruitful in general and decisive in the cases of somatic illnesses, where the client often has the feeling that the therapist cannot know what it feels like to carry this or that disease.
3. The relationship between client and therapist is one of attempted equality. The therapist is not looking at something in the client. The client and the therapist are standing side by side looking together at something out there (or in there), discussing how to interpret the phenomenon they are watching and studying.
4. When working with groups, the therapist has a special protective function in relation to the individual towards world-views presented loudly by other group members. The therapist facilitates new insights and understandings within the individual which are initially quite vulnerable, since they are coming forth *in statu nascendi*.

On the following pages I report experiences from two types of group work, *existential–analytic group therapy* and *existential workshops with structured exercises*.[2]

EXISTENTIAL–ANALYTIC GROUP THERAPY

Existential–analytic group therapy is developed from group analysis (Foulkes, 1948; Pines, 1983) with a special focus on existential issues, and sometimes with a special initial selection of clients pointing towards common existential problems.

Important elements from the group analytic tradition are the frame and the roles. The frame consists in a group of eight people not knowing each other beforehand, plus one or two therapists (or group conductors). The group meet for one (or two) period(s) of 90 minutes every week. Punctuality and formality are maintained in starting and stopping on time, registering presence and absence, etc. The role of the participants is to express themselves as freely as possible in relation to whatever subjects emerge in the group. The participants are encouraged to explore their own feelings, thoughts, modes of relating to each other, and modes of relating to the world. The role of the therapist(s) is quite well-defined and restricted to listening, suggesting interpretations as to what is happening in the group, and now and then intervening by drawing in silent members or putting questions for reflection. These well-defined limits are thought of as facilitating a fruitful therapeutic space.

When the existential dimension is added to this analytic form, the therapist does to a higher degree show him/herself as a spontaneous and present human being, allowing them to make fun, show feelings of sadness, share thoughts and feelings, etc. Furthermore, the content of the interpretations and interventions moves from a preoccupation with dependency, power, roles and various psychodynamic mechanisms to a preoccupation with existential phenomena like death, choice, freedom, life meaning, being alone vs. being with others, being oneself vs. playing roles, etc. Also, the level of interpretation changes. Whereas in the analytic tradition so-called analytic interpretations are encouraged (which may appear quite enigmatic or mystical to the participants), in the existential group the interpretations are descriptive (Spinelli, 1994) or at least very close to the surface. The ideal is that the interpretation expands what is already seen or sensed by the participants, but does not "hit below the belt". Openness and transparency are what is aimed at, together with a clear commitment towards the basic questions of life.

Case Example

A group of eight people, all with some sort of somatic complaint, were collected through GPs and offered participation in a 10-week once-a-week existential–analytic group therapy.[3] Only clients who after an initial interview were thought suitable for group therapy were included.

The first session opened up with the therapists inviting the participants to tell each other: "What brings me here?" The participants related their physical problems, such as overweight, attacks of hyperventilation, drug addiction and consecutive liver disease, as well as psychological problems like having to live up to the expectations of other people and letting themselves be dominated by others.

After the presentational round, a rather long period of free conversation began. The common theme which developed was *problems of being oneself in relation to others*, consequences of showing oneself as the person one really is. The fear of rejection and loss of friends was contrasted with the possibility of getting friends and experiencing nearness precisely through showing who you are in a clear way. Some of the time the participants discussed the matter as something happening "out there". When this happened, one of the therapists tried to intervene to steer the focus to the here-and-now situation in the group: "Maybe some of you are considering how much of yourself you may disclose right now . . .".

The usual claim within analytic group therapy seems to be valid here, i.e. the subject of the conversation is a reflection of the ongoing group process: to get to know each other as persons. It should be remarked that already after 1 hour of therapy (in a group of strangers) a central existential problem emerged as the discussion theme—*the problem of authenticity*: being oneself vs. playing a role.

During the following two sessions, the group were occupied with subjects like: one's relation to one's own body, relations with the other sex, sexuality, one's relation to one's mother. From Session 4 and onwards, some core existential themes emerged and occupied the group.

One such theme was: *our relation to death*. This theme was introduced by a middle-aged actress, Anna, whose father was dying. She had been weeping together with the father, to whom she is very attached. In reviewing their life story she had experienced a new kind of nearness to him. She was very preoccupied with the phenomenon of death, and she feared what happens afterwards. She wondered whether reincarnation was a possibility. The other group members participated eagerly.

Two weeks later, Anna announced her father's death. Their parting had been the best possible, but she was very vulnerable, in a kind of crisis. Another group member, Beate, a young female teacher, had just lost her nephew, aged 4, who was born deaf and with a congenital heart defect. She had been very close to the little boy and related her rapidly shifting emotions.

Everybody in the group became absorbed by what it means when somebody dies. How can one draw conclusions or learn lessons when a close person dies? Anna had made the decision to consciously carry on certain traditions from her father's way of living in order to commemorate him. Beate had decided to pursue a career as a teacher of deaf children. In the group this thought is crystallised and formulated: "When someone dies, we want what they stood for to be continued".

A related existential theme that emerged was: *to have wasted one's own life*. Donald, a middle-aged previous drug addict, told about his remorse for having wasted his life and not having offered his three children (aged 4, 16 and 17) decent living conditions. He might have only 1–2 years left of his life (due to a liver disease)—was that enough to try to find a meaning to life and to try to change his current lifestyle in an increasing isolation? He had not dared to tell his children about his previous life, but had often wanted to. He found it very hard to tell this to the group, was anxious about being seen as different from the others and feared condemnation by the group.

His courageous input provided a lot of stimulus to the group. Everybody in the group knew of non-lived life (or existential guilt) and wanted to discuss what is important and what matters in the project of living and when facing possible death.

Donald was not the only group member to know what it means *to be alone* and to suffer from feelings of isolation. Cecile, a young female nurse, was experiencing panic if she was not constantly very close to her mother or her son. She seemed unable to be herself unless she was almost fused with others. Anna always had to read a book when on her own. If she did not read, losses and longings without words poured out and made her cry violently. Earl, a middle-aged locksmith, also found it extremely hard to be on his own without the television on. All kinds of old unsettled accounts took hold of his mind. He had a son whom he never saw and had begun to reflect whether he had been right in brutally telling him off at their last encounter many years before. Earl found it very hard to be alone and "open up towards himself", but he was encouraged by the group to do so. The existential theme of aloneness, in its negative and positive aspects, was worked through by the group.

In summary, the existential–analytic group form is suitable for persons who are not against the idea of participating in a therapeutic process in a group. It is less expensive than individual therapy. The existential themes may come and go, but such is the case also with individual therapy (Yalom, 1995). It is possible in the group form to do existential and personal work of considerable depth, although not so tailored to individual needs as in individual therapy.

EXISTENTIAL WORKSHOPS WITH STRUCTURED EXERCISES

This form, which has been developed by the author, differs in a number of ways from the previous one. Although the activities are deeply personal, they are not formally defined as therapy but as course or workshop activities with an emphasis on deep personal reflection. Thereby the activities become open to people who don't think of themselves as in need of treatment, but who welcome an opportunity for personal development. In this way the potential range of people with whom one can do existential work expands very considerably. There are today thousands of people who would say "no, thanks" to an offer of treatment or counselling, but "yes, please" to an offer of personal development.

The workshops or courses may be offered to and tailored to the needs of people in a specific situation, e.g. cancer patients, people with AIDS, arthritis patients, the nearest relatives to young schizophrenics, smokers or overweight people who want to change their health habits, people who have been exposed to an important loss, people working in the same enterprise, etc.—in short, people having a common destiny with existential implications. In addition, the workshops may be offered to the general public or tailored to the needs of nurses and other professionals for whom existential problems arise during their work.

The frame of the workshop consists of a group of 6–15 people meeting for at least one 3-hour period weekly or, alternatively, for 2 or more whole days. The central role of exercises makes it possible to go straight to the core of existential themes.

In what follows I will present the method systematically, step by step. It should be noted that one may go through the sequence of steps several times with the same group, but also that to do it once is entirely in accordance with the method.

Step 1. Describing a Central Life Experience

Apart from initial information, the workshop starts with the group leader proposing a working theme and then formulating a task. The theme may be proposed in a rather broad way, whereas the task has to be structured and formulated in a concise way. A typical formulation of the task will be something like: "Write about an experience you have had of . . . which has really impressed you". The empty space can be filled with an item reflecting the basic life situation of the participants, e.g. "being unemployed", "being an immigrant", or with an item reflecting an existential theme like "contracting a disease", "facing death" or "being totally on your own". The participants are encouraged to write personally in detail and to cover also the feelings which were involved. The group is given about 5 minutes to do this writing. The rationale of the arrangements is that it encourages the participants to dive into themselves in a process of inner concentration, to retrieve a story from their personal life that is really significant to them, and to bring that story to a preliminary formulation.

Case Example

Under the auspices of the Danish Cancer Society, one of the counselling centres announced workshops with the title "The Art of Living with Cancer". The workshops were announced in the local newspapers as an occasion to be together with equals in order to get on with life in spite of a cancer diagnosis. One such group[5] were to meet for one 4-hour session weekly for 3 weeks.

On the first day, the programme was introduced and there was a round of presentations. Then the first task was given: "Write down an experience you have had of what it means to live with cancer, an experience that has really impressed you". After a brief period of reflection one could observe the attention of the participants turn inward and soon everybody was writing their story down in a characteristic thoughtful mood, trying to remember how the incident in question really was, what really happened, and how it was really felt.

Later, this writing down and the consecutive round and deepening of the experiences was remembered as an extremely significant and emotionally full activity. The stories were loaded with personal significance and vivacity and pointed to basic existential themes for the participants. One such theme was: is it possible to live fully here and now, or do I have to fill my mind with preoccupations about the future? The activity and commitment was remarkable, and many participants who contributed in a very personal way said they would never have dared to confront these problems in the form of individual counselling!

Step 2. The Round

The experience having been written down, the group leader now suggests a round where everybody recounts what is on his/her paper.

A basic rule is formulated: it is always up to the individual how much or how little they want to reveal from their private life. But from the point of view of the other participants it is clearly desirable that the individual relates their story in a personal way, since this will enrich the understanding of everybody and enhance what everybody gets out of the workshop. The purpose of this rule is to create a climate without coercion and it is in fact very rare that individuals want to avoid relating their private and personal experiences.

During the first round the group leader maintains an attitude of treating everybody equally and finding interest in all stories. At this stage the participants will still be very sensitive as to the interest and value of their contributions.

Step 3. Deepening the Life Experiences

After the round the leader invites some of the participants to deepen their stories (the leader's criterion for selection being colourfulness and liveliness of the story plus a judgement of the narrator as having the capability to become the centre of attention for some time). In order to uncover the life experience in question the group leader puts a number of questions aiming at the different layers of the experience.

The structure of layers of the life experience can be pictured by the onion-like Figure 12.1 (Jacobsen, 1994). The words and the thoughts are closest to the surface. They come out most easily. But these layers are not very interesting if they are allowed to stand alone. It is essential to reach the deeper layers, and to get feelings and values into the foreground so that the whole life experience is expressed in the classroom and can later become an object of reflection. Feelings, values and basic conceptions of phenomena have a special interest. When a person talks about their values ("I am really against X"; "I deeply believe in Y") and identity ("I am Z kind of person"; "to behave like this is not me"), we come very close to what could be called the existential core within the person, and the atmosphere of the group usually becomes attentive, resonant and respectful.

The method of questioning by the group leader when uncovering the life experiences is phenomenological questioning (Spinelli, 1989). The questions aim at a concrete, specific, detailed account of what happened in the situation, who said and did what, in what manner, how the scene

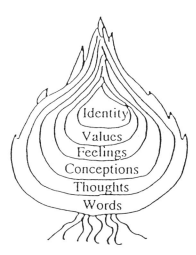

Figure 12.1:   The layers of the life experience

looked, which sense impressions were there, how the bodily reactions were, what the person felt in the situation, what the after-effects of the incident were, how the person thinks and feels now when looking at the event, what kind of value stance the person actually takes in relation to the event, whether the event affected the person lastingly. One especially fruitful way of asking is to uncover the basic conception (or world-view) of the person by problematising it, that is, confronting the person with the opposite view. If, for instance, a person through their story shows that they vehemently believe that one naturally always has to be worried and tired in one's job, it may have a powerful effect to ask the person why one couldn't just relax when at work and enjoy all the funny situations that pop up during the day. "You can't," the person may reply. "But why can't you?" the group leader continues, "What would happen?" This kind of questioning is a way of "taking stock" (van Deurzen-Smith, 1988) of the person's outlook on life.

Case Example

A group of nurses on a 3-day workshop on existential problems were working with the theme "Our Relation to Death". Each of them had been writing down a story relating ". . . an episode where you faced death and which made a particularly strong impression upon you". They shared their stories in groups of three. A few of the stories were then selected for further exploration. One of these, told by a middle-aged nurse, ran as follows (slightly reconstructed):

> I was working in an oncological hospital ward. I was attending a woman of about 30 with oesophageal cancer. Her boyfriend was visiting her. She knew that she was very ill. Both of them knew that the condition was terminal. They went to stay for a while in the sitting-room of the ward, while I was taking care of other patients. Suddenly the boyfriend came rushing in: "Come immediately, it's all wrong." As we entered the sitting-room, the woman was coughing and hacking up all the blood she contained in her body out through her mouth. It was a total explosion. She died within 1 or 2 minutes.

After having listened to this account and having made sure that everybody in the room had taken it in and was "with" the participant, the group leader cautiously posed a number of questions that all aimed at letting this central experience "stand out" for everybody as clearly as possible in its raw, vibrating, living quality. The group leader started by conveying to the participant that he understood her feelings:

GL (group leader): It must have been a harsh experience, it must have been hard to witness this.

P (participant): It sure was (appears quite affected).

GL: I see it is still living strongly within you, although it's some years since.

P: It is (still affected, but a little more calm).

GL: Is it OK if I pose a number of questions as to what happened, in order that we shall all see it as clearly as possible?

P: Yes, I'm willing to answer (is very cooperative).

GL: Can you describe the physical appearance of your patient?

P: She had become very thin, you almost saw her bones through the skin, she was extremely pale.

GL: What happened more precisely at the moment of her death?

P (describes again the explosion of blood, then continues): In dying she collapsed on the floor. I was sitting there on the floor holding her arms and legs. Her boyfriend stood beside me (is quite affected).

GL: Do you remember what you thought or felt at that moment?

P: Yes. I thought: why should she die like this? I thought it was a horrible thing to have to die this way. And I was scared! (still quite affected, but somewhat more calm).

GL: I understand you consider it a horrible thing to have to die the way this woman died. I am sitting here wondering: why is it actually so horrible to die in this way? What would be a better way to die?

P: It would have been better if she had died slower, in her bed. Not so violently. In a more calm way.

Another participant: I don't understand this. She died in the midst of her life, together with her boyfriend! That is much better than just lying in one's bed becoming weaker and weaker, gradually languishing.

GL to P: How do you consider that idea?

P: I don't agree. She should have seen this . . .

It appeared that it was the violent situation with blood everywhere that had impressed P so strongly. She had recalled the scene vividly for a long period after the event. We analysed the event further and reached the conclusion that it was the shock, the violent happenings, the explosive character, that impressed P so much.

After having dwelled on this story, this little piece of life which had entered the meeting room for a while, and having communicated to P our respect and thanks for her story, we proceeded to elaborate on a couple of other stories. At this moment the climate of the group was very close, intimate, consensual, and everybody seemed to be grappling with the question: What is the best way to die? And why?

Step 4. Studying Similarities and Differences

When some of the life experiences have been unfolded in this way, i.e. they stand out alive and in full detail, it is time for the group to try to connect the stories. One way is to encourage the group to explore differences and similarities of the stories. Another way is to try to analyse each story in common and to represent it with catchwords or diagrams at the blackboard.

During this activity the group leader has an important role, that of protecting the uniqueness and integrity of the individual. The individual participant has the ownership of their own experiences and stories; they belong to the life of that individual! If another participant or the group leader wants to talk about, discuss or comment on the story in question, they will have to do it in a way that is accepted by the individual. Nobody is allowed to re-interpret or re-word a story in a way which makes it foreign to the narrator. This applies to the group leader too, if they discuss it or make blackboard representations of a story, they have to make sure that the "story-owner" approves that version. A story is always also a world-view or a world interpretation, and it is up to the holder of that view to decide when time is ripe for change. This is where the systemic perspective enters and fuses with the existential–phenomenological perspective: although the group participants apparently look at and discuss the same subject (e.g. what is the best way to die), they still live each in their own world, having each one of them their own world view and view of the subject under discussion. The more this is respected, the more they can learn from each other and the richer in understanding they will become.

Step 5. Generalising and Preparing for Action

It is possible at this stage to try to formulate generalisations as to the kind of understanding which has developed in the group. Also at this stage it is possible with some groups to include knowledge in book form, and to discuss the relation between generalised theories from books and the more situational knowledge which has developed in the group.

Finally, with some groups it is fruitful to end up with a discussion of how the understanding which has developed in the group may be translated into action.

Case Example

To the story (previously quoted) of the young woman dying of cancer were added experiences with death from other participants. One case was about being with an old lady. Her eyesight was failing. Otherwise she was healthy. She went to bed and announced that she was not going to get up any more. I have had my life, she announced. She lay in bed for 8 days and then calmly stopped living. The participant who was there had never seen a more peaceful face. It was described as incredibly dignified. To finish life this way was the woman's own choice. The group remarked that the body and soul of the old woman seemed to have left earth simultaneously, which is certainly not always the case.

Another case was about the death of the baby of the participant's sister. There was terrible grief. Suddenly a big and up till now dispersed family moved closely together under the notion that the baby should not have died in vain. They developed a clearly increased family cohesion, and it became very meaningful to everybody to think that such a death has to have a meaning and a consequence.

The group now explored the similarities and differences of the stories. This led to new personal examples from other participants. And it led to a common, committed consideration of the questions: Does death always carry a meaning? Can one always find meaning in somebody else's death, or is it sometimes meaningless? What is the difference between timely and untimely death? Is untimely death so hard because it is an example of the unlived or the unfulfilled life? But do we ourselves live our lives in a full way?

In summary, the method of structured existential exercises can be applied to a wide range of people and situations. It is advisable that the participants should receive some idea beforehand as to the kind of process to expect. The method has a somewhat more preplanned character than the existential–analytic group method, but not more than, for instance, cognitive therapy.

SUMMARY AND APPLICATION

In this chapter, existential therapy with more than one person is explored. Two types of existential group work are accounted for in detail each with its own style, method and types of participants.

There is a vast potential field of work in applying the existential approach to more than one person. The main loci of intervention transcending the individual are: the family, the group, the organisation. It is argued that when you transcend the level of the individual you need a supplementary theory combined with the existential–phenomenological one. The systemic theory approach is suggested as the most suitable.

Working with groups as here described, or with families or organisations, is seen as having a number of assets: (a) you may reach a range of people not reachable through individual therapy; (b) some people may be able to afford group therapy, but not individual therapy; and (c) when you deal with families and organisations, you deal with individuals in their natural social contexts.

DISCUSSION WITH THE EDITOR

SIMON: You begin your chapter by summarising what you consider to be the main strengths and weaknesses of working with existential problems in groups. I want to resonate with this for a moment, and also suggest that the possibility of engagement with others which groups provide can in itself prove enormously therapeutic. Time and again I have been struck by the isolation and lack of involvement with life which seems to be central to the problems clients bring and the fear of engagement, of commitment, which accompanies and reinforces this. I wonder whether it is necessary to combine an existing theory of group psychology with a phenomenological–existential base. Existentialism isn't, of course, individualistic: Heidegger and Sartre are both very clear on this, emphasising that Being can only be understood as Being-with-others. So our relatedness with others is at the heart of the existential approach and examination of the way individuals enter into or deny this must be present in existential therapy. Cohn (1996) has recently outlined an existential–phenomenological approach to group work. And going on from this, I wonder if you feel there are problems in the idea of applying "existential approaches" to group work as a sort of add-on?

BO: Yes, participating in a group may have a therapeutic value in itself. This effect is especially visible in the existential–analytic groups where the relation between participants is often observed and reflected upon. To be a member of a group gives you a unique occasion to experiment with and develop your *ways of relating* with others, and even to study the relationship between this way of relating on one hand and your self-construct on the other. There are many possibilities to be explored with existential group therapy, especially when the therapy is seen not so much as individuals exchanging their inner worlds but as individuals-in-relation exploring their common world.

Is the existential–phenomenological approach sufficient for understanding groups and organisations? I agree that existentialism is about being-with-others. Especially the European thinkers emphasize this clearly. But existentialism has its point of observation within the individual. Even if the individual is seen as a being-in-the-world or a being-with-others, they are seen as such from the inside. Therefore, I suggest, there is a need for a complementary theory that uses flexible and varied observation points, like the systemic approach. It is always difficult work to try to combine two theories or theoretical approaches; it is an enterprise that requires detailed reflection. But, in principle, it is legitimate and often desirable, since "theories" as a rule only cover some part of "the world".

SIMON: I'm very struck by the fact, it seems to me, that "existential themes" do not "come and go" but are constantly present, in the sense that the groups are necessarily about how it is to be an individual, what it means to be a group member, the extent to which people are willing to be with each other. So I end up wondering what work the word "analytic" is doing in your term "existential–analytic group" . . . are we perhaps here talking about Daseinsanalysis rather than psychoanalysis?

BO: Can one say that "existential themes" "come and go" in the existential–analytic groups? It depends on what you mean by "theme". In a deeper sense, the themes are there all the time, but they may not be present in our consciousness. In this sense we always know, some-where, that one day we are going to die, or that we don't live as fully as we could, but we often don't want to think of it or talk about it. In a less deep sense, the themes—understood as conversation subjects—do come and go. Like an individual therapy, talk about seemingly every-day phenomena fills the space some of the time, but suddenly gives way to more penetrating and shivering insights into the depths of existence. The term "analytic" points to the free-floating process of exploring what comes up, what is there, what emerges, what "shines forth" as Boss (1994) says. In this sense, "analytic" is the contrary of preplanned and structured. Hopefully, it is more "daseinsanalytic" than "psychoanalytic", but "Daseinanalysis" is a demanding term which should not be used too loosely.

SIMON: Your pioneering work in making the existential approach to problems of living available to people who might not in the normal run of events see themselves as candidates for psychotherapy echoes, I think, the core message of this book, and at the same time it brings up moves around the extent to which there is a temptation to "existen-tialise" existing ways of delivering therapy. As one of the most experi-enced practitioners in Denmark, where do you see this trend going in the next, say, 15 or 20 years? How do you think Denmark and Britain compare in their willingness to take up such initiatives?

BO: The existential approach to problems of living does, I think, have many possibilities and important messages for people in our countries in the coming decades. These years are really a period with a need to find our roots, our ground, our values in a complex world. This can be done through therapy, through workshops and also in other ways. However, there is always the risk of a new vogue. If the existential way becomes fashion, it is no longer existential. We will have to fight continually against fixed methods and recipes, which is the very opposite of "being there".

NOTES

1. In Denmark (5 million inhabitants) there are 30–40 full-time psychologists working with counselling with these three groups, often with an existential approach. They are mainly applied by the patient societies (like the Danish Cancer Society). This type of work is expanding rapidly in many countries.
2. There exists a third method which is existentially related: the confrontational, gestalt-oriented bereavement therapy (Leick & Davidsen-Nielsen, 1991), which often deals with existential issues but in which, however, the client–therapist relationship does not meet some of the basic requirements of an existential relationship (Spinelli, 1994).
3. The group met at the University of Copenhagen, Department of Clinical Psychology. The other therapist was Vibeke Nathan, who is an experienced group analyst. Usually groups like these are not time-limited. It is not unusual to participate for 2–3 years, which is for many people a useful—and affordable—alternative to individual therapy.
4. Although the existential work is the central part of the process, it is not precluded to use a certain amount of time for giving information. For example, in working with AIDS patients or the families of schizophrenics, they would have the double need of receiving information and working with their existential situations.
5. The group leaders were psychologists Sussie Brandrup and Paul Gandil from the Lyngby Cancer Counselling Centre, with the author acting as a consultant.

REFERENCES

Bateson G. (1972). *Steps to an Ecology of Mind*. New York: Ballantine.
Boss, M. (1994). *Existential Foundations of Medicine and Psychology*. London: Jason Aronson.
Campbell, D. et al. (1989). *A Systemic Approach to Consultation*. London: DC Publishing.
Cohn, H.W. (1994). What is existential psychotherapy? *British Journal of Psychiatry*, **164**, 699–701.
Cohn, H.W. (1996). Existential–phenomenological dimensions of groups. *Journal of the Society for Existential Analysis*, **7**(1), 117–28.
Foulkes, S.H. (1948). *Introduction to Group-analytic Psychotherapy*. London: Heinemann.
Frankl, V.E. (1955). *The Doctor and the Soul*. New York: Vintage Books.
Jacobsen, B. (1994). The role of participants' life experiences in adult education. In P. Jarvis & F. Pöggeler (eds), *Developments in the Education of Adults in Europe*. pp. 81–9. Frankfurt-am-Main: Peter Laing.

Leick, N. & Davidsen-Nielsen, M. (1991). *Healing Pain: Attachment, Loss and Grief Therapy*. London: Tavistock/Routledge.

Maturana, R. & Varela, F. (1987). *The Tree of Knowledge: the Biological Roots of Human Understanding*. Boston: Shambuala.

Mills, T.M. (1967). *The Sociology of Small Groups*. Englewood Cliffs, NJ: Prentice-Hall.

Morgan, G. (1986). *Images of Organization*, Chapter 8. London: Sage.

Palazolli, M.S. et al. (1978). *Paradox and Counterparadox. A New Model in the Therapy of the Family in Schizophrenic Transaction*. New York: Jason Aronson.

Pines, M. (ed.) (1983). *The Evolution of Group Analysis*. London: Routledge.

Spinelli, E. (1989). *The Interpreted World: an Introduction to Phenomenological Psychology*. London: Sage.

Spinelli, E. (1994). *Demystifying Therapy*. London: Constable.

Tame, J. (1995). Looking existentially at counselling in organizations. *Journal of the Society of Existential Analysis*, **6**(2), 127–39.

van Deurzen-Smith, E. (1988). *Existential Counselling in Practice*. London: Sage.

Watzlawick, P. et al. (1974). *Change*. New York: Norton.

Yalom, I.D. (1980). *Existential Psychotherapy*. New York: Basic Books.

Yalom, I.D. (1995). Regarding Rollo May. Interview with Irvin Yalom. *Journal of the Society of Existential Analysis*, **6**(2), 159–64.

13

THERAPY IN THE LATTER HALF OF LIFE

June Roberts
Institute of Psychotherapy and Social Studies

INTRODUCTION

In this chapter I will offer a brief account of the backgrounds of both client and therapist, and the context in which the therapy took place. Three phases of work will be described, in conjunction with an examination of three basic assumptions which were originally conceived by Bion (1961; cited in Cohn, 1994). These are:

> The fear and denial of death as undisputed certainty is of crucial importance.

> All experience is both physical and mental, and the body–mind dichotomy is an abstraction of our own making, imposing on us the impossible task of finding a link between aspects of existence which were never apart.

> If we accept that we are capable of choosing our response to what is "given", we need to introduce new dimensions of anxiety and guilt into our work as psychotherapists. Being confronted with choice engenders a kind of anxiety which is different from neurotic anxiety, and avoiding choice engenders a kind of guilt which is different from neurotic guilt feelings. These new dimensions we call "existential" anxiety and guilt.

> (Cohn, 1994)

Case Studies in Existential Psychotherapy and Counselling. Edited by S. du Plock
© 1997 John Wiley & Sons Ltd

Finally, a critical analysis will be attempted, with the benefit of hindsight, to see how far the writer's psychotherapeutic background, founded on a developmental rather than a philosophical view of human existence, informed or constrained the process of therapy. In recent years an increased understanding of differential forms of time has been central to my approach.

> Time must be brought to light, and genuinely conceived, as the horizon for all understanding of Being and for any way of interpreting it.
>
> (Heidegger, 1927/1962)

CASE STUDY

The client, a 62-year-old woman who I shall call Gwen, arrived at a London counselling centre with an air of determination and muted hostility. I received her with some trepidation, 3 weeks after she had been assessed by a colleague, who reported that Gwen's teenage daughter had committed suicide about 9 months earlier. My own experience included a dire week spent at the bedside of a heavily comatose cousin who only just made it back to full recovery, and a hospital-based research project which dealt with the management of parasuicide patients within the NHS. In hearing Gwen's story I was conscious of a strong empathy and of intense anxiety engendered by the knowledge that someone was suspended in the half-way zone between life and death and the outcome was uncertain. Perhaps it was something of a relief to me to ask how long she envisaged our work would take: at least this could be planned. We agreed on 4 months, by which time her hope was that she would have been admitted to a religious order with whom she was testing her vocation. Here again there was a common ground between client and therapist, not in church membership, but in a common allegiance to sacramental Christianity.

I asked her to tell me anything which she thought I should know as her therapist, and I explained that I would not be referring to the interview with my colleagues unless she specifically wanted me to. She seemed to take this in her stride and began to tell me about the main landmarks in her life. She described a family in which everything was well ordered, and relationships were distant; boarding school was an accepted part of childhood, and achievement was rated much more highly than feelings. I was surprised by the lack of rancour in this account and invited her to feel free, in her time with me, not to censor her feelings or thoughts, as therapy offers the opportunity to bring these into the foreground as they arise.

Gwen's career had been in the media, where she had attained a senior position with scope for her very considerable organising ability. Her marriage had been one which worked well at the practical level, and there were four children, all now grown up. Her husband had died some 10 years earlier. When she came to speak of the youngest child, Amy, her voice and her eyes were lowered and a feeling of distance seemed to arise, in which my own anxiety became a major preoccupation. At this point I must acknowledge that I am some 12 years younger than Gwen, that a daughter of mine came near to death some 5 years before after being run over by a car—through which I learned that notions of surrender and hope are not at opposite poles but rather a closely connected means of living. In extremes of fear and loss:

> . . . one is given a (last) chance to actualise the highest value, to fulfil the deepest meaning, the meaning of suffering.
>
> (Frankl, 1946/1962)

Gwen continued to rehearse the story of her daughter's death, letting me know that they had been close, closer perhaps than the other three children, but that Amy was rebellious and did not always keep contact after she had left home to go into nursing. It was clear that mother and daughter had been fully occupied at this time, and if there were regrets about this they were kept at bay in the narrative. For me, however, the pain was palpable, and thinking back I am reminded of William James's (1842–1910) caution that involuntary identification can involve the risk of becoming ungrounded, and that a good therapeutic presence allows the "attentional focus to wax and wane". Whether or not I was able to achieve this, Gwen slowly recounted the events of the last week of Amy's life, about which little was known until they were together in intensive care, where it gradually became apparent that were she to survive, Amy would have sustained major damage to the brain and to her liver and kidneys. The mother surrendered her hope. Small details, which Gwen recalled, suggested that the course was set some months beforehand, when she first realised that her youngest was beyond her reach, or perhaps beyond her control, I reflected to myself.

The highly disciplined family mores which permeated Gwen's description of her own upbringing, the arbitrary partings and the low expectation of love or encouragement led me to feel a sense of fatalism in my client and an inverse absence of railing or bitterness. Again, these were feelings with which I was not unfamiliar. This, together with our mutual agreement to meet for 4 months, formed the beginning of the therapy. Gwen's commitment to seeking acceptance by a religious community was also a theme which was visited and re-visited over the weeks—my commitment was to her in the present and I was necessarily agnostic as to the meaning, and the wisdom, of looking for security, if such it was, within the walls of a convent. It had not escaped us, however, that the counselling room in which we met was also housed in the grounds of a convent.

Whilst the detail of these early sessions is now at a distance and escapes me, reflection on them does continue and I find myself wondering whether the loss of her husband and her youngest child had not impelled Gwen to seek the completion of her own death, not by suicide but by an "activism of the future," whereby she would live out her life within the community, loving her Maker and caring for the sisters who would take her into their family. If this sounds euphemistic, then her humour and ready ability to debunk and make fun would certainly make a very great impact in the lives of people she would live with.

During the middle phase of the therapy, a situation arose in which Gwen and I found ourselves confronted with another potentially morbid challenge, and one which allowed for a full frontal challenge of the mind–body dichotomy which is so often implied in modern medicine. She arrived at her session with the news that a lump had appeared in one of her breasts and that tests were being carried out which seemed likely to confirm that this was malignant. She was angry with the suspected diagnosis, and even more angry with what she thought was a disregarding manner which she encountered in the outpatients' clinic. What interests me in retrospect, is the growing conviction that Gwen was well ahead of me in the realisation that on the one hand death comes to us all, and on the other, that faced with this immediate threat her need of the therapeutic alliance was great. Furthermore, by this time our mutuality was well developed, hostility had given way to a willingness to ask for support and to receive it. Once more, my own life experience and recent events were to put me in a strong position to hear what this client was bringing to me, and to respond in a neutral but hopeful manner. About 3 years beforehand, I had had an advanced adenocarcinoma which was surgically removed, although histology was to reveal that the cells had spread to my lymphatic system. It seemed to me that there were better strategies for driving out the cells than chemotherapy and radiation, and friends supported me in this.

Gwen, it appeared, was full of fight as far as her survival was concerned, and more than a little controlled ire in her rather minimal encounters with doctors. I was encouraging as far as the anger went, knowing that a correlation has been found between holding it in and certain forms of cancer. As to the doctors, I offered the idea that accurate diagnosis helps you to know what you are dealing with, but thereafter the decisions most properly remain your own. It was this stance, in which I strove to bracket all preconceptions, which kept me calm enough to enable Gwen to explore not only her thoughts and feelings about the lump, but also her connection to the "abstract and absolute aspect of living"—the *Überwelt* (van Deurzen-Smith, 1988). Some of our discussion was "down-to-earth" and practical, much of it was elliptical and even non-verbal, for it concerned God.

When the result of the biopsy came through, Gwen dwelt more on her dislike of the doctor who told her that the lump was malignant than she did on the life-threatening implications. In reflecting this back I was careful to make plain that these feelings mattered, indeed that they could be channelled in whatever direction she wished. There followed a period of weeks in which she came regularly to therapy but failed to attend the hospital. This caused me anxiety, since studies suggest that removing the lump is an essential prerequisite to full recovery. Gwen, however, seemed confident in our alliance and intent upon examining her subjective existence, often alluding in passing to God, who presumably knew what he was up to! She continued her preparation for entering an order. It is hard for me to remember, at 6 years' distance, exactly what my responses were, except that I felt close to my client in experience and in belief. I knew that it was vital for her to discover her own resources, and that this can be greatly helped by trust, in a combination of the human and the divine.

One thing was very clear, Gwen's will to live was palpable, as was the lump; she told me in graphic detail how she had found it and what procedures she underwent during the diagnosis. The "felt sense" of all of this was important, as it seemed to provide the vehicle for her anger and for a lifetime's disregard by the parental figures of her earlier life. Also of interest was the simultaneous bridge-building in which she was engaged. I found myself reflecting that her spiritual directors were the authority figures in her present life, while I was the person to whom she brought her more intimate concerns. She had been at some pains to ensure that I was trustworthy, telling me how she was interviewed by a priest/ therapist as part of the testing of her vocation, and that he had taped the interview without telling her. She had discovered this when the tape finished with a loud click. Through all of this she was vigilant and attentive to my presence and I felt that we were forging something new in her *Eigenwelt*, namely comfort in proximity.

An issue for me now was whether or not to disclose my own experience of cancer, the outcome of which seemed hopeful at the time, although technically I was still in the period where recurrence was predicted, from a scientific point of view. All I can say is that congruence seemed to demand it and I told her the facts of my bill of health and by inference conveyed my hope and confidence. It was in the week after this disclosure that Gwen began to consider returning to the hospital, although her angry defence, an absolute obduracy in the face of authority, manifested itself in a fearful determination to wage war with the doctor at the slightest opportunity. I maintained calmness and neutrality as far as I was able. With hindsight, the words of S.H. Foulks seem relevant:

> "The therapist is himself the instrument of observation and treatment, and psychotherapy depends on 'experience', understanding, and communion—such as is only possible between two fully engaged persons."
>
> (Foulks, 1961)

In the light of this, I feel able to acknowledge my own need, if not urgency, at that particular time, for Sartre's third manner of being— "being for others". This is most helpfully described by Spinelli:

> *Being*-for-others views its relationship with others not as a competitive "you *or* me" relationship but as a cooperative "you *and* me" one. By implication, what this perspective leads to is the understanding that being-for-others cannot attach greater (or lesser) importance or significance to itself in relation to others (or *vice versa*). As such, any action taken or construed definition made by a being-for-others must take into account the effects it may have upon others.
>
> (Spinelli, 1989)

Where Gwen and I seemed to be in "communion" was precisely in a "being-for-others" by conviction and belief, and in a profound agnosticism towards scientific determinism. For a discussion of this which has informed me over the years, I refer first to Paul Halmos (1965), who comprehensively documents the role of love in therapy, and fearlessly elucidates the dialectic as between the hegemony of science on the one hand, and the tendency to manipulation which may arise on the therapist's side, where the client's own phenomena are not given the primacy which being-for-others would seem to demand. As might be expected in the middle phase of a well established therapy, much of my internal process was necessarily tacit, Gwen for her part was working things out within the parameters of her chronological stage of life and her own belief system. Surprisingly, her manner with me remained cheerful and largely optimistic.

During this time her progress towards acceptance into the religious order was maintained, but I was not told whether any of her mentors were taken into her confidence about the lump. Our sessions were quietly

reflective but more buoyant than might have been expected in the circumstances. Subjectively, it seemed that our relationship was more important
to Gwen than the malignancy. Eventually she returned to the hospital, as
she thought, to be booked in for an operation to remove the lump. She
was understandably militant around the issue of signing the consent form
and whether the surgery would be radical or simply a lumpectomy. As
she was well informed in these matters I was saved from having to
discuss the latest state of research into breast cancer, although it was on
my mind.

There was a planned break in the sessions after which she returned
with some extraordinary news. She had been to the hospital, where the
doctor examined her breast again and was unable to feel the lump. He
ordered the tests to be repeated and nothing was found. This came as a
shock to me, and although I was able to reciprocate Gwen's apparent
relief, I was actually thrown into a maelstrom by the challenge to my own
situation: was it possible that physical strategies, whether medical or
"alternative", were not actually needed to rid the body of cancer? With
hindsight it appears that being still within the critical period for recurrence of my own cancer, I needed to accept Gwen's account without
question. Henry Peter Wilburg (1992) wrote of the practice of therapy
being an:

> "Inner voice communication" to explore and heal disturbances of
> being and communication by enhanced awareness of inner vibra-
> tional touch . . . our *felt sense* of what our own stance embodies in its
> feeling tone and posture, is itself part of that stance and of what we
> communicate by it.
>
> (Wilburg, 1992)

I can only conclude, whatever the whys and wherefores of the situation,
that my own commitment to self-healing and to reliance on the spiritual
and metaphysical sources of support must have been powerfully conveyed at some level of our communication. The vibrations were of joy and
of relief.

In the final weeks of this therapy, as client and therapist prepared to
part, another happening occurred which was to throw my avowed therapeutic framework into relief. The larger part of my practice is time-limited
and owes a great deal to the American psychoanalyst James Mann, who
regards the planned ending as a notable catalyst in the resolution of
internal conflicts (see Kierkegaard, 1985). It was not, therefore, a great
surprise to me when Gwen arrived expectantly but more nervously than
usual for the third session from the last. She was hesitant and tentative in
a way which I had not seen before, and very much needing to test the

waters and how I might receive her. Gradually she revealed her feelings of love, strong but not demanding and prompting the words, which she voiced, "Do you think I am a lesbian?"

To me this felt like easier territory, coming as I do from an approach which places an appreciative emphasis on developmental stages. My self-supervision ranged immediately over Gwen's acknowledged, highly controlled emotional history, replicated in the early phase of her work with me—virtually the "permission to speak" ethos which I imagined her to be heading for when she joined the religious community. Added to this, she described herself as highly disciplined, and somewhat hierarchical by background and paying the price of severe distancing from her children, the older of whom were keen for her to return home rather than to pursue her vocation. I asked her to tell me more about her love, and we sat at ease with silence for some of the time. She seemed content to leave the issue of lesbianism, perhaps because I said I welcomed this new way of being and saw it as an essential part of her character, but one which may have been frozen in its infancy at an earlier stage of her life. Gwen's mood in the succeeding session was friendly, open and even somewhat celebratory. I felt confident in her well-being and glad toh ear her range over the weeks of our work, saying that it had brought her to the point where she could look back as well as forwards without too much pain. For the first time she announced that she would visit her children and grandchildren before taking up an offer to live in community with nuns, whilst waiting for the hierarchy to agree to her being admitted as a postulant. She said that she would make the best of London while she had the chance. We took our leave of each other, very much on equal terms, and I noticed that I no longer felt suspicious of her motives for becoming a nun!

What seems very important, in looking back on this final phase, is the role of guilt and anxiety. Whilst Gwen was never one to complain of either, it might be thought that there was an element of self-immolation in her whole trajectory towards an enclosed life. Furthermore, the forbearing way in which she revealed her loving feelings for me, just in time for us to talk about them without my being burdened by them, might also be seen as highly conscientious, and not a little self-sacrificial. What was apparent, however, was her growing confidence, the freedom with which she talked in the latter half of the therapy, by contrast with her heavily controlled presentation at the beginning. A further reflection that I would make was that she brought a relative absence of grief to the sessions, which I tended to assume might be because her capacity for strong affectional ties was not very great, as evidence by the coolness and amused cynicism with which she described her relationships. At all events, her relationship with me had become noticeably warmer as the weeks went by, and there was a sense of completion as we said goodbye to each other.

REVIEW

The fear and denial of death as an undisputed certainty, is of crucial importance.

(Cohn, 1994, p. 701)

As I review Gwen's work with me at 5 years' distance, two factors seem to dominate my reflections and these are different from the usual analytical framework to which I owe the main substance of my approach to therapy and counselling. The first is that we were both faced with a real threat to our lives in the form of cancer, and that therapeutic work was in two different ways, a part of our strategy for dealing with the possibility of dying in the shortest term. Secondly, I am struck by the fact that the application of phenomenological principles to our dialogue might have revealed a radically different set of meanings, as weil as the ones of which I was aware at the time. This is not to say that this methodology is necessarily at variance with the best of analytical psychotherapy. What is clear, however, is that our alliance was strengthened by a common commitment to taking responsibility for our own health, and that my defences against impending death were the stronger for having watched my daughter struggle back from the brink, and my cousin recover from a serious suicide attempt. Gwen, on the other hand, had lost her youngest daughter through suicide, and had survived her husband's death by some 10 years. The way of life which she had chosen in the aftermath of these losses seemed to exemplify the wish and the hope that she would become herself most fully as she entered what must be the last quarter of her life.

As I write, I am conscious that this interpretation of her decision to enter a religious order goes further than Victor Frankl's (1946/1962) ontology of continuous becoming, and enters the realm more graphically described by Kierkegaard, namely faith:

> "... that every man has; it is inherent in him, every man has it if he wills to have it; and this is the glory of faith, that it can only be had on this condition; therefore it is the only unfailing good, because it can only be had through being constantly acquired, and can only be acquired through being constantly developed."

(Kierkegaard, 1985)

In my consciousness, a conviction that death is not the end of life had always seemed to pre-date any awareness of faith, and a Christian education only confirmed for me Kierkegaard's dictum, "one man can do much for another, but he cannot give him faith"! (Kierkegaard, 1985).

Nevertheless, it does seem possible that Gwen was able to apprehend in me the particular faith which enabled me to refuse chemotherapy and radiation after my tumour was removed. As far as I can remember, we spoke of survival but not of death.

> All experience is both physical and mental, and the mind–body dichotomy is an abstraction of our own making, imposing on us the impossible task of finding a link between aspects of existence which were never apart. Although this cannot be said to be an axiomatic tenet of existential therapy, it certainly does inform our thinking as far as psychiatric diagnosis goes.
>
> (Kierkegaard, 1985)

Phenomenological therapists argue that, rather than being problems open to medical treatment, mental disturbances reveal primarily onto-logical (that is, "being"-related) issues (Kierkegaard, 1985). Can we extend this to amplify our understanding of physical disease? Certainly, oncologists are beginning to recognise a link between loss and stress, and failures of the immune system. this has implications not just for under-standing the aetiology of cancer, but also for apprehending the extent to which mind and emotions can be influential in making the body well:

> One of the greatest advances in modern medicine, is the new vision that doctors and others are gaining in regard to the amount of control a person may learn to exert over the mental processes that influence a wide variety of physical processes.
>
> (Simonton et al., 1978)

Returning to the specific psychotherapeutic work described in this chapter, all I can be sure of is that I was committed to the view that the immune system can drive out cancerous cells, and this has subsequently been proved to be so in my own case. It was therefore relatively straight-forward for me to support Gwen in the idea that faith might play a significant part in the removal of her lump, just as losses may have played a part in its generation. The emphasis in my own mind must always be on meaning; it is not my contention that psychotherapy can offer a placebo effect, powerful though placebos have been shown to be. However, if existential therapy were to extend the refutation of the mind–body dicho-tomy to embrace the idea that bodily phenomena are susceptible to being changed by mental process, then the previously inexplicable "spon-taneous remission' may be brought into focus by looking at the role played by the client's belief system, and in psychotherapy that of the therapist as well.

The alarming concomitant of this thinking is that current affective states, as they are experienced in day-to-day life and in psychotherapeutic work, might be as likely to cause a lump as to assist in its disappearance. Also, it goes without saying, on this basis, that the therapist's chosen responses to the "givens" in his/her own life will have a direct beating on the intersubjective process, the feelings experienced and the interpretations offered. Hence a phenomenological analysis of an accurate record of the dialogue of the sessions, had this been possible, may have yielded deeper or different meanings than those which I am offering here.

Once again, five years' hindsight, and a recent exposure to some of the existential literature, allows me a very different process of reflection than would have been possible had I confined myself to the analytical literature with which I was more familiar at the time when I encountered Gwen. In particular it must be acknowledged that the assumptions derived from the developmental aspect of my training, as well as the urgency with which I was involving my personal beliefs in response to the perceived threat imposed by the cancers, were in the forefront of my thinking and my experiencing, as I sat with Gwen through 16 sessions. My expectations were by no means fixed, on gaining an initial impression of my client, but certain hypotheses undoubtedly crossed my mind; the first of these concerned the pain and anger which seemed likely to persist after losing a daughter by suicide. The possible corollary to this, I speculated, might be that Gwen would contact an earlier loss and in so doing reintegrate an important part of her psyche. Whilst all clients must be regarded as self-determining during therapy, it did seem likely that the work which we would do together might ultimately have a bearing on some of the decisions with which she was faced. If I am honest, I must also admit to wondering about the nature of her motivation for joining a religious order. Perhaps I was anxious as to how far neurotic guilt may have been the precipitating factor.

My surmise is that a combination of forces has influenced this decision, the strongest of which may well have been existential anxiety about her own death, or even more powerfully about the feared loss of any one of her surviving children or grandchildren. This might have led to offering her own life to God as some kind of bargaining. The fact that she still experienced guilt in relation to her own sexuality, might also have played a part in her wish to make a promise in favour of chastity.

Although my intention was to reserve judgement, I am sure these ideas were influential in my way of responding to Gwen's account of her situation. What I was not so fully prepared for was the transcendent effect of suffering, suffering in the past, suffering through cancer in the Now. This engendered conversations between us which concerned the soul, and its qualifying attribute, that:

Makes meaning possible, turns events into experiences, is communicated in love—and had a religious concern.

(James Hillman, 1967, p. 42)

The words were brief but their inference was strong and hopeful, even when she was in flight from the hospital. Gwen was undeniably strong and seems to have made choices following her daughter's death, which were in keeping with her beliefs and allowed her to begin to put her painful experiences into the past. Therapy played a small part in this project until deeply feared feelings of intimacy welled up—throwing Gwen into a wave of neurotic guilt and concomitant malignant anxiety. The re-framing of these feelings in the context of a trusting relationship, was both healing and restorative beyond our expectations.

Where I believe I may have failed her, however, is in the area of existential anxiety about death. I was too busy dealing with my own, and had experienced an analytical therapy which was almost exclusively concerned with an entrenched transference neurosis! It seems highly likely, in retrospect, that Gwen was further advanced in facing her mortality than I was, since she seemed able to look to the future, whatever it might hold, with greater equanimity.

POSTSCRIPT

Finally, I will address myself to Gwen's disclosure about the lump in her breast, and advance three possible hypotheses as to the meaning of this part of our therapeutic dialogue. These are not intended to be in conflict with each other, but I will leave readers to make their own interpretation of the phenomena as I recall them.

In the context of her avowed intention to spend the last part of her life under vows of poverty, chastity and obedience, it is tempting first of all to suggest that Gwen's primary defence against death anxiety conforms remarkably closely to Yalom's notion of the "ultimate rescuer" (Yalom, 1980, 129–41). She might not see herself as leading a sacrificial life, seeking redemption, and gaining the ultimate reward of salvation through embracing an established spiritual path and submitting herself to the authority of superiors of the same persuasion. Seen in this light, the lump takes on a biblical connotation and puts Gwen (and myself) directly in line for divine healing and for confirmation of her specialness in the eyes of God. A continuation, one might believe on some level, of the New Testament tradition, and a powerful defence. The implication of this as far as our work together is concerned might suggest that she saw me as another instrument or sign, my own woundedness lending confirmation of a sacrificial view of life, predicated on a belief in ultimate resurrection.

A second possible explanation is that Gwen, far from being defended against the impending certainty of her own death, was actively wishing it. On this hypothesis a malignancy would simply be a means to an end—hence her reluctance to receive medical treatment. If this were the case, one might hazard the guess that Gwen, being conscientious, would not have wished to compromise her psychotherapist. Fearing that I might pressure her to be treated, or that I would be upset by her illness, she told me that the lump had disappeared. She certainly appeared to be strong enough to take such a stance and I have known a number of women who found it more authentic to accept a morbid diagnosis than to resist it.

A third hypothesis came into my mind as I was recalling the feeling "in the room" as Gwen talked with me about cancer. It runs like this. Since the therapy was planned in terms of time, and had a desired outcome, which Gwen expressed as being in a good state to act positively on the success, or the failure, of her application to become a nun and live in community, the ingredients were all in place for a very dynamic time-limited therapy.

At the time of working with her I was relatively inexperienced in this approach and certainly had not assimilated the relevant literature, but subsequently I have participated in many time-limited therapies and have noticed, in more than a handful of cases, a phenomenon which may bear some relation to the particular dynamic transaction which took place in the latter half of Gwen's therapy. It is concerned with conflict resolution and the re-experience of unbearable anger; perhaps akin to implosion in ontological terms. The client bonds closely with the therapist, yet knows from the beginning that separation will ensue, thus there is an inbuilt incentive to aim high by risking the "lowest" or the most anxiety-provoking feelings. In Gwen's case, her anger towards those who left her seems always to have been sublimiated in hard work and not externalised. Might the cancerous lump, on this theory, have been the most malignant metaphor which she could bring me (whether or not she could intimate my own situation)?

Furthermore, she knew that I was committed to receiving her feelings and I did indeed maintain our alliance; what greater gift could she give me on nearing the end of our sessions, than a symbolic healing and a loving resolution of long-felt inhibition and resentment?

As I prepare to close this chapter, which reads far more seriously than the actual dialogue of the sessions, I am reminded of some words in the epilogue to *The Facts of Life*, by Ronnie Laing:

I am myself perplexed. But I have tried, as best I can, to convey the nature of my perplexity!

(Laing, 1977)

DISCUSSION WITH THE EDITOR

SIMON: It is very interesting to see what a therapist like yourself who has been working in the field for many years and who was trained primarily psychodynamically takes from the existential tradition. There is clearly a fundamental distinction between the two approaches. You quote Cohn at the beginning of your chapter and I know he sees the two as diametrically opposed . . .

JUNE: As you say, I am a practitioner of long standing; such learning as I have was derived from doing first, then seeking out theoretical bases and beginning the long process of integrating theoretical insights with a constantly evolving therapeutic methodology. My understanding of the existential tradition is that first and foremost they seek to honour the underlying epistomology; it is rooted in philosophy, and in practice existential therapists aspire to a genuinely phenomenological stance. As a trainer, I learn much from this, and this discipline amplifies my analytically-oriented stance and enables deeper congruence with my client. My own theory-building, however, owes more to the careful, naturalistic observation of selected phenomena, as in sociology, and is often informed by the expressed need of clients to bring the concerns of an earlier stage of life directly into the "now" of psychotherapy.

SIMON: In your experience is it the case that many psychodynamically-trained therapists are incorporating existential concepts into their work, and if this is so how happy do you think the outcome is?

JUNE: Perhaps the best of them are, but the snag is that their tradition comes out of medicine to a great extent, and may involve an unhealthy preoccupation with psychopathology, which is sometimes taught as though it were a "given". Usually it takes a very good personal therapy or familiarity with a non-positivistic academic methodology to engender existential awareness and open the mind to more than a narrowly conceived developmental theory. I speak as one who sees the knowledge of developmental conflicts and stages as a fundamental part of the therapist's equipment.

In time-limited psychotherapy it is the degree of trust engendered at the beginning, and the knowledge of impending parting, which form the crucible in which the particular conflict at the heart of the client's difficulties is reworked as thoroughly as the therapeutic dyad are capable. Only an awareness of the commonality of experience will enable the therapist to provide an open and unbiased presence as the central conflict is brought, together with the pain of separation evoked by the planned ending.

For many people, the event which precipitates their entry into therapy is but one manifestation or evocation of a recurring pattern which may have endured from an early, unresolved separation, insult or confusion, which constituted their unique response to the significant other through whom they experienced and learned about the complexity of relationship. In our approach we operate a dual strategy by allying ourselves with the client's declared wish for resolution of this difficulty, and by actively addressing the meaning, within the working alliance, of all their communications, and, of course, our own.

Where phenomenology helps us is in looking at the material of the session without preconceptions, as far as this is possible, and discovering the meaning by attending to both sides of the interaction.

Where we diverge from the existential stance is in the manner in which we week to understand matters of which the client is consciously aware, his/her current concerns, and to apprehend those with which he/she may have lost contact. I think it must be owned that our position owes more to that of Robert Lang's communicative psychotherapy, in that the major tool at our disposal is that of listening to both the client's and the therapist's subjective response, or "counter-transference", to the dynamics of the session. It is our hope and aspiration that our own experiences in therapy and in supervision enable the systematic unravelling of the central conflict, within an agreed period of time. We also seek to facilitate a more manageable separation at the end of therapy, and to allow for the integration of earlier losses in a context in which the client will have been encouraged in the expectation that positive change will occur.

The small piece of formal research with which a cohort of our clients cooperated revealed a high standard of recall and articulacy about the process they had been through. Quantitatively, our findings are very much in line with those of other brief, dynamic therapists, in that there is a minimal rate of drop-out, and the rate of return for further work, as far as we can establish it, is similarly small and runs at less than a quarter of clients who accept a time-limited agreement.

While answering your questions, I have been recalling a conversation with Ernesto Spinelli and can only repeat my earlier assertion that the long process of acquiring, reviewing and integrating theoretical insights with experience gained alongside clients is continuous, and that there is always room for radical rethinking, as well as for consolidation.

As to the nature of brief psychotherapy, I leave the last word to James Mann (1973):

Time sense and reality are co-conspirators in repeating an existential trauma in the patient . . .

and this provides us with a rational and a therapeutic incentive to offer a time-limited contract as a genuinely hopeful therapeutic option for people who want to change.

REFERENCES

Cohn, H. (1994). What is existential psychotherapy? *British Journal of Psychiatry,* **165**, 700–701.

Foulks, S.H. (1961). Psychotherapy. *British Journal of Medical Psychology,* **XXXV**(11).

Frank., V. (1946, revised 1962). *An Introduction to Logotherapy—Man's Search for Maning.* London: Hodder and Stoughton.

Halmos, P. (1965). *The Faith of Counsellors.* London: Constable.

Heidegger, M. (1927, revised 1962). In J. Macquarrie & E. Robinson (eds) *Being and Time.* New York: Harper & Row.

Hillman, J. (1967). *In Search: Psychology and Religion.* Fourth Spring Publications.

Kierkegaard, S. (1955). In P. Homer (ed.), *The Edifying Discourses.* London: Collins.

Laing, R.D. (1977). *The Facts of Life.* Harmondsworth: Penguin.

Mann, J. (1973). *Time-Limited Psychotherapy.* Harmondsworth, MA: Harvard University Press.

Simonton, C., Simonton, S. & Creighton, J. (1978). *Getting Well Again.* London: Bantam.

Spinelli, E. (1989). *The Interpreted World.* London: Sage.

van Deurzen-Smith, E. (1988). *The Überwelt.* In *Existential Counselling in Practice.* London: Sage.

Yalom, I.D. (1980). *Existential Psychotherapy.* New York: Basic Books.

Wilburg, H.P. (1992). The language of listening. *Journal of the Society for Existential Analysis,* **3**.

INDEX

Related titles of interest...

Paradox and Passion in Psychotherapy
An Existential Approach to Therapy and Counselling
Emmy Van Deurzen

This book considers a number of crucial concerns that are often brought to psychotherapists or counsellors in a disguised form and that these professionals frequently have trouble addressing squarely.

0-471-96191-4 170pp Publication due April 1998 Hardback
0-471-97390-4 170pp Publication due April 1998 Paperback

Existential Time-Limited Therapy
The Wheel of Existence
Freddie Strasser and Alison Strasser

While there are various brief therapy models on the market, this book combines existential ideas into a structured time-limited modular approach. It represents an overview of the principal existential ideas and then applies them to the model, using case vignettes throughout.

0-471-96308-9 170pp September 1997 Hardback
0-471-97571-0 170pp September 1997 Paperback

Psychology in Counselling and Therapeutic Practice
Jill D. Wilkinson, Elizabeth A. Campbell, with contributions by Adrian Coyle and Alyson Davis

This book is a concise text and accessible reference book dealing with the areas of psychology which particularly support and enlighten the practice of counselling and psychotherapy. By bringing psychology into the consulting room, the authors ensure that psychological theory and research are accessible and applicable to the therapist's work with clients.

0-471-95562-0 286pp February 1997 Paperback

Brief Rational Emotive Behaviour Therapy
Windy Dryden

Provides concepts in the context of a brief therapy process. Practitioners will find useful insights and guidance on applying these methods throughout the process of therapy, including building the working alliance, assessment, formulation, and work in sessions and outside the sessions. The whole process is illustrated by a case study which reflects the problems of real life work with a client.

0-471-95786-0 244pp 1995 Paperback

Visit the Wiley Home Page at http://www.wiley.co.uk